Amanda Corday

THE DRAMATIC WORKS OF G. E. LESSING MISS SARA SAMPSON, PHILOTAS, EMILIA GALOTTI, NATHAN THE WISE

Gotthold Ephraim Lessing

www.GeneralBooksClub.com

Publication Data:
Title: The Dramatic Works of G. E. Lessing Miss Sara Sampson, Philotas, Emilia Galotti, Nathan the Wise;
Author: Lessing, Gotthold Ephraim, 1729-1781
Reprinted: 2010, General Books LLC, Memphis, Tennessee, USA
Contact the publisher: http://generalbooksclub.com/contactus.cfm

THE DRAMATIC WORKS OF G. E. LESSING MISS SARA SAMPSON, PHILOTAS, EMILIA...

Produced by Charles Bowen, from page scans provided by Google Books

Transcriber's Note:

1. Page scan source: http:books.google.combooks?id=BPQIAAAAQAAJ pg

Lessing

Lessing.

THE DRAMATIC WORKS

OF

G. E. LESSING.

Translated from the German.

EDITED BY

ERNEST BELL, M.A.,

TRINITY COLLEGE, CAMBRIDGE.

WITH A SHORT MEMOIR BY HELEN ZIMMERN.

MISS SARA SAMPSON, PHILOTAS, EMILIA GALOTTI,

NATHAN THE WISE.

LONDON:

GEORGE BELL AND SONS, YORK STREET,

COVENT GARDEN.

1878.
LONDON:
PRINTED BY WILLIAM CLOWES ANB SONS,
STAMFORD STREET AND CHARING CROSS.

PREFACE.

A Translation of some of Lessing's works has long been contemplated for 'Bonn's Standard Library,' and the publishers are glad to be able to bring it out at a time when an increased appreciation of this writer has become manifest in this country.

The publication of Mr. Sime's work on Lessing, and the almost simultaneous appearance of Miss Helen Zimmern's shorter but probably more popular biographical study, will, without doubt, tend to spread amongst English-speaking people a knowledge of a writer who is held in peculiar reverence by his own countrymen; and there is little, if anything, of what he wrote that does not appeal in some way or other to the sympathies of Englishmen.

In this translation it is purposed to include the most popular of his works--the first two volumes comprising all the finished dramatic pieces, whilst the third will contain the famous 'Laokoon,' and a large portion of the 'Hamburg Dramaturgy' (here called 'Dramatic Notes'), and some other smaller pieces.

The arrangement of the plays is as follows:--The first volume contains the three tragedies and the "dramatic poem," 'Nathan the Wise.' This last piece and 'Emilia Galotti' are translated by Mr. R. Dillon Boylan, whose English versions of Schiller's 'Don Carlos,' Goethe's 'Wilhelm Meister,' c., had previously distinguished him in this path of literature.

The second volume will be found to consist entirely of comedies, arranged according to the date of composition; and as it happens that all these comedies, with the exception of the last and best, 'Minna von Barnhelm,' were written before he published any more serious dramatic composition, we have, by reversing the order of the first two volumes, an almost exactly chronological view of Lessing's dramatic work. The later section of it has been placed at the commencement of the series, simply because it was more convenient to include in it the introductory notice which Miss Zimmern kindly consented to write.

York Street, Covent Garden

.

June 1878.

LESSING.

Since Luther, Germany has produced no greater or better man than Gotthold Ephraim Lessing; these two are Germany's pride and joy.

This is the witness of Heine, and with Goethe in memory, none would pronounce the statement too bold. Luther and Lessing are Germany's representative men; each inaugurates an epoch the very existence of which would not have been possible without him. Nor is this the only point of analogy. Lessing was the Luther of the eighteenth century. Like Luther, Lessing is distinguished by earnestness, ardour, true manliness, fierce hatred of dissimulation, largeness of mind, breadth, and profundity of thought. Like Luther, he stands in history a massive presence whereon the weak may lean. Like Luther, he led the vanguard of reform in every department of human learning into which he penetrated. Like Luther, he was true to every conviction, and did not shrink from its expression. Like

Luther, he could have said, "I was born to fight with devils and storms, and hence it is that my writings are so boisterous and stormy." Like Luther, he became the founder of a new religion and of a new German literature. And again, like Luther, his life labours were not for Germany alone, but spread over all Europe; and few of us know how much of our present culture we owe directly or indirectly to Lessing's influence.

In this country he has not been sufficiently known. Up to the present, his name has been familiar to Englishmen only as the author of the 'Laokoon,' 'Nathan the Wise,' and, possibly also, of 'Minna von Barnhelm.' In knowing these, we certainly know the names of some of his masterpieces, but we cannot thence deduce the entire cause of the man's far-spreading influence.

Fully to understand Lessing's influence, and fully to understand the bearing of his works, some slight previous acquaintance with German literature is absolutely requisite. For unless we comprehend the source whence an author's inspirations have sprung, we may often misconceive his views. And Lessing's writings, above all, essentially sprang from the needs of his time. The subject is a large one, and can only be briefly indicated here; but we venture to remark, for those whose interest may be aroused in the subject of this volume, that the fuller their knowledge of the man and the motive force that evoked his works, the keener will be their enjoyment of these works themselves.

In naming Lessing, Goethe, and Schiller, we utter the three greatest names that German literature can boast. And between the three runs a connecting link of endeavour; the efforts of none can be conceived without the efforts of the others; but Lessing was the leader. He was the mental pathfinder who smoothed the way for Goethe's genius, and prepared the popular understanding for Schiller, the poetical interpreter of Kant.

Lessing was born in the early years of the eighteenth century, at a time therefore when Germany may be said practically to have had no literature. For the revival of learning, the interest in letters that arose with the Reformation, and had been fostered by the emancipating spirit of Protestantism, had been blighted and extinguished by the terrible wars that ravaged the country for thirty years, impoverishing the people, destroying the homesteads and farms, and utterly annihilating the mental repose needful to the growth and to the just appreciation of literature. Books were destroyed as relentlessly in those sad times as flourishing cornfields were down-trodden by the iron heel of the invader. It was a fearful period of anarchy and retrogression, under the baneful effects of which Germany still labours. Peace was at last restored in 1648 by the Treaty of Westphalia, but it found the nation broken in spirit and vigour, and where material needs entirely absorb the mental energies of a people the Muses cannot flourish. And not only was the spirit of the people broken by the war, their national feeling seemed totally extinct. The bold fine language wherewith Luther had endowed them was neglected and despised by the better classes, who deemed servile imitation of the foreigner the true and only criterion of good taste. It grew, at last, to be held quite a distinction for a German to be unable to speak his own language correctly, and it seems probable that but for the religious utterances of the hymn-writers, who thus provided the poor oppressed people with ideal consolations, the very essence of the language, in all its purity, might have perished. It is among these hymn-writers that we must seek and shall find the finest, truest, and most national expressions of that time. Shortly before Lessing's birth there had awakened a sense of this national degradation, and some princes and nobles formed themselves into a society to suppress the fashionable Gallicisms and reinstate the people's language. Their efforts met with some little success, but their powers were too limited, and their attempts too artificial and jejune to exert any considerable influence either in the direction of conservation or of reform. It needed something stronger, bolder, to dispel the apathy of a century. Still these associations, known as the two Silesian schools, bore their part in sowing the good seed, and though most of it fell on stony ground, because there was little other ground for it whereon to fall, still some fell on fruitful earth, and brought forth in due season. An excessive interest in French literature was opposed by an equal interest in English literature. The adherents of these two factions formed what was known as the Swiss and Leipzig schools. They waged a fierce paper warfare, that had the good effect of once more attracting popular attention to the claims of letters, as well as showing the people that in French manners, French language, and French literature, the Alpha and Omega of culture need not of necessity be sought. The leader of the Leipzig faction, who stood by the French, was Gottsched, a German professor of high pretensions and small merits, who put his opponents on their mettle by his pedantic and arrogant attacks. He had instituted himself a national dictator of good taste, and for a long time it seemed probable that he and his party would triumph. His ultimate defeat was accomplished by Lessing, whose early boyhood was contemporaneous with the fiercest encounters of these antagonists. It was he who gave the death-blow to their factious disputes, and referred the nation back to itself and its own national glory and power. He found Germany without original literature, and, before his short life was ended, the splendid genius of Goethe shed its light over the land. Who and what was the man who effected so much?

Gotthold Ephraim Lessing was born on the twenty-second of January, 1729, at Camentz, a small town in Saxony, of which his father was head pastor. For several generations Lessing's ancestors had been distinguished for their learning, and with few exceptions they had all held ecclesiastical preferment. The father of Gotthold Ephraim was a man of no inconsiderable talents and acquirements. His upright principles, breadth of vision and scholarly attainments, made him a venerated example to his son, with whom he maintained through life the most cordial relationship, though the son's yet more enlightened standpoint came to transcend the comprehension of the father. Their first divergence occurred on the choice of a profession. It had been traditional among the Lessings that the eldest son should take orders, and accordingly Gotthold Ephraim was silently assumed to be training for the ministry. He was sent for this end, first to the Grammar-school of his native town, then to a public school at Meissen, and finally to the University of Leipzig. At Meissen he distinguished himself in classical studies, and attempted some original German verses. He outstripped his compeers, and before he had accomplished his curriculum, the rector recommended his removal, inasmuch as he had exhausted the resources of the school. At Leipzig he appeared to turn his back on study. He deserted the class-rooms of the theologians and was the more constant attendant instead at the theatre, at that time the bête noire of all who affected respectability, and decried loudly by the clergy as a very hotbed of vice. News of their son's haunts reached the dismayed parents. They urged him to abandon his courses, that could only end in mental and moral destruction. In vain the son represented to them that he had lived in retirement too long, that he now wished to become acquainted with the world and men, and that he held the theatre to be a popular educator. In vain he represented that he did attend the philosophical courses of Professors Kaestner, Ernesti, and Christ. He was a playgoer, and what was still worse, he was a play-writer, for the directress of the Leipzig Theatre, Frau Neuber, a woman, of great taste and intelligence, had put on the stage Lessing's juvenile effort, 'The Young Scholar.' Nay more, he associated with a notorious freethinker, Mylius, and in concert with him had contributed to various journals and periodicals. And meanwhile the magistracy of Camentz was allowing Lessing a stipend on condition of studying theology. It was too much. His son was neglecting the dic cur hic, and to obviate this the father recalled him home by a stratagem, informing him that his mother was dying and desired once more to see her son. The ruse, intended also as a test of Lessing's filial obedience, succeeded in so far as to prove that this was at least unshaken; but his parents urged in vain that he should abandon his evil ways. He once more expressed with great decision his disinclination towards a theological career. But he was also firmly resolved to be no longer a burden to his parents, whose large family was a great drain on their resources. He determined to follow Mylius, who had gone to Berlin in the capacity of editor, convinced that a good brain and steadfast will would force their own way in the world.

Accordingly Lessing settled in Berlin in 1748, a youth of barely twenty years, prepared to fight a hand-to-hand struggle for existence. Frederick the Great at that time ruled in Prussia, and his capital was in ill repute as a hotbed of frivolity and atheism. If anything could be worse in the parents' eyes than their son's attendance at the theatre, it was his presence at Berlin. They urged his return home. He refused respectfully but decidedly. He had found employment that remunerated him. Voss's Gazette had appointed him literary editor, he wrote its critical feuilletons, and here he had the first opportunity of attacking the Swiss and Leipzig factions, and of exposing the absurdities of both schools. He was able to teach himself Spanish and Italian, he translated for the booksellers, he catalogued a library; and while thus earning his livelihood tant bien que mal, he indirectly prosecuted his studies and enlarged his knowledge of literature and life. For at Berlin he was not forced to associate only with books, he also came in contact with intellectual men, his views expanded, his judgment became sure. A volume of minor poems that he published in 1751 excited attention.

The essays he contributed to Voss's Gazette gave him notoriety on account of their independent spirit, their pregnant flashes of originality and truth. This unknown youth ventured alone and unsupported to attack Gottsched's meretricious writings, and so successfully that even the vain dictator trembled, and the rival schools asked each other who was this Daniel that had come to judgment? With pitiless subtlety he exposed the crudity, the inflation of Klopstock's 'Messiah,' which at that time one half the world extolled, the other half abused, while he alone could truly distinguish in what respects the poem fell short of its pretensions to be a national epic, and where its national importance and merit really lay.

For two years Lessing remained at Berlin; busy years, in which he scattered these treatises teeming with discernment and genius. Then at the end of that time he felt himself exhausted, he craved seclusion, in which he could once more live for himself and garner up fresh stores of knowledge. The city and his numerous friends were too distracting. So one day he stole away without previous warning and installed himself in the quiet university town of Wittenberg. At Wittenberg he spent a year of quiet study. The

University library was freely opened to him, and he could boast that it did not contain a book he had not held in his hands. Wittenberg: being chiefly a theological university, Lessing's attention was principally attracted to that subject, and he here laid the foundations of the accurate knowledge that was in after years to stand him in great stead. When he had exhausted all that Wittenberg could offer, he one day (1752) reappeared at Berlin as unexpectedly as he had quitted it, and quickly resumed his old relations there, which proved as busy and significant as before. Lessing again maintained himself by authorship, but this time his productions were riper. He published several volumes of his writings. They contained treatises composed at Wittenberg, Rehabilitations (Rettungen) of distinguished men, whom he held the world had maligned, as well as several plays, among which were the 'Jews,' 'The Woman-hater,' 'The Freethinker,' 'The Treasure,' as well as the fragmentary play 'Samuel Henzi,' a novel attempt to treat of modern historical incidents on the stage. A somewhat savage attack, entitled 'Vade mecum,' in which he criticised unsparingly a certain Pastor Lange's rendering of 'Horace,' drew upon Lessing the attention of the learned world, and since he was in the right in his strictures, they regarded him with mingled fear and admiration. His renewed criticisms in Voss's Gazette further maintained his reputation as a redoubtable critic.

These were happy, hopeful years in Lessing's life; he enjoyed his work, and it brought him success. He had, moreover, formed some of the warmest friendships of his life with the bookseller Nicolai and the philosopher Moses Mendelssohn. With the former he discoursed on English literature, with the latter, on æsthetic and metaphysical themes. Their frequent reunions were sources of mental refreshment and invigoration to all three. What cared Lessing that his resources were meagre, he could live, and his father was growing more reconciled now that men of established repute lauded his son's works. Together with Mendelssohn, Lessing wrote an essay on a theme propounded by the Berlin Academy, 'Pope a Metaphysician!' that did not obtain the prize, as it ridiculed the learned body which had proposed a ridiculous theme, but it attracted notice.

In the year 1755 Lessing wrote 'Miss Sara Sampson,' a play that marks an epoch in his life and in German literature. It was the first German attempt at domestic drama, and was, moreover, written in prose instead of in the fashionable Alexandrines. The play was acted that same year at Frankfurt-on-the-Oder, and Lessing went to superintend in person. Its success was immense, and revived Lessing's love for the stage, which had rather flagged at Berlin from want of a theatre there. He accordingly resolved on this account to remove to Leipzig again, and disappeared from Berlin without announcing his intention to his friends.

At Leipzig he once more lived among the comedians, and carried on a lively correspondence with Mendelssohn on the philosophical theories of the drama in general, with especial reference to Aristotle. A proposal to act as travelling companion to a rich Leipzig merchant interrupted this life. The pair started early in the year 1756, intending a long absence that should include a visit to England. The trip, however, did not extend beyond Holland, as the Seven Years' War broke out. Prussian troops were stationed at Leipzig, and this caused Lessing's companion to desire return. Return they accordingly did, Lessing waiting all the winter for the resumption of their interrupted project. But as the prospects of peace grew more distant, their contract was annulled, much to Lessing's regret, and also to his severe pecuniary loss. He found himself at Leipzig penniless, the theatre closed by the war, and interest in letters deadened from the same cause. He contrived, however, to maintain himself by hack-work for the booksellers; but it was a dismal time, not devoid, however, of some redeeming lights. The poet Von Kleist was then stationed at Leipzig, and with him Lessing formed a friendship that proved one of his warmest and tenderest. On the removal of Kleist to active service, Lessing determined to quit Leipzig, which had grown distasteful to him in its military hubbub. In May 1758 he once more appeared at Berlin, and fell into his former niche. He worked at his 'Fables,' wrote a play on the Greek models, 'Philotas,' began a life of Sophocles, and edited and translated several works of minor importance. But the chief labour of the period was the establishment of a journal dealing with contemporary literature. It was to be written tersely, as was suited to a time of war and general excitement; and to connect it with the war, it was couched in the form of letters purporting to be addressed to an officer in the field, who wished to be kept acquainted with current literature. Kleist was certainly in Lessing's mind when he began. The letters were to be written by Mendelssohn, Nicolai, and Lessing, but nearly all the earlier ones are from Lessing's pen. The papers made a great mark, from their bold strictures and independence. They did not belong to either of the recognised coteries, plainly placing themselves on a footing outside and above them. Though they were issued anonymously, Lessing was now sufficiently known, and it was not long before they were universally attributed to him. Their peculiar merit was that they did not merely condemn the contemporary productions, but showed the way to their improvement. They are throughout written with dialectic brilliancy, vigour, and lively wit, so that they are classics to this day, although their immediate themes are long removed from our interests From these 'Letters Concerning Contemporary Literature' our modern science of criticism may be said to date. After this, works were no longer merely judged by ancient standards, but by their application to the demands of the age in which they were written.

The news of Kleist's death affected Lessing severely, and so broke down his energies that he felt the imperative need of a change of scene. He therefore accepted an offer to act as secretary to General Tauentzien, who had been appointed Governor of Breslau. He followed him to that city in 1760, hoping to find renewed energies in a fixed employment that gave him good emolument and left him free time for self-culture.

Lessing remained at this post for nearly five years, until the conclusion of the Seven Years' War, and though his letters of that period are very scanty, and though he gained evil repute at Breslau as a gambler and a tavern haunter, they were really the busiest and most studious years of his life. Here he read Spinoza and the Church Fathers, studied æsthetics and Winckelmann's newly issued 'History of Art,' wrote his 'Minna von Barnhelm,' and the 'Laokoon.' Their publication did not occur till his return to Berlin after the peace of Hubertsburg, when Lessing threw up his appointment, greatly to the dismay of his family, who had reckoned on it as a permanent resource. But Lessing had had enough of soldiers and military life, he had exhausted all they could teach him, and he craved to resume his studious and independent existence. He did not like it on resumption so well as he had thought he should at a distance. Restlessness seized him. He wanted to travel; to see Italy. His friends desired an appointment for him as royal librarian. He applied for the post, and was kept for some time in uncertainty. He failed, however, owing to Frederick's dislike to German learned men, and it was in vain that Lessing's friends pleaded that he was anything but the typical German pedant, uncouth, unkempt, who was Frederick's bête noire. To prove his efficiency for the post, Lessing had published his 'Laokoon.' He published it as a fragment, and, like too many of Lessing's works, it never grew beyond that stage.

But torso as it is, its influence has been far spreading. The science of æsthetics was in its infancy when Lessing wrote. Pedantic and conventional rules were laid down regarding beauty, and the greatest confusion of ideas existed concerning the provinces and limits of the respective arts. Poetry and painting were treated as arts identical in purpose and scope; indeed each was advised to borrow aid from the resources of the other. Simonides' dictum that "Painting is silent poetry, and poetry eloquent painting," was regarded as an incontrovertible axiom. Winckelmann's lately published 'History of Art' had supported this view of the matter; a point of view that encouraged allegorical painting and didactic poetry. The 'Laokoon' strove to expose the radical error of this idea, as its second title, 'or the boundaries of Poetry and Painting,' proves. The conclusions established by the 'Laokoon' have become to-day the very groundwork of cultured art criticism, and though the somewhat narrow scope of its æsthetic theory has been extended, the basis remains untouched and unshaken. The book is of as much value now as upon its first appearance. Its luminous distinctions, its suggestive utterances, point the way to exact truth, even where they do not define it. Like the celebrated Torso of the Vatican, it can be made an object of constant study, and every fresh investigation will reveal new beauties, new subtle traits of artistic comprehension hitherto overlooked.

This work, so grand and ultimately fruitful, fell, nevertheless, very flat on its first issue, and only gradually assumed the position that was its due. It had indeed to educate its public, so new were the principles it enunciated. Three years after its publication, Lessing told a friend that hardly any one seemed to know at what goal he had aimed in his 'Laokoon.' Critics arose in plenty, but their criticism was of such a character that Lessing, usually so combative, did not hold them worthy of a reply. Little wonder, therefore, that even the discerning Frederick did not recognise the value of its author, and finally decided against Lessing's appointment as royal librarian.

In November 1766 Lessing describes himself as standing idly in the market-place waiting for hire. He was discontented with his surroundings, eager to find himself in a wider and more congenial mental atmosphere than that of Berlin, uncertain whither to turn, and hampered by money difficulties, private debts and family demands. At this juncture an invitation from Hamburg reached him, which at the first aspect seemed to open out a future peculiarly suited to Lessing's tastes and idiosyncrasies. An association of rich burghers had conceived the idea of founding a national theatre, which, liberally endowed, and thus removed from the region of pecuniary speculation, could devote itself exclusively to the cultivation of high art, and thus raise the national standard of taste. A dramatic critic and adviser was to belong to the establishment, and this post was offered to Lessing with a salary of 800 thalers. He accepted with alacrity, and repaired to Hamburg in the confidence of having at last found a niche well suited to his capacity. At the worst, he had nothing to lose and everything to gain by this step, and he gladly turned his back on Berlin, now distasteful to him. He hoped to throw himself once more into dramatic labours, and to find himself in contact with the living stage. Only too speedily his hopes were destined to disappointment. He had not been long at Hamburg before, notwithstanding all his power of illusion, he could not disguise from himself the fact that the project that sounded so noble and disinterested really rested on no higher basis than that of miserable stage cabals.

Before issuing the first number of his paper, the 'Hamburger Dramaturgie,' a critical journal, which was to accompany the art of the author and actor throughout the representations, he already knew that the project begun with such high hopes must end in a miserable fiasco. Still he set to work upon his journal undauntedly, determined that it should, as far as it lay in his power, serve the purposes of the drama and instruct the populace as to the full import and aim of this noble art. The paper was a weekly one, the criticisms, therefore, had the merit of being thoroughly thought out and digested, not written like our modern theatrical criticisms under the very glare of the foot-lights. Lessing analysed the plays and their performance; he pointed out not only where, but why actors had erred; his sure perception and accurate knowledge of stage routine made him an invaluable guide to the performers. His criticisms, had they been continued, would have laid the basis of a science of histrionics, but unhappily for the world, the wretched vanity of the artistes, some of whom he had ventured gently to condemn, caused him to desist from this portion of his criticism. He confined himself solely to the play performed. After a while, however, even this did not suffice; bad management, stage cabals, private jealousy, and clerical intrigues, had undermined the slender popularity of the theatre. Before the end of its first year, the house saw itself forced to close its doors, thanks to creditors and to the rival and superior attractions of a company of French comedians. It is true the German troupe returned in the spring to make a final effort, but this also proved a failure; the debts were only increased, and the throng of creditors who besieged the box-office was so great that the public could not have entered if it had tried. In November (1768) the theatre finally closed its doors.

Transeat cum cæteris erroribus, was Lessing's comment on the event. He was the poorer by another hope, and not only poorer in spirit but in fact. The promised salary had not been paid, the sale of his rich library would not suffice for his debts and needs, and he had moreover hampered himself with a printing-press that only helped yet more to cripple his means. His position was a sorry one. Literary work was once more his only resource. It happened that he had from the first been in arrears with his journal, first advisedly, then from a tendency to procrastination that befell him whenever the first white heat of interest had been expended. He now determined to continue it, employing it as a vehicle for his own opinions under the cover of criticisms of the national theatre, which he still hoped against hope might not be utterly defunct.

The 'Dramaturgy' is the permanent result of this shipwrecked undertaking, itself a fragment--for after a while Lessing wearied of it, and piratical reprints robbed him of the slender profit--but a fragment like the 'Laokoon,' full of suggestive truths and flashes of elucidation. As an entire work it is not as homogeneous in design as the 'Laokoon'; no connected or definite thread of reasoning pervades it, its perusal requires more independent thought from the reader, who must form his own conclusions, they are not worked out before him as in the 'Laokoon.' But in its ultimate results it is no less valuable, and has been no less effective. It freed the German stage from bondage to French pseudo-classicisms by its scornful exposure of the perversions practised by the Gallic authors under the cloak of Aristotelian laws. Lessing showed the divergence between real and absolute, and fanciful and perverted rules. He pointed out how the three unities insisted on by the French had been often violated by them in the spirit if not in the letter. He demonstrated the real meaning of Aristotle; and enabled, by his exact classical knowledge, to place himself on the actual stand-point of the ancients, he exposed the meretricious imitations of the French, that had been too long passed off as genuine. He referred the Germans to Shakespeare as a far truer follower of Sophocles than Voltaire or Corneille, and he illustrated his conclusions by excerpts and digressions remote from the subject presumed to be under treatment, and which had first started this train of thought. Until now the French had prescribed the sole standard of good taste. Lessing wished to destroy this unthinking veneration, and lead his nation back to the true sources of inspiration, and he fought with an iconoclastic zeal against all distortions, and all confusions of æsthetic boundaries. In a measure, indeed, the 'Dramaturgy' supplements the 'Laokoon', for in the latter work Lessing had distinctly referred to the drama as the highest expression of poetry, and he had placed poetry above the arts of design in its results and capacities. Once more he displays his subtlety in discriminating between the various constituents of the complex feelings produced by art, and his rare faculty of combining æsthetic sensibility with logical criticism constitutes one of his grand claims to originality. The 'Dramaturgy' must be regarded rather as a collection of [Greek: epea pteroenta], than a systematic book. This remark applies, indeed, to all Lessing's prose writings.

The 'Dramaturgy' was not the only work that occupied Lessing at Hamburg. A certain Professor Klotz had been for some time past attacking Lessing's writings, and had done this in a spirit of arrogant superiority that roused his ire. A remark that Lessing had been guilty of "an unpardonable fault," in an archaeological matter, wherein Klotz himself was plainly in error, brought matters to a crisis, and drew down on Klotz a series of 'Letters treating of Antiquarian Subjects,' that utterly demolished both the man and his conclusions. A private feud gave occasion to this publication, but, like all that Lessing wrote, it is full of matter of permanent worth. Cameos and engraved gems form the ground-work of the controversy that was waged fast and furiously for some months, until at last Lessing silenced his adversary. The archaeological studies that it necessitated had awakened afresh Lessing's artistic interests and provoked the charming little essay, 'How the Ancients represented Death,' that starting as a polemic against Klotz, ended in becoming a finished and exquisite whole.

About this time (1772) Lessing received encouragement from Vienna to settle in the Austrian dominions, but as the offers concerned the theatre he declined compliance, still feeling sore from his late experiences. The old desire to visit Italy was once more uppermost, his restless activity had exhausted the slender intellectual resources of Hamburg. But he was once more hampered by money difficulties. He vacillated for a while between remaining and leaving, and finally accepted an appointment at the Brunswick Court as librarian of the Wolfenbüttel Library, with the proviso that this appointment should not permanently interfere with his projected Italian journey. His salary was to be 600 thalers, with an official residence; his duties were undefined. The Duke, who recognised Lessing's eminence, wished to attach him to his Court, and desired that Lessing should use the library for his personal convenience rather than as its custodian. The post promised well, though Lessing entered on it with reluctance; his love of freedom causing him at any time to shrink from any definite appointment. He loved, as he himself expressed it, to be like the sparrow on the housetops, but considerations hitherto unknown contributed to induce him to seek a settled post and establish his affairs on a more permanent basis than heretofore. The wish to marry had become awakened in him at the mature age of forty; he had made the acquaintance in Hamburg of a Madame Koenig, a widow, the first woman who had seriously roused his interest. Business complications of her late husband's and the charge of a family made union impossible for some little time, but Lessing had not been long at Wolfenbüttel before a formal engagement was entered upon whose ultimate fulfilment it was confidently expected would not be too long deferred. It was deferred, however, for the space of six years--years that were the weariest and saddest in Lessing's life, and mark the only time when his healthful optimism, his sanguine cheerfulness broke into complaint and yielded to depression of mind. Physical causes were at work as well as mental. Wolfenbüttel was an old deserted capital, devoid of society, and Lessing, who loved to mingle with his fellow-creatures, saw himself banished from any intelligent human intercourse, unless he undertook the somewhat expensive journey to Brunswick. At Hamburg he had lived in an active and intellectual circle; here he found himself thrown back upon himself and books. His heart and thoughts were with Madame Koenig, her business affairs went badly; their rare meetings only further strengthened his desire to claim as his own this the only woman who understood him and felt with him. The promised leave of absence, too, for Italy, was constantly deferred under futile prbooks, and thus depressed, dispirited, Lessing could not feel within himself the capability of original production. At the same time he did not feel it right or wise to neglect the resources placed within his reach by the excellent library of which he was custodian; he ransacked its manuscript treasures, and published some of them. He also in a brief period of renewed happiness and mental vigour, that followed a visit to Hamburg and a meeting with Madame Koenig, wrote his famous tragedy 'Emilia Galotti.'

This drama is an illustration of the principles enunciated by Lessing in his 'Dramaturgy;' its condensation is a protest against the verbosity of the French, its form an approach to Shakespeare; while its tendency is a stricture on the abuses practised at petty Courts. The latter was a bold innovation, considering that at the time Lessing wrote and produced this play he was himself the servant of a Court, enlightened and liberal it is true, but libertine and despotic; and that parallels could not fail to be drawn by the malevolent between Brunswick and Guastalla. The story is a modernised version of that of Virginia, but the catastrophe is not equally harmonious, because not so absolutely necessitated by the conditions of modern society as by those of the ancient world. Still the play is in many respects inimitable; the manner in which the story is developed and unravelled renders it a model to young dramatists; nothing superfluous, nothing obscure, no needless retrogressions, no violent transitions. Lessing's contemporaries were not slow to recognise that he had presented them with a master-piece. He himself after its completion had sunk back into his former mood of irritated depression, and he would not even be present at the first representation. This mood was in great part physical, but was also the result of circumstances. He was anxious and uneasy. The hereditary prince had held out hopes to him, but their fulfilment was too long deferred; Madame Koenig's affairs grew more and more involved, the solitude of Wolfenbüttel more and more arid.

At last his restless spirit could brook this position no longer. Heedless of Madame Koenig's warning prayers not to bring matters to an abrupt crisis, to have patience with the Court whose financial position at the time was truly a sorry one, Lessing one day broke away from Wolfenbüttel and appeared at Berlin, whence he applied for an extended leave of absence to Vienna, where Madame Koenig's business had lately required her presence. He reassures her that he has not burnt his ships behind him, and this was true, but he wished to ascertain for himself how matters stood with her, and also if there was, any opening for him in that capital. He arrived at Vienna in March 1775, and found Madame Koenig's affairs so far advanced towards settlement as to justify him in entertaining hopes of a speedy union.

But the evil fortune that seemed to run like a fatal thread through Lessing's life whenever he found himself near the fulfilment of an ardent desire again asserted itself. He had not been ten days in Vienna before one of the younger princes of the house of Brunswick arrived there also on his way to Italy. He wished to have Lessing as his travelling companion. Thus a long cherished desire was to be realised at the moment when a far stronger one had usurped its place. Lessing debated for some time what he should do, but on consideration with Madame Koenig, it was decided to be unwise to offend the prince whose earnest wish for Lessing's companionship was supported by the Empress Maria Theresa, and moreover the projected journey was only to extend over eight weeks; consequently the parting and delay would be brief, while the ultimate consequences of having obliged the ducal house at personal inconvenience might be incalculable. The journey extended to nine months, and was a period of misery to Lessing. He never received a line from Madame Koenig all this time, her letters having all miscarried, thanks to the officious zeal of her Vienna acquaintances, and he tortured himself with fears lest she were ill or dead. Neither did he write to her, nor keep a diary, beyond the very briefest records of some discoveries in libraries. Not a word about the art, the scenery of the land he had so craved to see. He perceived quickly enough that it could offer all, and more than he had anticipated, but, added to his private anxieties, this travelling in the suite of a prince was not propitious to the proper enjoyment of Italy. Receptions, formal dinners, deputations, at all of which Lessing had to be present, engrossed the precious time that should have been devoted to more intellectual pursuits.

Transeat cum cæteris erroribus, Lessing might again have written when he returned to Germany in December. He hastened to Vienna to learn news of his beloved, and there a whole packet of her letters were put into his hands--those letters the want of which had preyed upon his heart. He was now more fully determined than ever to bring matters to a crisis; if the Brunswick Court would not improve his position he would seek employment elsewhere; at the very worst he could not fare worse than he was at present faring. His resolution triumphed, his salary was raised, his position improved, and on the 8th of October, 1776, he was at last united to the woman of his choice.

Then followed a very heyday of happiness to Lessing; he was at last content, at peace; his wife understood him and felt with him; she was his stay, his pride, his joy. But once more the evil fate was at work, and could not permit of ease to this poor victim she pursued so relentlessly. Early in January (1778) Lessing saw his wife and baby boy laid in the grave. The brief sunshine which had illumined his path had vanished for ever.

The letters written by him at the time are more pathetic in their stoic brevity than folios of lamentations. There were no further hopes of happiness for him on earth; he must just resign himself and work on at his appointed labour until he too should be laid to rest. He turned with an ardour that was almost furious to encounter the assailants of his last literary publication. Since his appointment as Wolfenbüttel librarian Lessing had from time to time published some of its manuscript treasures, and among these he had inserted portions of a work that had been intrusted to him, and which he deemed ought not to be withheld from the light of day. These were the famous Wolfenbüttel Fragments issued anonymously by Lessing, but really the work of a deceased Hamburger, Professor Reimarus. Their publication drew down upon Lessing a fury of rancorous abuse, and involved him in a vortex of controversy that lasted till his death. The chief and most vehement of his opponents was Pastor J. M. Goeze, whose insulting polemic reached him by the bedside of his dying wife. Its malignant and unjustified attacks roused Lessing's energy. He assailed Goeze with all the strength of his grief, for which he was thankful to find a safety-valve in controversy. The work of Reimarus had advocated rationalism; Lessing had distinctly placed himself in position of editor, and pronounced that he did not of necessity subscribe to the opinions therein enunciated, but he found in their reasoning much food for thought, and with his almost romantic passion for truth he deemed that such matter should not be withheld from the world. Goeze chose to consider that Lessing was sailing under false colours, that the fragments were his own composition, and that he was undermining the national faith. Lessing replied to Goeze's insults by a series of fourteen letters, entitled 'Anti-Goeze,' which actually silenced his opponent, who had never been known before to allow an adversary the last word. They are written in a serio-comic tone, and for sparkling wit, trenchant sarcasm, and dramatic dialectics surpass anything ever penned by Lessing. No less admirable is his accurate theological knowledge and his large-minded comprehension of the purposes of religion.

The same noble spirit pervades his 'Nathan the Wise,' which he wrote about this time as a relief to his controversial discussions, and as another protest against the narrow-minded assumptions of the professional theologians. Lessing had ever contended that the stage might prove as useful a pulpit as the church, and in 'Nathan' he strove to preach the universal brotherhood of mankind; its hero is a Jew of ideal and pure morality. The whole purpose of the drama was a stricture on class prejudices and an enunciation of the innate truth that underlies all forms of creeds. The play is too well known even in this country to require much comment; it is a noble monument of toleration and large-mindedness, and the fact that he could produce it under the load of a crushing sorrow speaks volumes for the true earnest religious faith that dwelt in Lessing's nature. At the time its pure tendencies were not understood. Lessing had progressed beyond the comprehension of his age, and the inevitable consequences ensued,--misconstruction and mental loneliness. He began to be regarded with suspicion as a dangerous innovator; even old friends held aloof in doubt. Meanwhile his only comfort remained in his home, in the step-children, whom his wife had brought thither. His step-daughter was his tender and attentive companion, for since his wife's death Lessing's health had declined, and he required care. Though no trace of impaired vigour appears in his writings of the period, which indeed are animated by an exhilarating vitality, yet too evident traces of impaired vigour appeared in himself. He grew languid, an excessive inclination to sleep overpowered him; he suffered from attacks of vertigo. Yet as long as he could hold a pen he should write, he told his brother,--write in the cause of what he firmly held to be the truth.

A small pamphlet, consisting of a hundred propositions, entitled 'The Education of the Human Race,' was his next production, a work pregnant with thought that opens out wide vistas of knowledge and progress to mankind. Lessing indeed was the first man of his century to formulate the modern doctrine of progress; he preached a true millennium of toleration, love, and knowledge; he distinctly proclaimed his faith in the immortality of the soul. 'The Education of the Human Race' is a splendid disavowal of his enemies' calumnious assertions. It was a glorious swan-song, wherewith he lulled himself into eternal peace.

On one of his official visits to Brunswick, Lessing was overtaken by a paralytic stroke. On the 15th of February, 1781, he passed away. He died as he lived, nobly, in a reverent assurance that he had fought a good fight on earth in the cause of truth and enlightenment, progress and humanity.

Time, the true criterion of human fame, has not only left his glory undiminished, but has augmented it, as popular intelligence has gradually arisen to the comprehension of its many-sided significance. It will be long before we have outgrown Lessing, if indeed that time can ever come. And even if some things in his writings may seem narrow or antiquated to our vision, we may readily pass them over to arrive at matters eternally true, exalted, sublime. Truth was the main purpose of all he wrote, and truth is for all ages and all time. Lessing was one of the truly great ones of this earth, and petty cavillers should lay to heart the words of another wise man, the author of 'The Imitation:'

"All perfection in this world has some imperfection coupled with it, and none of our investigations are without some obscurity."

Helen Zimmern

.

MISS SARA SAMPSON.

A TRAGEDY IN FIVE ACTS.

Miss Sara Sampson, the first of Lessing's tragedies, was completed in the year 1755, while Lessing was at Potsdam. In the same year it was represented at Frankfort-on-the-Oder, and was very well received. It was afterwards translated and acted in France, where it also met with success.

The present is the first English translation which has appeared.

DRAMATIS PERSONÆ.

Sir William Sampson

.

Miss Sara Sampson

, his daughter.

Mellefont

.

Marwood

, formerly Mellefont's

mistress.

Arabella

, a child, daughter of Marwood

.

Waitwell

, an old servant of Sir William

.

Norton

, servant of Mellefont

.

Betty, Sara's

maid.

Hannah, Marwood's

maid.

The Innkeeper

and others.

MISS SARA SAMPSON.

ACT I.

Scene

I.--A room in an inn

.

Sir William Sampson, Waitwell

.

SIR WILLIAM.

My daughter, here? Here in this wretched inn?

WAITWELL.

No doubt, Mellefont has purposely selected the most wretched one in the town. The wicked always seek the darkness, because they are wicked. But what would it help them, could they even hide themselves from the whole world? Conscience after all is more powerful than the accusations of a world. Ah, you are weeping again, again, Sir!--Sir!

SIR WILLIAM.

Let me weep, my honest old servant! Or does she not, do you think, deserve my tears?

WAITWELL.

Alas! She deserves them, were they tears of blood.

SIR WILLIAM.

Well, let me weep!

WAITWELL.

The best, the loveliest, the most innocent child that ever lived beneath the sun, must thus be led astray! Oh, my Sara, my little Sara! I have watched thee grow; a hundred times have I carried thee as a child in these arms, have I admired thy smiles, thy lispings. From every childish look beamed forth the dawn of an intelligence, a kindliness, a----

SIR WILLIAM.

Oh, be silent! Does not the present rend my heart enough? Will you make my tortures more infernal still by recalling past happiness? Change your tone, if you will do me a service. Reproach me, make of my tenderness a crime, magnify my daughter's fault; fill me with abhorrence of her, if you can; stir up anew my revenge against her cursed seducer; say, that Sara never was virtuous, since she so lightly ceased to be so; say that she never loved me, since she clandestinely forsook me!

WAITWELL.

If I said that, I should utter a lie, a shameless, wicked lie. It might come to me again on my death-bed, and I, old wretch, would die in despair. No, little Sara has loved her father; and doubtless, doubtless she loves him yet. If you will only be convinced of this, I shall see her again in your arms this very day.

SIR WILLIAM.

Yes, Waitwell, of this alone I ask to be convinced. I cannot any longer live without her; she is the support of my age, and if she does not help to sweeten the sad remaining days of my life, who shall do it? If she loves me still, her error is forgotten. It was the error of a tender-hearted maiden, and her flight was the result of her remorse. Such errors are better than forced virtues. Yet I feel, Waitwell, I feel it, even were these errors real crimes, premeditated vices--even then I should forgive her. I would rather be loved by a wicked daughter, than by none at all.

WAITWELL.

Dry your tears, dear sir! I hear some one. It will be the landlord coming to welcome us.

Scene

II.

The Landlord, Sir William Sampson, Waitwell

.

LANDLORD.

So early, gentlemen, so early? You are welcome; welcome, Waitwell! You have doubtless been travelling all night! Is that the gentleman, of whom you spoke to me yesterday?

WAITWELL.

Yes, it is he, and I hope that in accordance with what we settled----

LANDLORD.

I am entirely at your service, my lord. What is it to me, whether I know or not, what cause has brought you hither, and why you wish to live in seclusion in my house? A landlord takes his money and lets his guests do as they think best. Waitwell, it is true, has told me that you wish to observe the stranger a little, who has been staying here for a few weeks with his young wife, but I hope that you will not cause him any annoyance. You would bring my house into ill repute and certain people would fear to stop here. Men like us must live on people of all kinds.

SIR WILLIAM.

Do not fear; only conduct me to the room which Waitwell has ordered for me; I come here for an honourable purpose.

LANDLORD.

I have no wish to know your secrets, my lord! Curiosity is by no means a fault of mine. I might for instance have known long ago, who the stranger is, on whom you want to keep a watch, but I have no wish to know. This much however I have discovered, that he must have eloped with the young lady. The poor little wife--or whatever she may be!--remains the whole day long locked up in her room, and cries.

SIR WILLIAM.

And cries?

LANDLORD.

Yes, and cries; but, my lord, why do your tears fall? The young lady must interest you deeply. Surely you are not----

WAITWELL.

Do not detain him any longer!

LANDLORD.

Come, come! One wall only will separate you from the lady in whom you are so much interested, and who may be----

WAITWELL.

You mean then at any cost to know, who----

LANDLORD.

No, Waitwell! I have no wish to know anything.

WAITWELL.

Make haste, then, and take us to our rooms, before the whole house begins to stir.

LANDLORD.

Will you please follow me, then, my lord? (Exeunt.)

Scene

III.--Mellefont's

room

.

Mellefont, Norton

.

MELLEFONT (in dressing-gown, sitting in an easy chair)

.

Another night, which I could not have spent more cruelly on the rack!--(calls) Norton!--I must make haste to get sight of a face or two. If I remained alone with my thoughts any longer, they might carry me too far. Hey, Norton! He is still asleep. But is not it cruel of me, not to let the poor devil sleep? How happy he is! However, I do not wish any one about me to be happy! Norton!

NORTON (coming)

.

Sir!

MELLEFONT.

Dress me!--Oh, no sour looks please! When I shall be able to sleep longer myself I will let you do the same. If you wish to do your duty, at least have pity on me.

NORTON.

Pity, sir! Pity on you? I know better where pity is due.

MELLEFONT.

And where then?

NORTON.

Ah, let me dress you and don't ask.

MELLEFONT.

Confound it! Are your reproofs then to awaken together with my conscience? I understand you; I know on whom you expend your pity. But I will do justice to her and to myself. Quite right, do not have any pity on me! Curse me in your heart; but--curse yourself also!

NORTON.

Myself also?

MELLEFONT.

Yes, because you serve a miserable wretch, whom earth ought not to bear, and because you have made yourself a partaker in his crimes.

NORTON.

I made myself a partaker in your crimes? In what way?

MELLEFONT.

By keeping silent about them.

NORTON.

Well, that is good! A word would have cost me my neck in the heat of your passions. And, besides, did I not find you already so bad, when I made your acquaintance, that all hope of amendment was vain? What a life I have seen you leading from the first moment! In the lowest society of gamblers and vagrants--I call them what they were without regard to their knightly titles and such like--in this society you squandered a fortune which might have made a way for you to an honourable position. And your culpable intercourse with all sorts of women, especially with the wicked Marwood----

MELLEFONT.

Restore me--restore me to that life. It was virtue compared with the present one. I spent my fortune; well! The punishment follows, and I shall soon enough feel all the severity and humiliation of want. I associated with vicious women; that may be. I was myself seduced more often than I seduced others; and those whom I did seduce wished it. But--I still had no ruined virtue upon my conscience. I had carried off no Sara from the house of a beloved father and forced her to follow a scoundrel, who was no longer free. I had----who comes so early to me?

Scene

IV.

Betty

, Mellefont

, Norton

.

NORTON.

It is Betty.

MELLEFONT.

Up already, Betty? How is your mistress?

BETTY.

How is she? (sobbing.) It was long after midnight before I could persuade her to go to bed. She slept a few moments; but God, what a sleep that must have been! She started suddenly, sprang up and fell into my arms, like one pursued by a murderer. She trembled, and a cold perspiration started on her pale face. I did all I could to calm her, but up to this morning she has only answered me with silent tears. At length she sent me several times to your door to listen whether you were up. She wishes to speak to you. You alone can comfort her. O do so, dearest sir, do so! My heart will break, if she continues to fret like this.

MELLEFONT.

Go, Betty! Tell her, I shall be with her in a moment,
BETTY.
No, she wishes to come to you herself.
MELLEFONT.
Well, tell her, then, that I am awaiting her----
(Exit Betty.)
Scene
V.
Mellefont
, Norton
.
NORTON.
O God, the poor young lady!
MELLEFONT.
Whose feelings is this exclamation of yours meant to rouse? See, the first tear which I have shed since my childhood is running down my cheek. A bad preparation for receiving one who seeks comfort. But why does she seek it from me? Yet where else shall she seek it? I must collect myself (drying his eyes). Where is the old firmness with which I could see a beautiful eye in tears? Where is the gift of dissimulation gone by which I could be and could say whatsoever I wished? She will come now and weep tears that brook no resistance. Confused and ashamed I shall stand before her; like a convicted criminal I shall stand before her. Counsel me, what shall I do? What shall I say?
NORTON.
You shall do what she asks of you!
MELLEFONT.
I shall then perpetrate a fresh act of cruelty against her. She is wrong to blame me for delaying a ceremony which cannot be performed in this country without the greatest injury to us.
NORTON.
Well, leave it, then. Why do we delay? Why do you let one day after the other pass, and one week after the other? Just give me the order, and you will be safe on board to-morrow! Perhaps her grief will not follow her over the ocean; she may leave part of it behind, and in another land may----
MELLEFONT.
I hope that myself. Silence! She is coming! How my heart throbs!
Scene
VI.
Sara
, Mellefont
, Norton
.
MELLEFONT (advancing towards her
).
You have had a restless night, dearest Sara.
SARA.

Alas, Mellefont, if it were nothing but a restless night.

MELLEFONT (to his servant)

.

Leave us!

NORTON (aside, in going)

.

I would not stay if I was paid in gold for every moment.

Scene

VII.

Sara

, Mellefont

.

MELLEFONT.

You are faint, dearest Sara! You must sit down!

SARA (sits down)

.

I trouble you very early! Will you forgive me that with the morning I again begin my complaints?

MELLEFONT.

Dearest Sara, you mean to say that you cannot forgive me, because another morning has dawned, and I have not yet put an end to your complaints?

SARA.

What is there that I would not forgive you? You know what I have already forgiven you. But the ninth week, Mellefont! the ninth week begins to-day, and this miserable house still sees me in just the same position as on the first day.

MELLEFONT.

You doubt my love?

SARA.

I doubt your love? No, I feel my misery too much, too much to wish to deprive myself of this last and only solace.

MELLEFONT.

How, then, can you be uneasy about the delay of a ceremony?

SARA.

Ah, Mellefont! Why is it that we think so differently about this ceremony! Yield a little to the woman's way of thinking! I imagine in it a more direct consent from Heaven. In vain did I try again, only yesterday, in the long tedious evening, to adopt your ideas, and to banish from my breast the doubt which just now--not for the first time, you have deemed the result of my distrust. I struggled with myself; I was clever enough to deafen my understanding; but my heart and my feeling quickly overthrew this toilsome structure of reason. Reproachful voices roused me from my sleep, and my imagination united with them to torment me. What pictures, what dreadful pictures hovered about me! I would willingly believe them to be dreams----

MELLEFONT.

What? Could my sensible Sara believe them to be anything else? Dreams, my dearest, dreams!--How unhappy is man!--Did not his Creator find tortures enough for him in the realm of reality? Had he also to create in him the still more spacious realm of imagination in order to increase them?

SARA.

Do not accuse Heaven! It has left the imagination in our power. She is guided by our acts; and when these are in accordance with our duties and with virtue the imagination serves only to increase our peace and happiness. A single act, Mellefont, a single blessing bestowed upon us by a messenger of peace, in the name of the Eternal One, can restore my shattered imagination again. Do you still hesitate to do a few days sooner for love of me, what in any case you mean to do at some future time? Have pity on me, and consider that, although by this you may be freeing me only from torments of the imagination, yet these imagined torments are torments, and are real torments for her who feels them. Ah! could I but tell you the terrors of the last night half as vividly as I have felt them. Wearied with crying and grieving--my only occupations--I sank down on my bed with half-closed eyes. Sly nature wished to recover itself a moment, to collect new tears. But hardly asleep yet, I suddenly saw myself on the steepest peak of a terrible rock. You went on before, and I followed with tottering, anxious steps, strengthened now and then by a glance which you threw back upon me. Suddenly I heard behind me a gentle call, which bade me stop. It was my father's voice--I unhappy one, can I forget nothing which is his? Alas if his memory renders him equally cruel service; if he too cannot forget me!--But he has forgotten me. Comfort! cruel comfort for his Sara!--But, listen, Mellefont! In turning round to this well-known voice, my foot slipped; I reeled, and was on the point of falling down the precipice, when just in time, I felt myself held back by one who resembled myself. I was just returning her my passionate thanks, when she drew a dagger from her bosom. "I saved you," she cried, "to ruin you!" She lifted her armed hand--and--! I awoke with the blow. Awake, I still felt all the pain which a mortal stab must give, without the pleasure which it brings--the hope for the end of grief in the end of life.

MELLEFONT.

Ah! dearest Sara, I promise you the end of your grief, without the end of your life, which would certainly be the end of mine also. Forget the terrible tissue of a meaningless dream!

SARA.

I look to you for the strength to be able to forget it. Be it love or seduction, happiness or unhappiness which threw me into your arms, I am yours in my heart and will remain so for ever. But I am not yet yours in the eyes of that Judge, who has threatened to punish the smallest transgressions of His law----

MELLEFONT.

Then may all the punishment fall upon me alone!

SARA.

What can fall upon you, without touching me too? But do not misinterpret my urgent request! Another woman, after having forfeited her honour by an error like mine, might perhaps only seek to regain a part of it by a legal union. I do not think of that, Mellefont, because I do not wish to know of any other honour in this world than that of loving you. I do not wish to be united to you for the world's sake but for my own. And I will willingly bear the shame of not appearing to be so, when I am united to you. You need not then, if you do not wish, acknowledge me to be your wife, you may call me what you will! I will not bear your name; you shall keep our union as secret as you think good, and may I always be unworthy of it, if I ever harbour the thought of drawing any other advantage from it than the appeasing of my conscience.

MELLEFONT.

Stop, Sara, or I shall die before your eyes. How wretched I am, that I have not the courage to make you more wretched still! Consider that you have given yourself up to my guidance; consider that it is my duty to look to our future, and that I must at present be deaf to your complaints, if I will not hear you utter more grievous complaints throughout the rest of your life. Have you then forgotten what I have so often represented to you in justification of my conduct?

SARA.

I have not forgotten it, Mellefont! You wish first to secure a certain bequest. You wish first to secure temporal goods, and you let me forfeit eternal ones, perhaps, through it.

MELLEFONT.

Ah, Sara! If you were as certain of all temporal goods as your virtue is of the eternal ones----

SARA.

My virtue? Do not say that word! Once it sounded sweet to me, but now a terrible thunder rolls in it!

MELLEFONT.

What? Must he who is to be virtuous, never have committed a trespass? Has a single error such fatal effect that it can annihilate a whole course of blameless years? If so, no one is virtuous; virtue is then a chimera, which disperses in the air, when one thinks that one grasps it most firmly; if so, there is no Wise Being who suits our duties to our strength; if so, there is----I am frightened at the terrible conclusions in which your despondency must involve you. No, Sara, you are still the virtuous Sara that you were before your unfortunate acquaintance with me. If you look upon yourself with such cruel eyes, with what eyes must you regard me!

SARA.

With the eyes of love, Mellefont!

MELLEFONT.

I implore you, then, on my knees I implore you for the sake of this love, this generous love which overlooks all my unworthiness, to calm yourself! Have patience for a few days longer!

SARA.

A few days! How long even a single day is!

MELLEFONT.

Cursed bequest! Cursed nonsense of a dying cousin, who would only leave me his fortune on the condition that I should give my hand to a relation who hates me as much as I hate her! To you, inhuman tyrants of our freedom, be imputed all the misfortune, all the sin, into which your compulsion forces us. Could I but dispense with this degrading inheritance. As long as my father's fortune sufficed for my maintenance, I always scorned it, and did not even think it worthy of mentioning. But now, now, when I should like to possess all the treasures of the world only to lay them at the feet of my Sara, now, when I must contrive at least to let her appear in the world as befits her station, now I must have recourse to it.

SARA.

Which probably will not be successful after all.

MELLEFONT.

You always forbode the worst. No, the lady whom this also concerns is not disinclined to enter into a sort of agreement with me. The fortune is to be divided, and as she cannot enjoy the whole with me, she is willing to let me buy my liberty with half of it. I am every hour expecting the final intelligence, the delay of which alone has so prolonged our sojourn here. As soon as I receive it, we shall not remain here one moment longer. We will immediately cross to France, dearest Sara, where you shall find new friends, who already look forward to the pleasure of seeing and loving you. And these new friends shall be the witnesses of our union----

SARA.

They shall be the witnesses of our union? Cruel man, our union, then, is not to be in my native land? I shall leave my country as a criminal? And as such, you think, I should have the courage to trust myself to the ocean. The heart of him must be calmer or more impious than mine, who, only for a moment, can see with indifference between himself and destruction, nothing but a quivering plank. Death would roar at me in every wave that struck against the vessel, every wind would howl its curses after me from my native shore, and the slightest storm would seem a sentence of death pronounced upon me. No, Mellefont, you cannot be so cruel to me! If I live to see the completion of this agreement, you must not grudge another day, to be spent here. This must be the day, on which you shall teach me to forget the tortures of all these tearful days. This must be the sacred day--alas! which day will it be?

MELLEFONT.

But do you consider, Sara, that our marriage here would lack those ceremonies which are due to it?

SARA.

A sacred act does not acquire more force through ceremonies.

MELLEFONT.

But----

SARA.

I am astonished. You surely will not insist on such a trivial prbook? O Mellefont, Mellefont! had I not made for myself an inviolable law, never to doubt the sincerity of your love, this circumstance might----But too much of this already, it might seem as if I had been doubting it even now.

MELLEFONT.

The first moment of your doubt would be the last moment of my life! Alas, Sara, what have I done, that you should remind me even of the possibility of it? It is true the confessions, which I have made to you without fear, of my early excesses cannot do me honour, but they should at least awaken confidence. A coquettish Marwood held me in her meshes, because I felt for her that which is so often taken for love which it so rarely is. I should still bear her shameful fetters, had not Heaven, which perhaps did not think my heart quite unworthy to bum with better flames, taken pity on me. To see you, dearest

Sara, was to forget all Marwoods! But how dearly have you paid for taking me out of such hands! I had grown too familiar with vice, and you know it too little----

SARA.

Let us think no more of it.

Scene

VIII.

Norton, Mellefont, Sara

.

MELLEFONT.

What do you want?

NORTON.

While I was standing before the house, a servant gave me this letter. It is directed to you, sir!

MELLEFONT.

To me? Who knows my name here? (looking at the letter). Good heavens!

SARA.

You are startled.

MELLEFONT.

But without cause, Sara, as I now perceive. I was mistaken in the handwriting.

SARA.

May the contents be as agreeable to you as you can wish.

MELLEFONT.

I suspect that they will be of very little importance.

SARA.

One is less constrained when one is alone, so allow me to retire to my room again.

MELLEFONT.

You entertain suspicions, then, about it?

SARA.

Not at all, Mellefont.

MELLEFONT (going with her to the back of the stage)

.

I shall be with you in a moment, dearest Sara.

Scene

IX.

Mellefont, Norton

.

MELLEFONT (still looking at the letter)

.

Just Heaven!

NORTON.

Woe to you, if it is only just!

MELLEFONT.

Is it possible? I see this cursed handwriting again and am not chilled with terror? Is it she? Is it not she? Why do I still doubt? It is she! Alas, friend, a letter from Marwood! What fury, what demon has betrayed my abode to her? What does she still want from me? Go, make preparations immediately that we may get away from here. Yet stop! Perhaps it is unnecessary; perhaps the contempt of my farewell letters has only caused Marwood to reply with equal contempt. There, open the letter; read it! I am afraid to do it myself.

NORTON (reads)

.

"If you will deign, Mellefont, to glance at the name which you will find at the bottom of the page, it will be to me as though I had written you the longest of letters."

MELLEFONT.

Curse the name! Would I had never heard it! Would it could be erased from the book of the living!

NORTON (reads on)

.

"The labour of finding you out has been sweetened by the love which helped me in my search."

MELLEFONT.

Love? Wanton creature! You profane the words which belong to virtue alone.

NORTON (continues)

.

"Love has done more still"----

MELLEFONT.

I tremble----

NORTON.

"It has brought me to you"----

MELLEFONT.

Traitor, what are you reading? (snatches the letter from his hand and reads himself). "I am here; and it rests with you, whether you will await a visit from me, or whether you will anticipate mine by one from you. Marwood." What a thunderbolt! She is here! Where is she? She shall atone for this audacity with her life!

NORTON.

With her life? One glance from her and you will be again at her feet. Take care what you do! You must not speak with her, or the misfortunes of your poor young lady will be complete.

MELLEFONT.

O, wretched man that I am! No, I must speak with her! She would go even into Sara's room in search of me, and would vent all her rage on the innocent girl.

NORTON.

But, sir----

MELLEFONT.

Not a word! Let me see (looking at the letter) whether she has given the address. Here it is! Come, show me the way!

(Exeunt).

ACT II.

Scene

I.--Marwood's

room in another inn

.

Marwood

(in negligée), Hannah

.

MARWOOD.

I hope Belfort has delivered the letter at the right address, Hannah?

HANNAH.

He has.

MARWOOD.

To him himself?

HANNAH.

To his servant.

MARWOOD.

I am all impatience to see what effect it will have. Do I not seem a little uneasy to you, Hannah? And I am so. The traitor! But gently! I must not on any account give way to anger. Forbearance, love, entreaty are the only weapons which I can use against him, if I rightly understand his weak side.

HANNAH.

But if he should harden himself against them?

MARWOOD.

If he should harden himself against them? Then I shall not be angry. I shall rave! I feel it, Hannah, and I would rather do so to begin with.

HANNAH.

Calm yourself! He may come at any moment.

MARWOOD.

I only hope he may come; I only hope he has not decided to await me on his own ground. But do you know, Hannah, on what I chiefly found my hopes of drawing away the faithless man from this new object of his love? On our Bella!

HANNAH.

It is true, she is a little idol to him; and there could not have been a happier idea than that of bringing her with you.

MARWOOD.

Even if his heart should be deaf to an old love, the language of blood will at least be audible to him. He tore the child from my arms a short time ago under the prbook of wishing to give her an education such as she could not have with me. It is only by an artifice that I have been able to get her again from the lady who had charge of her. He had paid more than a year in advance, and had given strict orders the very day before his flight that they should by no means give admission to a certain Marwood, who would perhaps come and give herself out as mother of the child. From this order I see the distinction which he draws between us. He regards Arabella as a precious portion of himself, and me as an unfortunate creature, of whose charms he has grown weary.

HANNAH.

What ingratitude!

MARWOOD.

Ah, Hannah! Nothing more infallibly draws down ingratitude, than favours for which no gratitude would be too great. Why have I shown him these fatal favours? Ought I not to have foreseen that they could not always retain their value with him; that their value rested on the difficulty in the way of their enjoyment, and that the latter must disappear with the charm of our looks which the hand of time imperceptibly but surely effaces?

HANNAH.

You, Madam, have not anything to fear for a long time from this dangerous hand! To my mind your beauty is so far from having passed the point of its brightest bloom, that it is rather advancing towards it, and would enchain fresh hearts for you every day if you only would give it the permission.

MARWOOD.

Be silent, Hannah! You flatter me on an occasion which makes me suspicious of any flattery. It is nonsense to speak of new conquests, if one has not even sufficient power to retain possession of those which one has already made.

Scene

II.

A Servant, Marwood, Hannah

.

SERVANT.

Some one wishes to have the honour of speaking with you.

MARWOOD.

Who is it?

SERVANT.

I suppose it is the gentleman to whom the letter was addressed. At least the servant to whom I delivered it is with him.

MARWOOD.

Mellefont!--Quick, bring him up! (Exit Servant

.) Ah, Hannah! He is here now! How shall I receive him? What shall I say? What look shall I put on? Is this calm enough? Just see!

HANNAH.

Anything but calm.

MARWOOD.

This, then?

HANNAH.

Throw a little sweetness into it.

MARWOOD.

So, perhaps?

HANNAH.

Too sad.

MARWOOD.

Would this smile do?

HANNAH.

Perfectly--only less constrained--He is coming.

Scene

III.

Mellefont, Marwood, Hannah

.

MELLEFONT (entering with wild gestures)

.

Ha! Marwood----
MARWOOD (running to meet him smiling, and with open arms)

.

Ah, Mellefont!
MELLEFONT (aside)

.

The murderess! What a look!
MARWOOD.
I must embrace you, faithless, dear fugitive! Share my joy with me! Why do you tear yourself from my caresses!
MELLEFONT.
I expected, Marwood, that you would receive me differently.
MARWOOD.
Why differently? With more love, perhaps? With more delight? Alas, how unhappy I am, that I cannot express all that I feel! Do you not see, Mellefont, do you not see that joy, too, has its tears? Here they fall, the offspring of sweetest delight! But alas, vain tears! His hand does not dry you!
MELLEFONT.
Marwood, the time is gone, when such words would have charmed me. You must speak now with me in another tone. I come to hear your last reproaches and to answer them.
MARWOOD.
Reproaches? What reproaches should I have for you, Mellefont? None!
MELLEFONT.
Then you might have spared yourself the journey, I should think.
MARWOOD.
Dearest, capricious heart. Why will you forcibly compel me to recall a trifle which I forgave you the same moment I heard of it? Does a passing infidelity which your gallantry, but not your heart, has caused, deserve these reproaches? Come, let us laugh at it!
MELLEFONT.
You are mistaken; my heart is more concerned in it, than it ever was in all our love affairs, upon which I cannot now look back but with disgust.
MARWOOD.
Your heart, Mellefont, is a good little fool. It lets your imagination persuade it to whatever it will. Believe me, I know it better than you do yourself! Were it not the best, the most faithful of hearts, should I take such pains to keep it?
MELLEFONT.
To keep it? You have never possessed it, I tell you.
MARWOOD.
And I tell you, that in reality I possess it still!
MELLEFONT.

Marwood! if I knew that you still possessed one single fibre of it, I would tear it out of my breast here before your eyes.

MARWOOD.

You would see that you were tearing mine out at the same time. And then, then these hearts would at last attain that union which they have sought so often upon our lips.

MELLEFONT (aside)

.

What a serpent! Flight will be the best thing here.--Just tell me briefly, Marwood, why you have followed me, and what you still desire of me! But tell it me without this smile, without this look, in which a whole' hell of seduction lurks and terrifies me.

MARWOOD (insinuatingly)

.

Just listen, my dear Mellefont! I see your position now. Your desires and your taste are at present your tyrants. Never mind, one must let them wear themselves out. It is folly to resist them. They are most safely lulled to sleep, and at last even conquered, by giving them free scope. They wear themselves away. Can you accuse me, my fickle friend, of ever having been jealous, when more powerful charms than mine estranged you from me for a time? I never grudged you the change, by which I always won more than I lost. You returned with new ardour, with new passion to my arms, in which with light bonds, and never with heavy fetters I encompassed you. Have I not often even been your confidante though you had nothing to confide but the favours which you stole from me, in order to lavish them on others. Why should you believe then, that I would now begin to display a capriciousness just when I am ceasing, or, perhaps have already ceased, to be justified in it. If your ardour for the pretty country girl has not yet cooled down, if you are still in the first fever of your love for her; if you cannot yet do without the enjoyment she gives you; who hinders you from devoting yourself to her, as long as you think good? But must you on that account make such rash projects, and purpose to fly from the country with her?

MELLEFONT.

Marwood! You speak in perfect keeping with your character, the wickedness of which I never understood so well as I do now, since, in the society of a virtuous woman, I have learned to distinguish love from licentiousness.

MARWOOD.

Indeed! Your new mistress is then a girl of fine moral sentiments, I suppose? You men surely cannot know yourselves what you want. At one time you are pleased with the most wanton talk and the most unchaste jests from us, at another time we charm you, when we talk nothing but virtue, and seem to have all the seven sages on our lips. But the worst is, that you get tired of one as much as the other. We may be foolish or reasonable, worldly or spiritual; our efforts to make you constant are lost either way. The turn will come to your beautiful saint soon enough. Shall I give you a little sketch? Just at present you are in the most passionate paroxysm over her. I allow this two or at the most three days more. To this will succeed a tolerably calm love; for this I allow a week. The next week you will only think occasionally of this love. In the third week, you will have to be reminded of it; and when you have got tired of being thus reminded, you will so quickly see yourself reduced to the most utter indifference, that I can hardly allow the fourth week for this final change. This would be about a month altogether. And this month, Mellefont,

I will overlook with the greatest pleasure; but you will allow that I must not lose sight of you.

MELLEFONT.

You try all the weapons in vain which you remember to have used successfully with me in bygone days. A virtuous resolution secures me against both your tenderness and your wit. However, I will not expose myself longer to either. I go, and have nothing more to tell you but that in a few days you shall know that I am bound in such a manner as will utterly destroy all your hope of my ever returning into your sinful slavery. You will have learned my justification sufficiently from the letter which I sent to you before my departure.

MARWOOD.

It is well that you mention this letter. Tell me, who did you get to write it?

MELLEFONT.

Did not I write it myself?

MARWOOD.

Impossible! The beginning of it, in which you reckoned up--I do not know what sums--which you say you have wasted with me, must have been written by an innkeeper, and the theological part at the end by a Quaker. I will now give you a serious reply to it. As to the principal point, you well know that all the presents which you have made are still in existence. I have never considered your cheques or your jewels as my property, and I have brought them all with me to return them into the hands which entrusted them to me.

MELLEFONT.

Keep them all, Marwood!

MARWOOD.

I will not keep any of them. What right have I to them without you yourself? Although you do not love me any more, you must at least do me justice and not take me for one of those venal females, to whom it is a matter of indifference by whose booty they enrich themselves. Come, Mellefont, you shall this moment be as rich again as you perhaps might still be if you had not known me; and perhaps, too, might not be.

MELLEFONT.

What demon intent upon my destruction speaks through you now! Voluptuous Marwood does not think so nobly.

MARWOOD.

Do you call that noble? I call it only just. No, Sir, no, I do not ask that you shall account the return of your gifts as anything remarkable. It costs me nothing, and I should even consider the slightest expression of thanks on your part as an insult, which could have no other meaning than this: "Marwood, I thought you a base deceiver; I am thankful that you have not wished to be so towards me at least."

MELLEFONT.

Enough, Madam, enough! I fly, since my unlucky destiny threatens to involve me in a contest of generosity, in which I should be most unwilling to succumb.

MARWOOD.

Fly, then! But take everything with you that could remind me of you. Poor, despised, without honour, and without friends, I will then venture again to awaken your pity. I will show you in the unfortunate Marwood only a miserable woman, who has sacrificed to you her person, her honour, her virtue, and her conscience. I will remind you of the first day, when you saw and loved me; of the first, stammering, bashful confession of your love, which you made me at my feet; of the first assurance of my return of your love, which you forced from me; of the tender looks, of the passionate embraces, which followed, of the eloquent silence, when each with busy mind divined the other's most secret feelings, and read the most hidden thoughts of the soul in the languishing eye; of the trembling expectation of approaching gratification; of the intoxication of its joys; of the sweet relaxation after the fulness of enjoyment, in which the exhausted spirits regained strength for fresh delights. I shall remind you of all this, and then embrace your knees, and entreat without ceasing for the only gift, which you cannot deny me, and which I can accept without blushing--for death from your hand.

MELLEFONT.

Cruel one! I would still give even my life for you. Ask it, ask it, only do not any longer claim my love. I must leave you, Marwood, or make myself an object of loathing to the whole world. I am culpable already in that I only stand here and listen to you. Farewell, farewell!

MARWOOD (holding him back)

.

You must leave me? And what, then, do you wish, shall become of me? As I am now, I am your creature; do, then, what becomes a creator; he may not withdraw his hand from the work until he wishes to destroy it utterly. Alas, Hannah, I see now, my entreaties alone are too feeble. Go, bring my intercessor, who will now, perhaps, return to me more than she ever received from me. (Exit Hannah

).

MELLEFONT.

What intercessor, Marwood?

MARWOOD.

Ah, an intercessor of whom you would only too willingly have deprived me. Nature will take a shorter road to your heart with her grievances.

MELLEFONT.

You alarm me. Surely you have not----

Scene

IV.

Arabella, Hannah, Mellefont, Marwood

.

MELLEFONT.

What do I see? It is she! Marwood, how could you dare to----

MARWOOD.

Am I not her mother? Come, my Bella, see, here is your protector again, your friend, your .... Ah! his heart may tell him what more he can be to you than a protector and a friend.

MELLEFONT (turning away his face)

.

God, what shall I have to suffer here?

ARABELLA (advancing timidly towards him)

.

Ah, Sir! Is it you? Are you our Mellefont? No, Madam, surely, surely it is not he! Would he not look at me, if it were? Would he not hold me in his arms? He used to do so. What an unhappy child I am! How have I grieved him, this dear, dear man, who let me call him my father?

MARWOOD.

You are silent, Mellefont? You grudge the innocent child a single look?

MELLEFONT.

Ah!

ARABELLA.

Why, he sighs, Madam! What is the matter with him? Cannot we help him? Cannot I? Nor you? Then let us sigh with him! Ah, now he looks at me! No, he looks away again! He looks up to Heaven! What does he want? What does he ask from Heaven? Would that Heaven would grant him everything, even if it refused me everything for it!

MARWOOD.

Go, my child, go, fall at his feet! He wants to leave us, to leave us for ever.

ARABELLA (falling on her knees before him)

.

Here I am already. You will leave us? You will leave us for ever? Have not we already been without you for a little "for ever." Shall we have to lose you again? You have said so often that you loved us. Does one leave the people whom one loves? I cannot love you then, I suppose, for I should wish never to leave you. Never, and I never will leave you either.

MARWOOD.

I will help you in your entreaties, my child! And you must help me too! Now, Mellefont, you see me too at your feet....

MELLEFONT (stopping her, as she throws herself at his feet)

.

Marwood, dangerous Marwood! And you, too, my dearest Bella (raising her up), you too are the enemy of your Mellefont?

ARABELLA.

I your enemy?

MARWOOD.

What is your resolve?

MELLEFONT.

What it ought not to be, Marwood; what it ought not to be.

MARWOOD (embracing him)

.

Ah, I know that the honesty of your heart has always overcome the obstinacy of your desires.

MELLEFONT.

Do not importune me any longer! I am already what you wish to make me; a perjurer, a seducer, a robber, a murderer!

MARWOOD.

You will be so in imagination for a few days, and after that you will see that I have prevented you from becoming so in reality. You will return with us, won't you?

ARABELLA (insinuatingly)

.

Oh yes, do!

MELLEFONT.

Return with you! How can I?

MARWOOD.

Nothing is easier, if you only wish it.

MELLEFONT.

And my Sara----

MARWOOD.

And your Sara may look to herself.

MELLEFONT.

Ha! cruel Marwood, these words reveal the very bottom of your heart to me. And yet I, wretch, do not repent?

MARWOOD.

If you had seen the bottom of my heart, you would have discovered that it has more true pity for your Sara than you yourself have. I say true pity; for your pity is egotistic and weak. You have carried this love-affair much too far. We might let it pass, that you as a man, who by long intercourse with our sex has become master in the art of seducing, used your superiority in dissimulation and experience against such a young maiden, and did not rest until you had gained your end. You can plead the impetuosity of your passion as your excuse. But, Mellefont, you cannot justify yourself for having robbed an old father of his only child, for having rendered to an honourable old man his few remaining steps to the grave harder and more bitter, for having broken the strongest ties of nature for the sake of your desires. Repair your error, then, as far as it is possible to repair it. Give the old man his support again, and send a credulous daughter back to her home, which you need not render desolate also, because you have dishonoured it.

MELLEFONT.

This only was still wanting--that you should call in my conscience against me also. But even supposing what you say were just, must I not be brazenfaced if I should propose it myself to the unhappy girl?

MARWOOD.

Well, I will confess to you, that I have anticipated this difficulty, and considered how to spare you it. As soon as I learned your address, I informed her old father privately of it. He was beside himself with joy, and wanted to start directly. I wonder he has not yet arrived.

MELLEFONT.

What do you say?

MARWOOD.

Just await his arrival quietly, and do not let the girl notice anything. I myself will not detain you any longer. Go to her again; she might grow suspicious. But I trust that I shall see you again to-day.

MELLEFONT.

Oh, Marwood! With what feelings did I come to you, and with what must I leave you! A kiss, my dear Bella.

ARABELLA.

That was for you, now one for me! But come back again soon, do!

(Exit Mellefont

).

Scene

V.

Marwood, Arabella, Hannah

.

MARWOOD (drawing a deep breath)

.

Victory, Hannah! but a hard victory! Give me a chair, I feel quite exhausted (sitting down). He surrendered only just in time, if he had hesitated another moment, I should have shown him quite a different Marwood.

HANNAH.

Ah, Madam, what a woman you are! I should like to Bee the man who could resist you.

MARWOOD.

He has resisted me already too long. And assuredly, assuredly, I will not forgive him that he almost let me go down on my knees to him.

ARABELLA.

No, no! You must forgive him everything. He is so good, so good----

MARWOOD.

Be silent, little silly!

HANNAH.

I do not know on what side you did not attack him! But nothing, I think, touched him more, than the disinterestedness with which you offered to return all his presents to him.

MARWOOD.

I believe so too. Ha! ha! ha! (contemptuously).

HANNAH.

Why do you laugh, Madam? You really risked a great deal, if you were not in earnest about it. Suppose he had taken you at your word?

MARWOOD.

Oh, nonsense, one knows with whom one has to deal.

HANNAH.

I quite admit that! But you too, my pretty Bella, did your part excellently, excellently!

ARABELLA.

How so? Could I do it, then, any other way? I had not seen him for such a long time. I hope you are not angry, Madam, that I love him so? I love you as much as him, just as much.

MARWOOD.

Very well, I will pardon you this time that you do not love me better than him.

ARABELLA (sobbing)

.

This time?

MARWOOD.

Why, you are crying actually? What is it about?

ARABELLA.

Ah, no! I am not crying. Do not get angry! I will love you both so much, so much, that it will be impossible to love either of you more.

MARWOOD.

Very well.

ARABELLA.

I am so unhappy.

MARWOOD.

Now be quiet----but what is that?

Scene

VI.

Mellefont, Marwood, Arabella, Hannah

.

MARWOOD.

Why do you come back again so soon, Mellefont? (rising).

MELLEFONT (passionately)

.

Because I needed but a few moments to recover my senses.

MARWOOD.

Well?

MELLEFONT.

I was stunned, Marwood, but not moved! You have had all your trouble in vain. Another atmosphere than this infectious one of your room has given me back my courage and my strength, to withdraw my foot in time from this dangerous snare. Were the tricks of a Marwood not sufficiently familiar to me, unworthy wretch that I am?

MARWOOD (impatiently)

.

What language is that?

MELLEFONT.

The language of truth and anger.

MARWOOD.

Gently, Mellefont! or I too shall speak in the same language.

MELLEFONT.

I return only in order not to leave you one moment longer under a delusion with regard to me, which must make me despicable even in your eyes.

ARABELLA (timidly)

.

Oh, Hannah!

MELLEFONT.

Look at me as madly as you like. The more madly the better! Was it possible that I could hesitate only for one moment between a Marwood and a Sara, and that I had well nigh decided for the former?

ARABELLA.
Oh, Mellefont!
MELLEFONT.
Do not tremble, Bella! For your sake too I came back. Give me your hand, and follow me without fear!
MARWOOD (stopping them)
.
Whom shall she follow, traitor?
MELLEFONT.
Her father!
MARWOOD.
Go, pitiable wretch, and learn first to know her mother.
MELLEFONT.
I know her. She is a disgrace to her sex.
MARWOOD.
Take her away, Hannah!
MELLEFONT.
Remain here, Bella (attempting to stop her).
MARWOOD.
No force, Mellefont, or----
(Exeunt Hannah and Arabella).
Scene
VII.
Mellefont, Marwood
.
MARWOOD.
Now we are alone! Say now once more, whether you are determined to sacrifice me for a foolish girl?
MELLEFONT (bitterly)
.
Sacrifice you? You recall to my mind that impure animals were also sacrificed to the ancient gods.
MARWOOD (mockingly)
.
Express yourself without these learned allusions.
MELLEFONT.
I tell you, then, that I am firmly resolved never to think of you again, but with the most fearful of curses. Who are you? And who is Sara? You are a voluptuous, egoistic, shameful strumpet, who certainly can scarcely remember any longer that she ever was innocent. I have nothing to reproach myself with but that I have enjoyed with you that which otherwise you would perhaps have let the whole world enjoy. You have sought me, not I you, and if I now know who Marwood is, I have paid for this knowledge dearly enough. It has cost me my fortune, my honour, my happiness----
MARWOOD.

And I would that it might also cost you your eternal happiness. Monster! Is the devil worse than you, when he lures feeble mortals into crimes and himself accuses them afterwards for these crimes which are his own work! What is my innocence to you? What does it matter to you when and how I lost it. If I could not sacrifice my virtue, I have at least staked my good name for you. The former is no more valuable than the latter. What do I say? More valuable? Without it the former is a silly fancy, which brings one neither happiness nor guilt. The good name alone gives it some value, and can exist quite well without it. What did it matter what I was before I knew you, you wretch! It is enough that in the eyes of the world I was a woman without reproach. Through you only it has learned that I am not so; solely through my readiness to accept your heart, as I then thought, without your hand.

MELLEFONT.

This very readiness condemns you, vile woman!

MARWOOD.

But do you remember to what base tricks you owed it? Was I not persuaded by you, that you could not be publicly united to me without forfeiting an inheritance which you wished to share with me only? Is it time now to renounce it? And to renounce it, not for me but for another!

MELLEFONT.

It is a real delight to me to be able to tell you that this difficulty will soon be removed. Content yourself therefore with having deprived me of my father's inheritance, and let me enjoy a far smaller one with a more worthy wife.

MARWOOD.

Ha! Now I see what it is that makes you so perverse. Well, I will lose no more words. Be it so! Be assured I shall do everything to forget you. And the first thing that I will do to this end, shall be this. You will understand me! Tremble for your Bella! Her life shall not carry the memory of my despised love down to posterity; my cruelty shall do it. Behold in me a new Medea!

MELLEFONT (frightened)

.

Marwood!----

MARWOOD.

Or, if you know a more cruel mother still, behold her cruelty doubled in me! Poison and dagger shall avenge me. But no, poison and dagger are tools too merciful for me! They would kill your child and mine too soon. I will not see it dead. I will see it dying! I will see each feature of the face which she has from you disfigured, distorted, and obliterated by slow torture. With eager hand will I part limb from limb, vein from vein, nerve from nerve, and will not cease to cut and burn the very smallest of them, even when there is nothing remaining but a senseless carcass! I--I shall at least feel in it--how sweet is revenge!

MELLEFONT.

You are raving, Marwood----

MARWOOD.

You remind me that my ravings are not directed against the right person. The father must go first! He must already be in yonder world, when, through a thousand woes the spirit of his daughter follows him (she advances towards him with a dagger which she draws from her bosom). So die, traitor!

MELLEFONT (seizing her arm, and snatching the dagger from her)

.

Insane woman! What hinders me now from turning the steel against you? But live, and your punishment shall be left for a hand void of honour.

MARWOOD (wringing her hands)

.

Heaven, what have I done? Mellefont----

MELLEFONT.

Your grief shall not deceive me. I know well why you are sorry--not that you wished to stab me, but that you failed to do so.

MARWOOD.

Give me back the erring steel! Give it me back, and you shall see for whom it was sharpened! For this breast alone, which for long has been too narrow for a heart which will rather renounce life than your love.

MELLEFONT.

Hannah!

MARWOOD.

What are you doing, Mellefont?

Scene

VIII.

Hannah

(in terror), Marwood, Mellefont

.

MELLEFONT.

Did you hear, Hannah, how madly your mistress was behaving? Remember that I shall hold you responsible for Arabella!

HANNAH.

Madam, how agitated you are!

MELLEFONT.

I will place the innocent child in safety immediately. Justice will doubtless be able to bind the murderous hands of her cruel mother (going).

MARWOOD.

Whither, Mellefont? Is it astonishing that the violence of my grief deprived me of my reason? Who forces me to such unnatural excess? Is it not you yourself? Where can Bella be safer than with me? My lips may rave, but my heart still remains the heart of a mother. Oh, Mellefont, forget my madness, and to excuse it think only of its cause.

MELLEFONT.

There is only one thing which can induce me to forget it.

MARWOOD.

And that is?

MELLEFONT.

That you return immediately to London! I will send Arabella there under another escort. You must by no means have anything further to do with her.

MARWOOD.

Very well! I submit to everything; but grant me one single request more. Let me see your Sara once.

MELLEFONT.

And what for?

MARWOOD.

To read in her eyes my future fate. I will judge for myself whether she is worthy of such a breach of faith as you commit against me; and whether I may cherish the hope of receiving again, some day at any rate, a portion of your love.

MELLEFONT.

Vain hope!

MARWOOD.

Who is so cruel as to grudge even hope to the unhappy? I will not show myself to her as Marwood, but as a relation of yours. Announce me to her as such; you shall be present when I call upon her, and I promise you, by all that is sacred, to say nothing that is in any way displeasing to her. Do not refuse my request, for otherwise I might perhaps do all that is in my power to show myself to her in my true character.

MELLEFONT.

Marwood! This request----(after a moment's reflection) might be granted.--But will you then be sure to quit this spot?

MARWOOD.

Certainly; yes I promise you. Even more, I will spare you the visit from her father, if that is still possible.

MELLEFONT.

There is no need of that! I hope that he will include me too in the pardon which he grants to his daughter. But if he will not pardon her, I too shall know how to deal with him. I will go and announce you to my Sara. Only keep your promise, Marwood. (Exit.)

MARWOOD.

Alas, Hannah, that our powers are not as great as our courage. Come, help me to dress. I do not despair of my scheme. If I could only make sure of him first. Come!

ACT III.

Scene

I. (A room in the first inn

.)

Sir William Sampson, Waitwell

.

SIR WILLIAM SAMPSON.

There, Waitwell, take this letter to her! It is the letter of an affectionate father, who complains of nothing but her absence. Tell her that I have sent you on before with it, and that I only await her answer, to come myself and fold her again in my arms.

WAITWELL.

I think you do well to prepare them for your arrival in this way.

SIR WILLIAM SAMPSON.

I make sure of her intentions by this means, and give her the opportunity of freeing herself from any shame or sorrow which repentance might cause her, before she speaks verbally with me. In a letter it will cost her less embarrassment, and me, perhaps, fewer tears.

WAITWELL.

But may I ask, Sir, what you have resolved upon with regard to Mellefont?

SIR WILLIAM SAMPSON.

Ah, Waitwell, if I could separate him from my daughter's lover, I should make some very harsh resolve. But as this cannot be, you see, he is saved from my anger. I myself am most to blame in this misfortune. But for me Sara would never have made the acquaintance of this dangerous man. I admitted him freely into my house on account of an obligation under which I believed myself to be to him. It was natural that the attention which in gratitude I paid him, should win for him the esteem of my daughter. And it was just as natural, that a man of his disposition should suffer himself to be tempted by this esteem to something more. He had been clever enough to transform it into love before I noticed anything at all, and before I had time to inquire into his former life. The evil was done, and I should have done well, if I had forgiven them everything immediately. I wished to be inexorable towards him, and did not consider that I could not be so towards him alone. If I had spared my severity, which came too late, I would at least have prevented their flight. But here I am now, Waitwell! I must fetch them back myself and consider myself happy if only I can make a son of a seducer. For who knows whether he will give up his Marwoods and his other creatures for the sake of a girl who has left nothing for his desires to wish for and who understands so little the bewitching arts of a coquette?

WAITWELL.

Well, Sir, it cannot be possible, that a man could be so wicked----

SIR WILLIAM SAMPSON.

This doubt, good Waitwell, does honour to your virtue. But why, at the same time, is it true that the limits of human wickedness extend much further still? Go now, and do as I told you! Notice every look as she reads my letter. In this short deviation from virtue she cannot yet have learned the art of dissimulation, to the masks of which only deep-rooted vice can have recourse. You will read her whole soul in her face. Do not let a look escape you which might perhaps indicate indifference to me--disregard of her father. For if you should unhappily discover this, and if she loves me no more, I hope that I shall be able to conquer myself and abandon her to her fate. I hope so, Waitwell. Alas! would that there were no heart here, to contradict this hope. (Exeunt on different sides.)

Scene

II.

Miss Sara, Mellefont

.

(Sara's

room.)

MELLEFONT.

I have done wrong, dearest Sara, to leave you in uneasiness about the letter which came just now.

SARA.

Oh dear, no, Mellefont! I have not been in the least uneasy about it. Could you not love me even though you still had secrets from me?

MELLEFONT.

You think, then, that it was a secret?

SARA.

But not one which concerns me. And that must suffice for me.

MELLEFONT.

You are only too good. Let me nevertheless reveal my secret to you. The letter contained a few lines from a relative of mine, who has heard of my being here. She passes through here on her way to London, and would like to see me. She has begged at the same time to be allowed the honour of paying you a visit.

SARA.

It will always be a pleasure to me to make the acquaintance of the respected members of your family. But consider for yourself, whether I can yet appear before one of them without blushing.

MELLEFONT.

Without blushing? And for what? For your love to me? It is true, Sara, you could have given your love to a nobler or a richer man. You must be ashamed that you were content to give your heart for another heart only, and that in this exchange you lost sight of your happiness.

SARA.

You must know yourself how wrongly you interpret my words.

MELLEFONT.

Pardon me, Sara; if my interpretation is wrong, they can have no meaning at all.

SARA.

What is the name of your relation?

MELLEFONT.

She is--Lady Solmes. You will have heard me mention the name before.

SARA.

I don't remember.

MELLEFONT.

May I beg you to see her?

SARA.

Beg me? You can command me to do so.

MELLEFONT.

What a word! No, Sara, she shall not have the happiness of seeing you. She will regret it, but she must submit to it. Sara has her reasons, which I respect without knowing them.

SARA.

How hasty you are, Mellefont! I shall expect Lady Solmes, and do my best to show myself worthy of the honour of her visit. Are you content?

MELLEFONT.

Ah, Sara! let me confess my ambition. I should like to show you to the whole world! And were I not proud of the possession of such a being, I should reproach myself with not being able to appreciate her value. I will go and bring her to you at once. (Exit.)

SARA (alone)

.

I hope she will not be one of those proud women, who are so full of their own virtue that they believe themselves above all failings. With one single look of contempt they condemn us, and an equivocal shrug of the shoulders is all the pity we seem to deserve in their eyes.

Scene

III.

Waitwell, Sara

.

BETTY (behind the scenes)

.

Just come in here, if you must speak to her yourself!

SARA (looking round)

.

Who must speak to me? Whom do I see? Is it possible? You, Waitwell?

WAITWELL.

How happy I am to see our young lady again!

SARA.

Good God, what do you bring me? I hear already, I hear already; you bring me the news of my father's death! He is gone, the excellent man, the best of fathers! He is gone, and I--I am the miserable creature who has hastened his death.

WAITWELL.

Ah, Miss----

SARA.

Tell me, quick! tell me, that his last moments were not embittered by the thought of me; that he had forgotten me; that he died as peacefully as he used to hope to die in my arms; that he did not remember me even in his last prayer----

WAITWELL.

Pray do not torment yourself with such false notions! Your father is still alive! He is still alive, honest Sir William!

SARA.

Is he still alive? Is it true? Is he still alive? May he live a long while yet, and live happily! Oh, would that God would add the half of my years to his life! Half! How ungrateful should I be, if I were not willing to buy even a few moments for him with all the years, that may yet be mine! But tell me at least, Waitwell, that it is not hard for him to live without me; that it was easy to him to renounce a daughter who could so easily renounce her virtue, that he is angry with me for my flight, but not grieved; that he curses me, but does not mourn for me.

WAITWELL.

Ah! Sir William is still the same fond father, as his Sara is still the same fond daughter that she was.

SARA.

What do you say? You are a messenger of evil, of the most dreadful of all the evils which my imagination has ever pictured to me! He is still the same fond father? Then he loves me still? And he must mourn for me, then! No no, he does not do so; he cannot do so? Do you not see how infinitely each sigh which he wasted on me would magnify my crime? Would not the justice of heaven have to charge me with every tear which I forced from him, as if with each one I repeated my vice and my ingratitude? I grow chill at the thought. I cause him tears? Tears? And they are other tears than tears of joy? Contradict me, Waitwell! At most he has felt some slight stirring of the blood on my account; some transitory emotion, calmed by a slight effort of reason. He did not go so far as to shed tears, surely not to shed tears, Waitwell?

WAITWELL (wiping his eyes)

.

No, Miss, he did not go so far as that.

SARA.

Alas! your lips say no, and your eyes say yes.

WAITWELL.

Take this letter Miss, it is from him himself----

SARA.

From whom? From my father? To me?

WAITWELL.

Yes, take it! You can learn more from it, than I am able to say. He ought to have given this to another to do, not to me. I promised myself pleasure from it; but you turn my joy into sadness.

SARA.

Give it me, honest Waitwell! But no! I will not take it before you tell me what it contains.

WAITWELL.

What can it contain? Love and forgiveness.

SARA.

Love? Forgiveness?

WAITWELL.

And perhaps a real regret, that he used the rights of a father's power against a child, who should only have the privileges of a father's kindness.

SARA.

Then keep your cruel letter.

WAITWELL.

Cruel? Have no fear. Full liberty is granted you over your heart and hand.

SARA.

And it is just this which I fear. To grieve a father such as he, this I have had the courage to do. But to see him forced by this very grief-by his love which I have forfeited, to look with leniency on all the wrong into which an unfortunate passion has led me; this, Waitwell, I could not bear. If his letter contained all the hard and angry words which an exasperated father can utter in such a case, I should read it--with a shudder it is true--but still I should be able to read it. I should be able to produce a shadow of defence against his wrath, to make him by this defence if possible more angry still. My consolation then would be this-that melancholy grief could have no place with violent wrath and that the latter would transform itself finally into bitter contempt. And we grieve no more for one whom we despise. My father would have grown calm again, and I would not have to reproach myself with having made him unhappy for ever.

WAITWELL.

Alas, Miss! You will have to reproach yourself still less for this if you now accept his love again, which wishes only to forget everything.

SARA.

You are mistaken, Waitwell! His yearning for me misleads him, perhaps, to give his consent to everything. But no sooner would this desire be appeased a little, than he would feel ashamed before himself of his weakness. Sullen anger would take possession of him, and he would never be able to look at me without silently accusing me of all that I had dared to exact from him. Yes, if it were in my power to spare him his bitterest grief, when on my account he is laying the greatest restraint upon himself; if at a moment when he would grant me everything I could sacrifice all to him; then it would be quite a different matter. I would take the letter from your hands with pleasure, would admire in it the strength of the fatherly love, and, not to abuse this love, I would throw myself at his feet a repentant and obedient daughter. But can I do that? I shall be obliged to make use of his permission, regardless of the price this permission has cost him. And then, when I feel most happy, it will suddenly occur to me that he only outwardly appears to share my happiness and that inwardly he is sighing--in short, that he has made me happy by the renunciation of his own happiness. And to wish to be happy in this way,--do you expect that of me, Waitwell?

WAITWELL.

I truly do not know what answer to give to that.

SARA.

There is no answer to it. So take your letter back! If my father must be unhappy through me, I will myself remain unhappy also. To be quite alone in unhappiness is that for which I now pray Heaven every hour, but to be quite alone in my happiness--of that I will not hear.

WAITWELL (aside)

.

I really think I shall have to employ deception with this good child to get her to read the letter.

SARA.

What are you saying to yourself?

WAITWELL.

I was saying to myself that the idea I had hit on to get you to read this letter all the quicker was a very clumsy one.

SARA.

How so?

WAITWELL.

I could not look far enough. Of course you see more deeply into things than such as I. I did not wish to frighten you; the letter is perhaps only too hard; and when I said that it contained nothing but love and forgiveness, I ought to have said that I wished it might not contain anything else.

SARA.

Is that true? Give it me then! I will read it. If one has been unfortunate enough to deserve the anger of one's father, one should at least have enough respect for it to submit to the expression of it on his part. To try to frustrate it means to heap contempt on insult. I shall feel his anger in all its strength. You see I tremble already. But I must tremble; and I will rather tremble than weep (opens the letter). Now it is opened! I sink! But what do I see? (she reads) "My only, dearest daughter"--ah, you old deceiver, is that the language of an angry father? Go, I shall read no more----

WAITWELL.

Ah, Miss! You will pardon an old servant! Yes, truly, I believe it is the first time in my life that I have intentionally deceived any one. He who deceives once, Miss, and deceives for so good a purpose, is surely no old deceiver on that account. That touches me deeply, Miss! I know well that the good intention does not always excuse one; but what else could I do? To return his letter unread to such a good father? That certainly I cannot do! Sooner will I walk as far as my old legs will carry me, and never again come into his presence.

SARA.

What? You too will leave him?

WAITWELL.

Shall I not be obliged to do so if you do not read the letter? Read it, pray! Do not grudge a good result to the first deceit with which I have to reproach myself. You will forget it the sooner, and I shall the sooner be able to forgive myself. I am a common, simple man, who must not question the reasons why you cannot and will not read the letter. Whether they are true, I know not, but at any rate they do not appear to me to be natural. I should think thus, Miss: a father, I should think, is after all a father; and a child may err for once, and remain a good child in spite of it. If the father pardons the error, the child may behave again in such a manner that the father may not even think of it any more. For who likes to remember what he would rather had never happened? It seems, Miss, as if you thought only of your error, and believed you atoned sufficiently in exaggerating it in your imagination and tormenting yourself with these exaggerated ideas. But, I should think, you ought also to consider how you could make up for what has happened. And how will you make up for it, if you deprive yourself of every opportunity of doing so. Can it be hard for you to take the second step, when such a good father has already taken the first?

SARA.

What daggers pierce my heart in your simple words! That he has to take the first step is just what I cannot bear. And, besides, is it only the first step which he takes? He must do all! I cannot take a single one to meet him. As far as I have gone from him, so far must he descend to me. If he pardons me, he must pardon the whole crime, and in addition must bear the consequences of it continually before his eyes. Can one demand that from a father?

WAITWELL.

I do not know, Miss, whether I understand this quite right. But it seems to me, you mean to say that he would have to forgive you too much, and as this could not but be very difficult to him, you make a scruple of accepting his forgiveness. If you mean that, tell me, pray, is not forgiving a great happiness to a kind heart? I have not been so fortunate in my life as to have felt this happiness often. But I still remember with pleasure the few instances when I have felt it. I felt something so sweet, something so tranquillising, something so divine, that I could not help thinking of the great insurpassable blessedness of God, whose preservation of miserable mankind is a perpetual forgiveness. I wished that I could be forgiving continually, and was ashamed that I had only such trifles to pardon. To forgive real painful insults, deadly offences, I said to myself, must be a bliss in which the whole soul melts. And now, Miss, will you grudge your father such bliss?

SARA.

Ah! Go on, Waitwell, go on!

WAITWELL.

I know well there are people who accept nothing less willingly than forgiveness, and that because they have never learned to grant it. They are proud, unbending people, who will on no account confess that they have done wrong. But you do not belong to this kind, Miss! You have the most loving and tender of hearts that the best of your sex can have. You confess your fault too. Where then is the difficulty? But pardon me, Miss! I am an old chatterer, and ought to have seen at once that your refusal is only a praiseworthy solicitude, only a virtuous timidity. People who can accept a great benefit immediately without any hesitation are seldom worthy of it. Those who deserve it most have always the greatest mistrust of themselves. Yet mistrust must not be pushed beyond limits!

SARA.

Dear old father! I believe you have persuaded me.

WAITWELL.

If I have been so fortunate as that it must have been a good spirit that has helped me to plead. But no, Miss, my words have done no more than given you time to reflect and to recover from the bewilderment of joy. You will read the letter now, will you not? Oh, read it at once!

SARA.

I will do so, Waitwell! What regrets, what pain shall I feel!

WAITWELL.

Pain, Miss! but pleasant pain.

SARA.

Be silent! (begins reading to herself).

WAITWELL (aside)

.

Oh! If he could see her himself!

SARA (after reading a few moments)

.

Ah, Waitwell, what a father! He calls my flight "an absence." How much more culpable it becomes through this gentle word! (continues reading and interrupts herself again). Listen! he flatters himself I shall love him still. He flatters himself! He begs me--he begs me? A father begs his daughter? his culpable daughter? And what does he beg then? He begs me to forget his over-hasty severity, and not to punish him any longer with my absence. Over-hasty severity! To punish! More still! Now he thanks me even, and thanks me that I have given him an opportunity of learning the whole extent of paternal love. Unhappy opportunity! Would that he also said it had shown him at the same time the extent of filial disobedience. No, he does not say it! He does not mention my crime with one single word. (Continues reading.) He will come himself and fetch his children. His children, Waitwell! that surpasses everything! Have I read it rightly? (reads again to herself) I am overcome! He says, that he without whom he could not possess a daughter deserves but too well to be his son. Oh that he had never had this unfortunate daughter! Go, Waitwell, leave me alone! He wants an answer, and I will write it at once. Come again in an hour! I thank you meanwhile for your trouble. You are an honest man. Few servants are the friends of their masters!

WAITWELL.

Do not make me blush, Miss! If all masters were like Sir William, servants would be monsters, if they would not give their lives for them. (Exit.)

Scene

IV.

SARA (sits down to write)

.

If they had told me a year ago that I should have to answer such a letter! And under such circumstances! Yes, I have the pen in my hand. But do I know yet what I shall write? What I think; what I feel. And what then does one think when a thousand thoughts cross each other in one moment? And what does one feel, when the heart is in a stupor from a thousand feelings. But I must write! I do not guide the pen for the first time. After assisting me in so many a little act of politeness and friendship, should its help fail me at the most important office? (She pauses, and then writes a few lines.) It shall commence so? A very cold beginning! And shall I then begin with his love? I must begin with my crime. (She scratches it out and writes again.) I must be on my guard not to express myself too leniently. Shame may be in its place anywhere else, but not in the confession of our faults. I need not fear falling into exaggeration, even though I employ the most dreadful terms. Ah, am I to be interrupted now?

Scene

V.

Marwood, Mellefont, Sara

.

MELLEFONT.

Dearest Sara, I have the honour of introducing Lady Solmes to you; she is one of the members of my family to whom I feel myself most indebted.

MARWOOD.

I must beg your pardon, Madam, for taking the liberty of convincing myself with my own eyes of the happiness of a cousin, for whom I should wish the most perfect of women if the first moment had not at once convinced me, that he has found her already in you.

SARA.

Your ladyship does me too much honour! Such a compliment would have made me blush at any time, but now I would almost take it as concealed reproach, if I did not think that Lady Solmes is much too generous to let her superiority in virtue and wisdom be felt by an unhappy girl.

MARWOOD (coldly)

.

I should be inconsolable if you attributed to me any but the most friendly feelings towards you. (Aside.) She is good-looking.

MELLEFONT.

Would it be possible Madam, to remain indifferent to such beauty, such modesty? People say, it is true, that one charming woman rarely does another one justice, but this is to be taken only of those who are over-vain of their superiority, and on the other hand of those who are not conscious of possessing any superiority. How far are you both removed from this. (To Marwood

, who stands in deep thought.) Is it not true, Madam, that my love has been anything but partial? Is it not true, that though I have said much to you in praise of my Sara, I have not said nearly so much as you yourself see? But why so thoughtful. (Aside to her.) You forget whom you represent.

MARWOOD.

May I say it? The admiration of your dear young lady led me to the contemplation of her fate. It touched me, that she should not enjoy the fruits of her love in her native land. I recollected that she had to leave a father, and a very affectionate father as I have been told, in order to become yours; and I could not but wish for her reconciliation with him.

SARA.

Ah, Madam! how much am I indebted to you for this wish. It encourages me to tell you the whole of my happiness. You cannot yet know, Mellefont, that this wish was granted before Lady Solmes had the kindness to wish it.

MELLEFONT.

How do you mean, Sara?

MARWOOD (aside)

.

How am I to interpret that?

SARA.

I have just received a letter from my father. Waitwell brought it to me. Ah, Mellefont, such a letter!

MELLEFONT.

Quick, relieve me from my uncertainty. What have I to fear? What have I to hope? Is he still the father from whom we fled? And if he is, will Sara be the daughter who loves me so tenderly as to fly again? Alas, had I but done as you wished, dearest Sara, we should now be united by a bond which no caprice could dissolve. I feel now all the misfortune which the discovery of our abode may bring upon me.--He will come and tear you out of my arms. How I hate the contemptible being who has betrayed us to him (with an angry glance at Marwood

).

SARA.

Dearest Mellefont, how flattering to me is this uneasiness I And how happy are we both in that it is unnecessary. Read his letter! (To Marwood

, whilst Mellefont

reads the letter.) He will be astonished at the love of my father. Of my father? Ah, he is his now too.

MARWOOD (perplexed)

.

Is it possible?

SARA.

Yes, Madam, you have good cause to be surprised at this change. He forgives us everything; we shall now love each other before his eyes; he allows it, he commands it. How has this kindness gone to my very soul! Well, Mellefont? (who returns the letter to her). You are silent? Oh no, this tear which steals from your eye says far more than your lips could say.

MARWOOD (aside)

.

How I have injured my own cause. Imprudent woman that I was!

SARA.

Oh, let me kiss this tear from your cheek.

MELLEFONT.

Ah, Sara, why was it our fate to grieve such a godlike man? Yes, a godlike man, for what is more godlike than to forgive? Could we only have imagined such a happy issue possible, we should not now owe it to such violent means, we should owe it to our entreaties alone. What happiness is in store for me! But how painful also will be the conviction, that I am so unworthy of this happiness!

MARWOOD (aside)

.

And I must be present to hear this.

SARA.

How perfectly you justify my love by such thoughts.

MARWOOD (aside.)

What restraint must I put on myself!

SARA.

You too, Madam, must read my father's letter. You seem to take too great an interest in our fate to be indifferent to its contents.

MARWOOD.

Indifferent? (takes the letter).

SARA.

But, Madam, you still seem very thoughtful, very sad----

MARWOOD.

Thoughtful, but not sad!

MELLEFONT (aside)

.

Heavens! If she should betray herself!

SARA.

And why then thoughtful?

MARWOOD.

I tremble for you both. Could not this unforeseen kindness of your father be a dissimulation? An artifice?

SARA.

Assuredly not, Madam, assuredly not. Only read and you will admit it yourself. Dissimulation is always cold, it is not capable of such tender words. (Marwood

reads.) Do not grow suspicious, Mellefont, I beg. I pledge myself that my father cannot condescend to an artifice. He says nothing which he does not think, falseness is a vice unknown to him.

MELLEFONT.

Oh, of that I am thoroughly convinced, dearest Sara! You must pardon Lady Solmes for this suspicion, since she does not know the man whom it concerns.

SARA (whilst Marwood

returns the letter to her)

.

What do I see, my lady? You are pale! You tremble! What is the matter with you?

MELLEFONT (aside)

.

What anxiety I suffer? Why did I bring her here?

MARWOOD.

It is nothing but a slight dizziness, which will pass over. The night air on my journey must have disagreed with me.

MELLEFONT.

You frighten me! Would you not like to go into the air? You will recover sooner than in a close room.

MARWOOD.

If you think so, give me your arm!

SARA.

I will accompany your ladyship!

MARWOOD.

I beg you will not trouble to do so! My faintness will pass over immediately.

SARA.

I hope then, to see you again soon.

MARWOOD.

If you permit me (Mellefont

conducts her out).

SARA (alone)

.

Poor thing! She does not seem exactly the most friendly of people; but yet she does not appear to be either proud or ill-tempered. I am alone again. Can I employ the few moments, while I remain so, better than by finishing my answer? (Is about to sit down to write.)

Scene

VI.

Betty, Sara

.

BETTY.

That was indeed a very short visit.

SARA.

Yes, Betty! It was Lady Solmes, a relation of my Mellefont. She was suddenly taken faint. Where is she now?

BETTY.

Mellefont has accompanied her to the door.

SARA.

She is gone again, then?

BETTY.

I suppose so. But the more I look at you--you must forgive my freedom, Miss--the more you seem to me to be altered. There is something calm, something contented in your looks. Either Lady Solmes must have been a very pleasant visitor, or the old man a very pleasant messenger.

SARA.

The latter, Betty, the latter! He came from my father. What a tender letter I have for you to read! Your kind heart has often wept with me, now it shall rejoice with me, too. I shall be happy again, and be able to reward you for your good services.

BETTY.

What services could I render you in nine short weeks?

SARA.

You could not have done more for me in all the rest of my life, than in these nine weeks. They are over! But come now with me, Betty. As Mellefont is probably alone again, I must speak to him. It just occurs to me that it would be well if he wrote at the same time to my father, to whom an expression of gratitude from him could hardly come unexpectedly. Come! (Exeunt.)

Scene

VII.

Sir William Sampson, Waitwell

.

(The drawing-room.)

SIR WILLIAM.

What balm you have poured on my wounded heart with your words, Waitwell! I live again, and the prospect of her return seems to carry me as far back to my youth as her flight had brought me nearer to my grave. She loves me still? What more do I wish! Go back to her soon, Waitwell? I am impatient for the moment when I shall fold her again in these arms, which I had stretched out so longingly to death! How welcome would it have been to me in the moments of my grief! And how terrible will it be to me in my new happiness! An old man, no doubt, is to be blamed for drawing the bonds so tight again which still unite him to the world. The final separation becomes the more painful. But God who shows Himself so merciful to me now, will also help me to go through this. Would He, I ask, grant me a mercy in order to let it become ray ruin in the end? Would He give me back a daughter, that I should have to murmur when He calls me from life? No, no! He gives her back to me that in my last hour I may be anxious about myself alone. Thanks to Thee, Eternal Father! How feeble is the gratitude of mortal lips? But soon, soon I shall be ablc to thank Him more worthily in an eternity devoted to Him alone!

WAITWELL.

How it delights me, Sir, to know you happy again before my death! Believe me, I have suffered almost as much in your grief as you yourself. Almost as much, for the grief of a father in such a case must be inexpressible.

SIR WILLIAM.

Do not regard yourself as my servant any longer, my good Waitwell. You have long deserved to enjoy a more seemly old age. I will give it you, and you shall not be worse off than I am while I am still in this world. I will abolish all difference between us; in yonder world, you well know, it will be done. For this once be the old servant still, on whom I never relied in vain. Go, and be sure to bring me her answer, as soon as it is ready.

WAITWELL.

I go, Sir! But such an errand is not a service. It is a reward which you grant me for my services. Yes, truly it is so! (Exeunt on different sides of the stage.)

ACT IV.

Scene

I.--Mellefont's

room

.

Mellefont, Sara

.

MELLEFONT.

Yes, dearest Sara, yes! That I will do! That I must do.

SARA.

How happy you make me!

MELLEFONT.

It is I who must take the whole crime upon myself. I alone am guilty; I alone must ask for forgiveness.

SARA.

No, Mellefont, do not take from me the greater share which I have in our error! It is dear to me, however wrong it is, for it must have convinced you that I love my Mellefont above everything in this world. But is it, then, really true, that I may henceforth combine this love with the love of my father? Or am I in a pleasant dream? How I fear it will pass and I shall awaken in my old misery! But no! I am not merely dreaming, I am really happier than I ever dared hope to become; happier than this short life may perhaps allow. But perhaps this beam of happiness appears in the distance, and delusively seems to approach only in order to melt away again into thick darkness, and to leave me suddenly in a night whose whole terror has only become perceptible to me through this short illumination. What forebodings torment me! Are they really forebodings, Mellefont, or are they common feelings, which are inseparable from the expectation of an undeserved happiness, and the fear of losing it? How fast my heart beats, and how wildly it beats. How loud now, how quick! And now how weak, how anxious, how quivering! Now it hurries again, as if these were its last throbbings, which it would fain beat out rapidly. Poor heart!

MELLEFONT.

The tumult of your blood, which a sudden surprise cannot fail to cause, will abate, Sara, and your heart will continue its work more calmly. None of its throbs point to aught that is in the future, and we are to blame--forgive me, dearest Sara!--if we make the mechanic pressure of our blood into a prophet of evil. But I will not leave anything undone which you yourself think good to appease this little storm within your breast. I will write at once, and I hope that Sir William will be satisfied with the assurances of my repentance, with the expressions of my stricken heart, and my vows of affectionate obedience.

SARA.

Sir William? Ah, Mellefont, you must begin now to accustom yourself to a far more tender name. My father, your father, Mellefont----

MELLEFONT.

Very well, Sara, our kind, our dear father! I was very young when I last used this sweet name; very young, when I had to unlearn the equally sweet name of mother.

SARA.

You had to unlearn it, and I--I was never so happy, as to be able to pronounce it at all. My life was her death! O God, I was a guiltless matricide! And how much was wanting--how little, how almost nothing was wanting to my becoming a parricide too! Not a guiltless, but a voluntary parricide. And who knows, whether I am not so already? The years, the days, the moments by which he is nearer to his end than he would have been without the grief I have caused him--of those I have robbed him. However old and weary he may be when Fate shall permit him to depart, my conscience will yet be unable to escape the reproach that but for me he might have lived yet longer. A sad reproach with which I doubtless should not need to charge myself, if a loving mother had guided me in my youth. Through her teaching and her example my heart would--you look tenderly on me, Mellefont? You are right; a mother would perhaps have been a tyrant for very love, and I should not now belong to Mellefont. Why do I wish then for that, which a wiser Fate denied me out of kindness? Its dispensations are always best. Let us only make proper use of that which it gives us; a father who never yet let me sigh for a mother; a father who will also teach you to forget the parents you lost so soon. What a flattering thought. I fall in love with it, and forget almost, that in my innermost heart there is still something which refuses to put faith in it. What is this rebellious something?

MELLEFONT.

This something, dearest Sara, as you have already said yourself, is the natural, timid incapability to realize a great happiness. Ah, your heart hesitated less to believe itself unhappy than now, to its own torment, it hesitates to believe in its own happiness! But as to one who has become dizzy with quick movement, the external objects still appear to move round when again he is sitting still, so the heart which has been violently agitated cannot suddenly become calm again; there remains often for a long time, a quivering palpitation which we must suffer to exhaust itself.

SARA.

I believe it, Mellefont, I believe it, because you say it, because I wish it. But do not let us detain each other any longer! I will go and finish my letter. And you will let me read yours, will you not, after I have shown you mine?

MELLEFONT.

Each word shall be submitted to your judgment; except what I must say in your defence, for I know you do not think yourself so innocent as you are. (Accompanies Sara to the back of the stage.)

Scene

II.

MELLEFONT (after walking up and down several times in thought)

.

What a riddle I am to myself! What shall I think myself? A fool? Or a knave? Heart, what a villain thou art! I love the angel, however much of a devil I may be. I love her! Yes, certainly! certainly I love her. I feel I would sacrifice a thousand lives for her, for her who sacrificed her virtue for me; I would do so,--this very moment without hesitation would I do so. And yet, yet--I am afraid to say it to myself--and yet--how shall I explain it? And yet I fear the moment which will make her mine for ever before the world. It cannot be avoided now, for her father is reconciled. Nor shall I be able to put it off for long. The delay has already drawn down painful reproaches enough upon me. But painful as they were, they were still more supportable to me than the melancholy thought of being fettered for life. But am I not so already? Certainly,--and with pleasure! Certainly I am already her prisoner. What is it I want, then? At present I am a prisoner, who is allowed to go about on parole; that is flattering! Why cannot the matter rest there? Why must I be put in chains and thus lack even the pitiable shadow of freedom? In chains? Quite so! Sara Sampson, my beloved! What bliss lies in these words! Sara Sampson, my wife! The half of the bliss is gone! and the other half--will go! Monster that I am! And with such thoughts shall I write to her father? Yet these are not my real thoughts, they are fancies! Cursed fancies, which have become natural to me through my dissolute life! I will free myself from them, or live no more.

Scene

III.

Norton, Mellefont

.

MELLEFONT.

You disturb me, Norton!

NORTON.

I beg your pardon, Sir (withdrawing again).

MELLEFONT.

No, no! Stay! It is just as well that you should disturb me. What do you want?

NORTON.

I have heard some very good news from Betty, and have come to wish you happiness.

MELLEFONT.

On the reconciliation with her father, I suppose you mean? I thank you.

NORTON.

So Heaven still means to make you happy.

MELLEFONT.

If it means to do so,--you see, Norton, I am just towards myself--it certainly does not mean it for my sake.

NORTON.

No, no; if you feel that, then it will be for your sake also.

MELLEFONT.

For my Sara's sake alone. If its vengeance, already armed, could spare the whole of a sinful city for the sake of a few just men, surely it can also bear with a sinner, when a soul in which it finds delight, is the sharer of his fate.

NORTON.

You speak with earnestness and feeling. But does not joy express itself differently from this?

MELLEFONT.

Joy, Norton? (Looking sharply at him.) For me it is gone now for ever.

NORTON.

May I speak candidly?

MELLEFONT.

You may.

NORTON.

The reproach which I had to hear this morning of having made myself a participator in your crimes, because I had been silent about them, may excuse me, if I am less silent henceforth.

MELLEFONT.

Only do not forget who you are!

NORTON.

I will not forget that I am a servant, and a servant, alas, who might be something better, if he had lived for it. I am your servant, it is true, but not so far as to wish to be damned along with you.

MELLEFONT.

With me? And why do you say that now?

NORTON.

Because I am not a little astonished to find you different from what I expected.

MELLEFONT.

Will you not inform me what you expected?

NORTON.

To find you all delight.

MELLEFONT.

It is only the common herd who are beside themselves immediately when luck smiles on them for once.

NORTON.

Perhaps, because the common herd still have the feelings which among greater people are corrupted and weakened by a thousand unnatural notions. But there is something besides moderation to be read in your face--coldness, irresolution, disinclination.

MELLEFONT.

And if so? Have you forgotten who is here besides Sara? The presence of Marwood---

NORTON.

Could make you anxious, I daresay, but not despondent. Something else troubles you. And I shall be glad to be mistaken in thinking you would rather that the father were not yet reconciled. The prospect of a position which so little suits your way of thinking----

MELLEFONT.

Norton, Norton! Either you must have been, or still must be, a dreadful villain, that you can thus guess my thoughts. Since you have hit the nail upon the head, I will not deny it. It is true--so certain as it is that I shall love my Sara for ever so little does it please me, that I must--must love her for ever! But do not fear; I shall conquer this foolish fancy. Or do you think that it is no fancy? Who bids me look at marriage as compulsion? I certainly do not wish to be freer than she will permit me to be.

NORTON.

These reflections are all very well. But Marwood will come to the aid of your old prejudices, and I fear, I fear----

MELLEFONT.

That which will never happen! You shall see her go back this very evening to London. And as I have confessed my most secret--folly we will call it for the present--I must not conceal from you either, that I have put Marwood into such a fright that she will obey the slightest hint from me.

NORTON.

That sounds incredible to me.

MELLEFONT.

Look! I snatched this murderous steel from her hand (showing the dagger which he had taken from Marwood

) when in a fearful rage she was on the point of stabbing me to the heart with it. Will you believe now, that I offered her a stout resistance? At first she well nigh succeeded in throwing her noose around my neck again. The traitoress!--She has Arabella with her.

NORTON.

Arabella?

MELLEFONT.

I have not yet been able to fathom by what cunning she got the child back into her hands again. Enough, the result did not fall out as she no doubt had expected.

NORTON.

Allow me to rejoice at your firmness, and to consider your reformation half assured. Yet,--as you wish me to know all--what business had she here under the name of Lady Solmes?

MELLEFONT.

She wanted of all things to see her rival. I granted her wish partly from kindness, partly from rashness, partly from the desire to humiliate her by the sight of the best of her sex. You shake your head, Norton?

NORTON.

I should not have risked that.

MELLEFONT.

Risked? I did not risk anything more, after all, than what I should have had to risk if I had refused her. She would have tried to obtain admittance as Marwood; and the worst that can be expected from her incognito visit is not worse than that.

NORTON.

Thank Heaven that it went off so quietly.

MELLEFONT.

It is not quite over yet, Norton. A slight indisposition came over her and compelled her to go away without taking leave. She wants to come again. Let her do so! The wasp which has lost its sting (pointing to the dagger) can do nothing worse than buzz. But buzzing too shall cost her dear, if she grows too troublesome with it. Do I not hear somebody coming? Leave me if it should be she. It is she. Go! (Exit Norton

.)

Scene

IV.

Mellefont, Marwood

.

MARWOOD.

No doubt you are little pleased to see me again.

MELLEFONT.

I am very pleased, Marwood, to see that your indisposition has had no further consequences. You are better, I hope?

MARWOOD.

So, so.

MELLEFONT.

You have not done well, then, to trouble to come here again.

MARWOOD.

I thank you, Mellefont, if you say this out of kindness to me; and I do not take it amiss, if you have another meaning in it.

MELLEFONT.

I am pleased to see you so calm.

MARWOOD.

The storm is over. Forget it, I beg you once more.

MELLEFONT.

Only remember your promise, Marwood, and I will forget everything with pleasure. But if I knew that you would not consider it an offence, I should like to ask----

MARWOOD.

Ask on, Mellefont! You cannot offend me any more. What were you going to ask?

MELLEFONT.

How you liked my Sara?

MARWOOD.

The question is natural. My answer will not seem so natural, but it is none the less true for that. I liked her very much.

MELLEFONT.

Such impartiality delights me. But would it be possible for him who knew how to appreciate the charms of a Marwood to make a bad choice?

MARWOOD.

You ought to have spared me this flattery, Mellefont, if it is flattery. It is not in accordance with our intention to forget each other.

MELLEFONT.

You surely do not wish me to facilitate this intention by rudeness? Do not let our separation be of an ordinary nature. Let us break with each other as people of reason who yield to necessity; without bitterness, without anger, and with the preservation of a certain degree of respect, as behoves our former intimacy.

MARWOOD.

Former intimacy! I do not wish to be reminded of it. No more of it. What must be, must, and it matters little how. But one word more about Arabella. You will not let me have her?

MELLEFONT.

No, Marwood!

MARWOOD.

It is cruel, since you can no longer be her father, to take her mother also from her.

MELLEFONT.

I can still be her father, and will be so.

MARWOOD.

Prove it, then, now!

MELLEFONT.

How?

MARWOOD.

Permit Arabella to have the riches which I have in keeping for you, as her father's inheritance. As to her mother's inheritance I wish I could leave her a better one than the shame of having been borne by me.

MELLEFONT.

Do not speak so! I shall provide for Arabella without embarrassing her mother's property. If she wishes to forget me, she must begin by forgetting that she possesses anything from me. I have obligations towards her, and I shall never forget that really--though against her will--she has promoted my happiness. Yes, Marwood, in all seriousness I thank you for betraying our retreat to a father whose ignorance of it alone prevented him from receiving us again.

MARWOOD.

Do not torture me with gratitude which I never wished to deserve. Sir William is too good an old fool; he must think differently from what I should have thought in his place. I should have forgiven my daughter, but as to her seducer I should have----

MELLEFONT.

Marwood!

MARWOOD.

True; you yourself are the seducer! I am silent. Shall I be presently allowed to pay my farewell visit to Miss Sampson?

MELLEFONT.

Sara could not be offended, even if you left without seeing her again.

MARWOOD.

Mellefont, I do not like playing my part by halves, and I have no wish to be taken, even under an assumed name, for a woman without breeding.

MELLEFONT.

If you care for your own peace of mind you ought to avoid seeing a person again who must awaken certain thoughts in you which----

MARWOOD (smiling disdainfully)

.

You have a better opinion of yourself than of me. But even if you believed that I should be inconsolable on your account, you ought at least to believe it in silence.--Miss Sampson would awaken certain thoughts in me? Certain thoughts! Oh yes; but none more certain than this--that the best girl can often love the most worthless man.

MELLEFONT.

Charming, Marwood, perfectly charming. Now you are as I have long wished to see you; although I could almost have wished, as I told you before, that we could have retained some respect for each other. But this may perhaps come still when once your fermenting heart has cooled down. Excuse me for a moment. I will fetch Miss Sampson to see you.

Scene

V.

MARWOOD (looking round)

.

Am I alone? Can I take breath again unobserved, and let the muscles of my face relax into their natural position? I must just for a moment be the true Marwood in all my features to be able again to bear the restraint of dissimulation! How I hate thee, base dissimulation! Not because I love sincerity, but because thou art the most pitiable refuge of powerless revenge. I certainly would not condescend to thee, if a tyrant would lend me his power or Heaven its thunderbolt.--Yet, if thou only servest my end! The beginning is promising, and Mellefont seems disposed to grow more confident. If my device succeeds and I can speak alone with his Sara; then-yes, then, it is still very uncertain whether it will be of any use to me. The truths about Mellefont will perhaps be no novelty to her; the calumnies she will perhaps not believe, and the threats, perhaps, despise. But yet she shall hear truths, calumnies and threats. It would be bad, if they did not leave any sting at all in her mind. Silence; they are coming. I am no longer Marwood, I am a worthless outcast, who tries by little artful tricks to turn aside her shame,--a bruised worm, which turns and fain would wound at least the heel of him who trod upon it.

Scene

VI.

Sara, Mellefont, Marwood

.

SARA.

I am happy, Madam, that my uneasiness on your account has been unnecessary.

MARWOOD.

I thank you! The attack was so insignificant that it need not have made you uneasy.

MELLEFONT.

Lady Solmes wishes to take leave of you, dearest Sara!

SARA.

So soon, Madam?

MARWOOD.

I cannot go soon enough for those who desire my presence in London.

MELLEFONT.

You surely are not going to leave to-day?

MARWOOD.

To-morrow morning, first thing.

MELLEFONT.

To-morrow morning, first thing? I thought to-day.

SARA.

Our acquaintance, Madam, commences hurriedly. I hope to be honoured with a more intimate intercourse with you at some future time.

MARWOOD.

I solicit your friendship, Miss Sampson.

MELLEFONT.

I pledge myself, dearest Sara, that this desire of Lady Solmes is sincere, although I must tell you beforehand that you will certainly not see each other again for a long time. Lady Solmes will very rarely be able to live where we are.

MARWOOD (aside)

.

How subtle!

SARA.

That is to deprive me of a very pleasant anticipation, Mellefont!

MARWOOD.

I shall be the greatest loser!

MELLEFONT.

But in reality, Madam, do you not start before tomorrow morning?

MARWOOD.

It may be sooner! (Aside.) No one comes.

MELLEFONT.

We do not wish to remain much longer here either. It will be well, will it not, Sara, to follow our answer without delay? Sir William cannot be displeased with our haste.

Scene

VII.

Betty, Mellefont, Sara, Marwood

.

MELLEFONT.

What is it, Betty?

BETTY.

Somebody wishes to speak with you immediately.

MARWOOD (aside)

.

Ha! now all depends on whether----

MELLEFONT.

Me? Immediately? I will come at once. Madam, is it agreeable to you to shorten your visit?

SARA.

Why so, Mellefont? Lady Solmes will be so kind as to wait for your return.

MARWOOD.
Pardon me; I know my cousin Mellefont, and prefer to depart with him.
BETTY.
The stranger, sir--he wishes only to say a word to you. He says, that he has not a moment to lose.
MELLEFONT.
Go, please! I will be with him directly. I expect it will be some news at last about the agreement which I mentioned to you. (Exit Betty.)
MARWOOD (aside)
.
A good conjecture!
MELLEFONT.
But still, Madam----
MARWOOD.
If you order it, then, I must bid you----
SARA.
Oh no, Mellefont; I am sure you will not grudge me the pleasure of entertaining Lady Solmes during your absence?
MELLEFONT.
You wish it, Sara?
SARA.
Do not stay now, dearest Mellefont, but come back again soon! And come with a more joyful face, I will wish! You doubtless expect an unpleasant answer. Don't let this disturb you. I am more desirous to see whether after all you can gracefully prefer me to an inheritance, than I am to know that you are in the possession of one.
MELLEFONT.
I obey. (In a warning tone.) I shall be sure to come back in a moment, Madam.
MARWOOD (aside)
.
Lucky so far.
(Exit Mellefont
.)
Scene
VIII.
Sara, Marwood
.
SARA.
My good Mellefont sometimes gives his polite phrases quite a wrong accent. Do not you think so too, Madam?
MARWOOD.
I am no doubt too much accustomed to his way already to notice anything of that sort.
SARA.
Will you not take a seat, Madam?
MARWOOD.

If you desire it. (Aside, whilst they are seating themselves.) I must not let this moment slip by unused.

SARA.

Tell me! Shall I not be the most enviable of women with my Mellefont?

MARWOOD.

If Mellefont knows how to appreciate his happiness, Miss Sampson will make him the most enviable of men. But----

SARA.

A "but," and then a pause, Madam----

MARWOOD.

I am frank, Miss Sampson.

SARA.

And for this reason infinitely more to be esteemed.

MARWOOD.

Frank--not seldom imprudently so. My "but" is a proof of it. A very imprudent "but."

SARA.

I do not think that my Lady Solmes can wish through this evasion to make me more uneasy. It must be a cruel mercy that only rouses suspicions of an evil which it might disclose.

MARWOOD.

Not at all, Miss Sampson! You attach far too much importance to my "but." Mellefont is a relation of mine----

SARA.

Then all the more important is the slightest charge which you have to make against him.

MARWOOD.

But even were Mellefont my brother, I must tell you, that I should unhesitatingly side with one of my own sex against him, if I perceived that he did not act quite honestly towards her. We women ought properly to consider every insult shown to one of us as an insult to the whole sex, and to make it a common affair, in which even the sister and mother of the guilty one ought not to hesitate to share.

SARA.

This remark----

MARWOOD.

Has already been my guide now and then in doubtful cases.

SARA.

And promises me--I tremble.

MARWOOD.

No, Miss Sampson, if you mean to tremble, let us speak of something else----

SARA.

Cruel woman!

MARWOOD.

I am sorry to be misunderstood. I at least, if I place myself in imagination in Miss Sampson's position, would regard as a favour any more exact information which one might give me about the man with whose fate I was about to unite my own for ever.

SARA.

What do you wish, Madam? Do I not know my Mellefont already? Believe me I know him, as I do my own soul. I know that he loves me----

MARWOOD.

And others----

SARA.

Has loved others. That I know also. Was he to love me, before he knew anything about me? Can I ask to be the only one who has had charm enough to attract him? Must I not confess it to myself, that I have striven to please him? Is he not so lovable, that he must have awakened this endeavour in many a breast? And isn't it but natural, if several have been successful in their endeavour?

MARWOOD.

You defend him with just the same ardour and almost the same words with which I have often defended him already. It is no crime to have loved; much less still is it a crime to have been loved. But fickleness is a crime.

SARA.

Not always; for often, I believe, it is rendered excusable by the objects of one's love, which seldom deserve to be loved for ever.

MARWOOD.

Miss Sampson's doctrine of morals does not seem to be of the strictest.

SARA.

It is true; the one by which I judge those who themselves confess that they have taken to bad ways is not of the strictest. Nor should it be so. For here it is not a question of fixing the limits which virtue marks out for love, but merely of excusing the human weakness that has not remained within those limits and of judging the consequences arising therefrom by the rules of wisdom. If, for example, a Mellefont loves a Marwood and eventually abandons her; this abandonment is very praiseworthy in comparison with the love itself. It would be a misfortune if he had to love a vicious person for ever because he once had loved her.

MARWOOD.

But do you know this Marwood, whom you so confidently call a vicious person?

SARA.

I know her from Mellefont's description.

MARWOOD.

Mellefont's? Has it never occurred to you then that Mellefont must be a very invalid witness in his own affairs?

SARA.

I see now, Madam, that you wish to put me to the test. Mellefont will smile, when you repeat to him how earnestly I have defended him.

MARWOOD.

I beg your pardon, Miss Sampson, Mellefont must not hear anything about this conversation. You are of too noble a mind to wish out of gratitude for a well-meant warning to estrange from him a relation, who speaks against him only because she looks upon his unworthy behaviour towards more than one of the most amiable of her sex as if she herself had suffered from it.

SARA.

I do not wish to estrange anyone, and would that others wished it as little as I do.

MARWOOD.

Shall I tell you the story of Marwood in a few words?

SARA.

I do not know. But still--yes, Madam! but under the condition that you stop as soon as Mellefont returns. He might think that I had inquired about it myself; and I should not like him to think me capable of a curiosity so prejudicial to him.

MARWOOD.

I should have asked the same caution of Miss Sampson, if she had not anticipated me. He must not even be able to suspect that Marwood has been our topic; and you will be so cautious as to act in accordance with this. Hear now! Marwood is of good family. She was a young widow, when Mellefont made her acquaintance at the house of one of her friends. They say, that she lacked neither beauty, nor the grace without which beauty would be nothing. Her good name was spotless. One single thing was wanting. Money. Everything that she had possessed,--and she is said to have had considerable wealth,--she had sacrificed for the deliverance of a husband from whom she thought it right to withhold nothing, after she had willed to give him heart and hand.

SARA.

Truly a noble trait of character, which I wish could sparkle in a better setting!

MARWOOD.

In spite of her want of fortune she was sought by persons, who wished nothing more than to make her happy. Mellefont appeared amongst her rich and distinguished admirers. His offer was serious, and the abundance in which he promised to place Marwood was the least on which he relied. He knew, in their earliest intimacy, that he had not to deal with an egoist, but with a woman of refined feelings, who would have preferred to live in a hut with one she loved, than in a palace with one for whom she did not care.

SARA.

Another trait which I grudge Miss Marwood. Do not flatter her any more, pray, Madam, or I might be led to pity her at last.

MARWOOD.

Mellefont was just about to unite himself with her with due solemnity, when he received the news of the death of a cousin who left him his entire fortune on the condition that he should marry a distant relation. As Marwood had refused richer unions for his sake, he would not now yield to her in generosity. He intended to tell her nothing of this inheritance, until he had forfeited it through her. That was generously planned, was it not?

SARA.

Oh, Madam, who knows better than I, that Mellefont possesses the most generous of hearts?

MARWOOD.

But what did Marwood do? She heard late one evening, through some friends, of Mellefont's resolution. Mellefont came in the morning to see her, and Marwood was gone.

SARA.

Whereto? Why?

MARWOOD.

He found nothing but a letter from her, in which she told him that he must not expect ever to see her again. She did not deny, though, that she loved him; but for this very reason she could not bring herself to be the cause of an act, of which he must necessarily repent some day. She released him from his promise, and begged him by the consummation of the union, demanded by the will, to enter without further delay into the possession of a fortune, which an honourable man could employ for a better purpose than the thoughtless flattery of a woman.

SARA.

But, Madam, why do you attribute such noble sentiments to Marwood? Lady Solmes may be capable of such, I daresay, but not Marwood. Certainly not Marwood.

MARWOOD.

It is not surprising, that you are prejudiced against her. Mellefont was almost distracted at Marwood's resolution. He sent people in all directions to search for her, and at last found her.

SARA.

No doubly because she wished to be found!

MARWOOD.

No bitter jests! They do not become a woman of such gentle disposition. I say, he found her; and found her inexorable. She would not accept his hand on any account; and the promise to return to London was all that he could get from her. They agreed to postpone their marriage until his relative, tired of the long delay, should be compelled to propose an arrangement. In the meantime Marwood could not well renounce the daily visits from Mellefont, which for a long time were nothing but the respectful visits of a suitor, who has been ordered back within the bounds of friendship. But how impossible is it for a passionate temper not to transgress these bounds. Mellefont possesses everything which can make a man dangerous to us. Nobody can be more convinced of this than you yourself, Miss Sampson.

SARA.

Alas!

MARWOOD.

You sigh! Marwood too has sighed more than once over her weakness, and sighs yet.

SARA.

Enough, Madam, enough! These words I should think, are worse than the bitter jest which you were pleased to forbid me.

MARWOOD.

Its intention was not to offend you, but only to show you the unhappy Marwood in a light, in which you could most correctly judge her. To be brief--love gave Mellefont the rights of a husband; and Mellefont did not any longer consider it necessary to have them made valid by the law. How happy would Marwood be, if she, Mellefont, and Heaven alone knew of her shame! How happy if a pitiable daughter did not reveal to the whole world that which she would fain be able to hide from herself.

SARA.

What do you say? A daughter----

MARWOOD.

Yes, through the intervention of Sara Sampson, an unhappy daughter loses all hope of ever being able to name her parents without abhorrence.

SARA.

Terrible words! And Mellefont has concealed this from me? Am I to believe it, Madam?

MARWOOD.

You may assuredly believe that Mellefont has perhaps concealed still more from you.

SARA.

Still more? What more could he have concealed from me?

MARWOOD.

This,--that he still loves Marwood.

SARA.

You will kill me!

MARWOOD.

It is incredible that a love which has lasted more than ten years can die away so quickly. It may certainly suffer a short eclipse, but nothing but a short one, from which it breaks forth again with renewed brightness. I could name to you a Miss Oclaff, a Miss Dorcas, a Miss Moore, and several others, who one after another threatened to alienate from Marwood the man by whom they eventually saw themselves most cruelly deceived. There is a certain point beyond which he cannot go, and as soon as he gets face to face with it he draws suddenly back. But suppose, Miss Sampson, you were the one fortunate woman in whose case all circumstances declared themselves against him; suppose you succeeded in compelling him to conquer the disgust of a formal yoke which has now become innate to him; do you then expect to make sure of his heart in this way?

SARA.

Miserable girl that I am! What must I hear?

MARWOOD.

Nothing less than that! He would then hurry back all the more into the arms of her who had not been so jealous of his liberty. You would be called his wife and she would be it.

SARA.

Do not torment me longer with such dreadful pictures! Advise me rather, Madam, I pray you, advise me what to do. You must know him! You must know by what means it may still be possible to reconcile him with a bond without which even the most sincere love remains an unholy passion.

MARWOOD.

That one can catch a bird, I well know; but that one can render its cage more pleasant than the open field, I do not know. My advice, therefore, would be that one should rather not catch it, and should spare oneself the vexation of the profitless trouble. Content yourself, young lady, with the pleasure of having seen him very near your net; and as you can foresee, that he would certainly tear it if you tempted him in altogether, spare your net and do not tempt him in.

SARA.

I do not know whether I rightly understand your playful parable----

MARWOOD.

If you are vexed with it, you have understood it. In one word. Your own interest as well as that of another--wisdom as well as justice, can, and must induce Miss Sampson to renounce her claims to a man to whom Marwood has the first and strongest claim. You are still in such a position with regard to him that you can withdraw, I will not say with much honour, but still without public disgrace. A short disappearance with a lover is a stain, it is true; but still a stain which time effaces. In some years all will be forgotten, and for a rich heiress there are always men to be found, who are not so scrupulous. If Marwood were in such a position, and she needed no husband for her fading charms nor father for her helpless daughter, I am sure she would act more generously towards Miss Sampson than Miss Sampson acts towards her when raising these dishonourable difficulties.

SARA (rising angrily)

.

This is too much! Is that the language of a relative of Mellefont's? How shamefully you are betrayed, Mellefont! Now I perceive, Madam, why he was so unwilling to leave you alone with me. He knows already, I daresay, how much one has to fear from your tongue. A poisoned tongue! I speak boldly--for your unseemly talk has continued long enough. How has Marwood been able to enlist such a mediator; a mediator who summons all her ingenuity to force upon me a dazzling romance about her; und employs every art to rouse my suspicion against the loyalty of a man, who is a man but not a monster? Was it only for this that I was told that Marwood boasted of a daughter from him; only for this that I was told of this and that forsaken girl--in order that you might be enabled to hint to me in cruel fashion that I should do well if I gave place to a hardened strumpet!

MARWOOD.

Not so passionate, if you please, young lady! A hardened strumpet? You are surely using words whose full meaning you have not considered.

SARA.

Does she not appear such, even from Lady Solmes's description? Well, Madam, you are her friend, perhaps her intimate friend. I do not say this as a reproach, for it may well be that it is hardly possible in this world to have virtuous friends only. Yet why should I be so humiliated for the sake of this friendship of yours? If I had had Marwood's experience, I should certainly not have committed the error which places me on such a humiliating level with her. But if I had committed it, I should certainly not have continued in it for ten years. It is one thing to fall into vice from ignorance; and another to grow intimate with it when you know it. Alas, Madam, if you knew what regret, what remorse, what anxiety my error has cost me! My error, I say, for why shall I be so cruel to myself any longer, and look upon it as a crime? Heaven itself ceases to consider it such; it withdraws my punishment, and gives me back my father.--But I am frightened, Madam; how your features are suddenly transformed! They glow-rage speaks from the fixed eye, and the quivering movement of the mouth. Ah, if I have vexed you, Madam, I beg for pardon! I am a foolish, sensitive creature; what you have said was doubtless not meant so badly. Forget my rashness! How can I pacify you? How can I also gain a friend in you as Marwood has done? Let me, let me entreat you on my knees (falling down upon her knees) for your friendship, and if I cannot have this, at least for the justice not to place me and Marwood in one and the same rank.

MARWOOD (proudly stepping back and leaving Sara on her knees)

.

This position of Sara Sampson is too charming for Marwood to triumph in it unrecognised. In me, Miss Sampson, behold the Marwood with whom on your knees you beg--Marwood herself--not to compare you.

SARA (springing up and drawing back in terror)

.

You Marwood? Ha! Now I recognise her--now I recognise the murderous deliverer, to whose dagger a warning dream exposed me. It is she! Away, unhappy Sara! Save me, Mellefont; save your beloved! And thou, sweet voice of my beloved father, call! Where does it call? Whither shall I hasten to it?--here?--there?--Help, Mellefont! Help, Betty! Now she approaches me with murderous hand! Help! (Exit.)

Scene

IX.

MARWOOD.

What does the excitable girl mean? Would that she spake the truth, and that I approached her with murderous hand! I ought to have spared the dagger until now, fool that I was! What delight to be able to stab a rival at one's feet in her voluntary humiliation! What now? I am detected. Mellefont may be here this minute. Shall I fly from him? Shall I await him? I will wait, but not in idleness. Perhaps the cunning of my servant will detain him long enough? I see I am feared. Why do I not follow her then? Why do I not try the last expedient which I can use against her? Threats are pitiable weapons; but despair despises no weapons, however pitiable they may be. A timid girl, who flies stupid and terror-stricken from my mere name, can easily take dreadful words for dreadful deeds. But Mellefont! Mellefont will give her fresh courage, and teach her to scorn my threats. He will! Perhaps he will not! Few things would have been undertaken in this world, if men had always looked to the end. And am I not prepared for the most fatal end? The dagger was for others, the drug is for me! The drug for me! Long carried by me near my heart, it here awaits its sad service; here, where in better times I hid the written flatteries of my lovers,--poison for us equally sure if slower. Would it were not destined to rage in my veins only! Would that a faithless one--why do I waste my time in wishing? Away! I must not recover my reason nor she hers. He will dare nothing, who wishes to dare in cold blood!

ACT V.

Scene

I.

Sara's

room.

Sara (reclining in an armchair), Betty.

BETTY.

Do you feel a little better, Miss?

SARA.

Better--I wish only that Mellefont would return! You have sent for him, have you not?

BETTY.

Norton and the landlord have gone for him.

SARA.

Norton is a good fellow, but he is rash. I do not want him by any means to be rude to his master on my account. According to his story, Mellefont is innocent of all this. She follows him; what can he do? She storms, she raves, she tries to murder him. Do you see, Betty, I have exposed him to this danger? Who else but me? And the wicked Marwood at last insisted on seeing me or she would not return to London. Could he refuse her this trifling request? Have not I too often been curious to see Marwood. Mellefont knows well that we are curious creatures. And if I had not insisted myself that she should remain with me until his return, he would have taken her away with him. I should have seen her under a false name, without knowing that I had seen her. And I should perhaps have been pleased with this little deception at some future time. In short, it is all my fault. Well, well, I was frightened; nothing more! The swoon was nothing. You know, Betty, I am subject to such fits.

BETTY.

But I had never seen you in so deep a swoon before.

SARA.

Do not tell me so, please! I must have caused you a great deal of trouble, my good girl.

BETTY.

Marwood herself seemed moved by your danger. In spite of all I could do she would not leave the room, until you had opened your eyes a little and I could give you the medicine.

SARA.

After all I must consider it fortunate that I swooned. For who knows what more I should have had to hear from her! She certainly can hardly have followed me into my room without a purpose! You cannot imagine how terrified I was. The dreadful dream I had last night recurred to me suddenly, and I fled, like an insane woman who does not know why and whither she flies. But Mellefont does not come. Ah!

BETTY.

What a sigh, Miss! What convulsions!

SARA.

God! what sensation was this----

BETTY.

What was that?

SARA.

Nothing, Betty! A pain! Not one pain, a thousand burning pains in one! But do not be uneasy; it is over now!

Scene

II.

Norton, Sara, Betty

.

NORTON.

Mellefont will be here in a moment.

SARA.

That is well, Norton! But where did you find him?

NORTON.

A stranger had enticed him beyond the town gate, where he said a gentleman waited for him, to speak with him about matters of the greatest importance. After taking him from place to place for a long time, the swindler slunk away from him. It will be bad for him if he lets himself be caught; Mellefont is furious.

SARA.

Did you tell him what has happened?

NORTON.

All.

SARA.

But in such a way!----

NORTON.

I could not think about the way. Enough! He knows what anxiety his imprudence has again caused you.

SARA.

Not so, Norton; I have caused it myself.

NORTON.

Why may Mellefont never be in the wrong? Come in, sir; love has already excused you.

Scene

III.

Mellefont, Norton, Sara, Betty

.

MELLEFONT.

Ah, Sara! If this love of yours were not----

SARA.

Then I should certainly be the unhappier of the two. If nothing more vexatious has happened to you in your absence than to me, I am happy.

MELLEFONT.

I have not deserved to be so kindly received.

SARA.

Let my weakness be my excuse, that I do not receive you more tenderly. If only for your sake, I would that I was well again.

MELLEFONT.

Ha! Marwood! this treachery too! The scoundrel who led me with a mysterious air from one street to another can assuredly have been a messenger of her only! See, dearest Sara, she employed this artifice to get me away from you. A clumsy artifice certainly, but just from its very clumsiness, I was far from taking it for one. She shall have her reward for this treachery! Quick, Norton, go to her lodgings; do not lose sight of her, and detain her until I come!

SARA.

What for, Mellefont? I intercede for Marwood.

MELLEFONT.

Go!
(Exit Norton
.)
Scene
IV.
Sara, Mellefont, Betty
.
SARA.
Pray let the wearied enemy who has ventured the last fruitless assault retire in peace! Without Marwood I should be ignorant of much----
MELLEFONT.
Much? What is the "much?"
SARA.
What you would not have told me, Mellefont! You start! Well, I will forget it again, since you do not wish me to know it.
MELLEFONT.
I hope that you will not believe any ill of me which has no better foundation than the jealousy of an angry slanderer.
SARA.
More of this another time! But why do you not tell me first of all about the danger in which your precious life was placed? I, Mellefont, I should have been the one who had sharpened the sword, with which Marwood had stabbed you.
MELLEFONT.
The danger was not so great. Marwood was driven by blind passion, and I was cool, so her attack could not but fail. I only wish that she may not have been more successful with another attack--upon Sara's good opinion of her Mellefont! I must almost fear it. No, dearest Sara, do not conceal from me any longer what you have learned from her.
SARA.
Well! If I had still had the least doubt of your love, Mellefont, Marwood in her anger would have removed it. She surely must feel that through me she has lost that which is of the greatest value to her; for an uncertain loss would have let her act more cautiously.
MELLEFONT.
I shall soon learn to set some store by her bloodthirsty jealousy, her impetuous insolence, her treacherous cunning! But Sara! You wish again to evade my question and not to reveal to me----
SARA.
I will; and what I said was indeed a step towards it. That Mellefont loves me, then, is undeniably certain. If only I had not discovered that his love lacked a certain confidence, which would be as flattering to me as his love itself. In short, dearest Mellefont--Why does a sudden anxiety make it so difficult for me to speak?--Well, I suppose I shall have to tell it without seeking for the most prudent form in which to say it. Marwood mentioned a pledge of love; and the talkative Norton--forgive him, pray--told me a name--a name, Mellefont, which must rouse in you another tenderness than that which you feel for me.
MELLEFONT.

Is it possible? Has the shameless woman confessed her own disgrace? Alas, Sara, have pity on my confusion! Since you already know all, why do you wish to hear it again from my lips? She shall never come into your sight,--the unhappy child, who has no other fault than that of having such a mother.

SARA.

You love her, then, in spite of all?

MELLEFONT.

Too much, Sara, too much for me to deny it.

SARA.

Ah, Mellefont! How I too love you, for this very love's sake! You would have offended me deeply, if you had denied the sympathy of your blood for any scruples on my account. You have hurt me already in that you have threatened me never to let her come into my sight. No, Mellefont! That you will never forsake Arabella must be one of the promises which you vow to me in presence of the Almighty! In the hands of her mother she is in danger of becoming unworthy of her father. Use your authority over both, and let me take the place of Marwood. Do not refuse me the happiness of bringing up for myself a friend who owes her life to you--a Mellefont of my own sex. Happy days, when my father, when you, when Arabella will vie in your calls on my filial respect, my confiding love, my watchful friendship. Happy days! But, alas! They are still far distant in the future. And perhaps even the future knows nothing of them, perhaps they exist only in my own desire for happiness! Sensations, Mellefont, sensations which I never before experienced, turn my eyes to another prospect. A dark prospect, with awful shadows! What sensations are these? (puts her hand before her face.)

MELLEFONT.

What sudden change from exultation to terror! Hasten, Betty! Bring help! What ails you, generous Sara! Divine soul! Why does this jealous hand (moving it away) hide these sweet looks from me? Ah, they are looks which unwillingly betray cruel pain. And yet this hand is jealous to hide these looks from me. Shall I not share your pain with you? Unhappy man, that I can only share it--that I may not feel it alone! Hasten, Betty!

BETTY.

Whither shall I hasten?

MELLEFONT.

You see, and yet ask? For help!

SARA.

Stay. It passes over. I will not frighten you again, Mellefont.

MELLEFONT.

What has happened to her, Betty? These are not merely the results of a swoon.

Scene

V.

Norton, Mellefont, Sara, Betty

.

MELLEFONT.

You are back again already, Norton? That is well! You will be of more use here.

NORTON.

Marwood is gone----

MELLEFONT.

And my curses follow her! She is gone? Whither? May misfortune and death, and, were it possible, a whole hell lie in her path! May Heaven thunder a consuming fire upon her, may the earth burst open under her, and swallow the greatest of female monsters!

NORTON.

As soon as she returned to her lodgings, she threw herself into her carriage, together with Arabella and her maid, and hurried away, at full gallop. This sealed note was left behind for you.

MELLEFONT (taking the note)

.

It is addressed to me. Shall I read it, Sara?

SARA.

When you are calmer, Mellefont.

MELLEFONT.

Calmer? Can I be calmer, before I have revenged myself on her, and before I know that you are out of danger, dearest Sara?

SARA.

Let me not hear of revenge! Revenge is not ours.--But you open the letter? Alas, Mellefont! Why are we less prone to certain virtues with a healthy body, which feels its strength, than with a sick and wearied one? How hard are gentleness and moderation to you, and how unnatural to me appears the impatient heat of passion! Keep the contents for yourself alone.

MELLEFONT.

What spirit is it that seems to compel me to disobey you? I opened it against my will, and against my will I must read it!

SARA (whilst Mellefont
reads to himself)

.

How cunningly man can disunite his nature, and make of his passions another being than himself, on whom he can lay the blame for that which in cold blood he disapproves.--The water, Betty! I fear another shock, and shall need it. Do you see what effect the unlucky note has on him? Mellefont! You lose your senses, Mellefont! God! he is stunned! Here, Betty. Hand him the water! He needs it more than I.

MELLEFONT (pushing Betty
back)

.

Back, unhappy girl! Your medicines are poison!

SARA.

What do you say? Recover yourself! You do not recognise her.

BETTY.

I am Betty,--take it!

MELLEFONT.

Wish rather, unhappy girl, that you were not she! Quick! Fly, before in default of the guiltier one you become the guilty victim of my rage.

SARA.

What words! Mellefont, dearest Mellefont----

MELLEFONT.

The last "dearest Mellefont" from these divine lips, and then no more for ever! At your feet, Sara----(throwing himself down). But why at your feet? (springing up again). Disclose it? I disclose it to you? Yes! I will tell you, that you will hate me, that you must hate me! You shall not hear the contents, no, not from me. But you will hear them. You will----Why do you all stand here, stock still, doing nothing? Run, Norton, bring all the doctors? Seek help, Betty! Let your help be as effective as your error! No, stop here! I will go myself----

SARA.

Whither, Mellefont? Help for what? Of what error do you speak?

MELLEFONT.

Divine help, Sara! or inhuman revenge! You are lost, dearest Sara! I too am lost! Would the world were lost with us!

Scene

VI.

Sara, Norton, Betty

.

SARA.

He is gone! I am lost? What does he mean? Do you understand him, Norton? I am ill, very ill; but suppose the worst, that I must die, am I therefore lost? And why does he blame you, poor Betty? You wring your hands? Do not grieve; you cannot have offended him; he will bethink himself; Had he only done as I wished, and not read the note! He could have known that it must contain the last poisoned words from Marwood.

BETTY.

What terrible suspicion! No, it cannot be. I do not believe it! NORTON (who has gone towards the back of the stage). Your father's old servant, Miss.

SARA.

Let him come in, Norton.

Scene

VII.

Waitwell, Sara, Betty, Norton

.

SARA.

I suppose you are anxious for my answer, dear Waitwell. It is ready except a few lines. But why so alarmed? They must have told you that I am ill.

WAITWELL.

And more still.

SARA.

Dangerously ill? I conclude so from Mellefont's passionate anxiety more than from my own feelings. Suppose, Waitwell, you should have to go with an unfinished letter from your unhappy Sara to her still more unhappy father! Let us hope for the best! Will you wait until to-morrow? Perhaps I shall find a few good moments to finish off the letter to your satisfaction. At present, I cannot do so. This hand hangs as if dead by my benumbed side. If the whole body dies away as easily as these limbs----you are an old man, Waitwell, and cannot be far from the last scene. Believe me, if that which I feel is the approach of death, then the approach of death is not so bitter. Ah! Do not mind this sigh! Wholly without unpleasant sensation it cannot be. Man could not be void of feeling; he must not be impatient. But, Betty, why are you so inconsolable?

BETTY.

Permit me, Miss, permit me to leave you.

SARA.

Go; I well know it is not every one who can bear to be with the dying. Waitwell shall remain with me! And you, Norton, will do me a favour, if you go and look for your master. I long for his presence.

BETTY (going)

.

Alas, Norton, I took the medicine from Marwood's hands!

Scene

VIII.

Waitwell, Sara

.

SARA.

Waitwell, if you will do me the kindness to remain with me, you must not let me see such a melancholy face. You are mute! Speak, I pray! And if I may ask it, speak of my father! Repeat all the comforting words which you said to me a few hours ago. Repeat them to me, and tell me too, that the Eternal Heavenly Father cannot be less merciful. I can die with that assurance, can I not? Had this befallen me before your arrival, how would I have fared? I should have despaired, Waitwell. To leave this world burdened with the hatred of him, who belies his nature when he is forced to hate--what a thought! Tell him that I died with the feelings of the deepest remorse, gratitude and love. Tell him--alas, that I shall not tell him myself--how full my heart is of all the benefits I owe to him. My life was the smallest amongst them. Would that I could yield up at his feet the ebbing portion yet remaining!

WAITWELL.

Do you really wish to see him, Miss?

SARA.

At length you speak--to doubt my deepest, my last desire!

WAITWELL.

Where shall I find the words which I have so long been vainly seeking? A sudden joy is as dangerous as a sudden terror. I fear only that the effect of his unexpected appearance might be too violent for so tender a heart!

SARA.

What do you mean? The unexpected appearance of whom?

WAITWELL.

Of the wished-for one! Compose yourself!

Scene

IX.

Sir William Sampson, Sara, Waitwell

.

SIR WILLIAM.

You stay too long, Waitwell! I must see her!

SARA.

Whose voice----

SIR WILLIAM.

Oh, my daughter!

SARA.

Oh, my father! Help me to rise, Waitwell, help me to rise that I may throw myself at his feet, (she endeavours to rise and falls back again into the arm-chair). Is it he, or is it an apparition sent from heaven like the angel who came to strengthen the Strong One? Bless me, whoever thou art, whether a messenger from the Highest in my father's form or my father himself!

SIR WILLIAM.

God bless thee, my daughter! Keep quiet (she tries again to throw herself at his feet). Another time, when you have regained your strength, I shall not be displeased to see you clasp my faltering knees.

SARA.

Now, my father, or never! Soon I shall be no more! I shall be only too happy if I still have a few moments to reveal my heart to you. But not moments--whole days--another life, would be necessary to tell all that a guilty, chastened and repentant daughter can say to an injured but generous and loving father. My offence, and your forgiveness----

SIR WILLIAM.

Do not reproach yourself for your weakness, nor give me credit for that which is only my duty. When you remind me of my pardon, you remind me also of my hesitation in granting it. Why did I not forgive you at once? Why did I reduce you to the necessity of flying from me. And this very day, when I had already forgiven you, what was it that forced me to wait first for an answer from you? I could already have enjoyed a whole day with you if I had hastened at once to your arms. Some latent spleen must still have lain in the innermost recesses of my disappointed heart, that I wished first to be assured of the continuance of your love before I gave you mine again. Ought a father to act so selfishly? Ought we only to love those who love us? Chide me, dearest Sara! Chide me! I thought more of my own joy in you than of you yourself. And if I were now to lose this joy? But who, then, says that I must lose it? You will live; you will still live long. Banish all these black thoughts! Mellefont magnifies the danger. He put the whole house in an uproar, and hurried away himself to fetch the doctors, whom he probably will not find in this miserable place. I saw his passionate anxiety, his hopeless sorrow, without being seen by him. Now I know that he loves you sincerely; now I do not grudge him you any longer. I will wait here for him and lay your hand in his. What I would otherwise have done only by compulsion, I now do willingly, since I see how dear you are to him. Is it true that it was Marwood herself who caused you this terror? I could understand this much from your Betty's lamentations, but nothing more. But why do I inquire into the causes of your illness, when I ought only to be thinking how to remedy it. I see you growing fainter every moment, I see it and stand helplessly here. What shall I do, Waitwell? Whither shall I run? What shall I give her? My fortune? My life? Speak!

SARA.

Dearest father! all help would be in vain! The dearest help, purchased with your life, would be of no avail.

Scene

X.

Mellefont, Sara, Sir William, Waitwell

.

MELLEFONT.

Do I dare to set my foot again in this room? Is she still alive?

SARA.

Step nearer, Mellefont!

MELLEFONT.

Am I to see your face again? No, Sara; I return without consolation, without help. Despair alone brings me back. But whom do I see? You, Sir? Unhappy father! You have come to a dreadful scene! Why did you not come sooner? You are too late to save your daughter! But, be comforted! You shall not have come too late to see yourself revenged.

SIR WILLIAM.

Do not remember in this moment, Mellefont, that we have ever been at enmity! We are so no more, and we shall never be so again. Only keep my daughter for me, and you shall keep a wife for yourself.

MELLEFONT.

Make me a god, and then repeat your prayer! I have brought so many misfortunes to you already, Sara, that I need not hesitate to announce the last one. You must die! And do you know by whose hand you die?

SARA.

I do not wish to know it--that I can suspect it is already too much----

MELLEFONT.

You must know it, for who could be assured that you did not suspect wrongly? Marwood writes thus: (he reads) "When you read this letter, Mellefont, your infidelity will already be punished in its cause. I had made myself known to her and she had swooned with terror. Betty did her utmost to restore her to consciousness. I saw her taking out a soothing-powder, and the happy idea occurred to me of exchanging it for a poisonous one. I feigned to be moved, and anxious to help her, and prepared the draught myself. I saw it given to her, and went away triumphant. Revenge and rage have made me a murderess; but I will not be like a common murderess who does not venture to boast of her deed. I am on my way to Dover; you can pursue me, and let my own handwriting bear witness against me. If I reach the harbour unpursued I will leave Arabella behind unhurt. Till then I shall look upon her as a hostage, Marwood." Now you know all, Sara! Here, Sir, preserve this paper! You must bring the murderess to punishment, and for this it is indispensable.--How motionless he stands!

SARA.

Give me this paper, Mellefont! I will convince myself with my own eyes (he hands it to her and she looks at it for a moment). Shall I still have sufficient strength? (tears it.)

MELLEFONT.

What are you doing, Sara!

SARA.

Marwood will not escape her fate; but neither you nor my father shall be her accusers. I die, and forgive the hand through which God chastens me. Alas, my father, what gloomy grief has taken hold of you? I love you still, Mellefont, and if loving you is a crime, how guilty shall I enter yonder world! Would I might hope, dearest father, that you would receive a son in place of a daughter! And with him you will have a daughter too, if you will acknowledge Arabella as such. You must fetch her back, Mellefont; her mother may escape. Since my father loves me, why should I not be allowed to deal with this love as with a legacy? I bequeath this fatherly love to you and Arabella. Speak now and then to her of a friend from whose example she may learn to be on her guard against love. A last blessing, my father!--Who would venture to judge the ways of the Highest?--Console your master, Waitwell! But you too stand there in grief and despair, you who lose in me neither a lover nor a daughter?

SIR WILLIAM.

We ought to be giving you courage, and your dying eyes are giving it to us. No more, my earthly daughter--half angel already; of what avail can the blessing of a mourning father be to a spirit upon whom all the blessings of heaven flow? Leave me a ray of the light which raises you so far above everything human. Or pray to God, who hears no prayer so surely as that of a pious and departing soul--pray to Him that this day may be the last of my life also!

SARA.

God must let the virtue which has been tested remain long in this world as an example; only the weak virtue which would perhaps succumb to too many temptations is quickly raised above the dangerous confines of the earth. For whom do these tears flow, my father? They fall like fiery drops upon my heart; and yet--yet they are less terrible to me than mute despair. Conquer it, Mellefont!--My eyes grow dim.--That sigh was the last! But where is Betty?--Now I understand the wringing of her hands.--Poor girl!--Let no one reproach her with carelessness, it is excused by a heart without falsehood, and without suspicion of it.--The moment is come! Mellefont--my father--(dies).

MELLEFONT.

She dies! Ah, let me kiss this cold hand once more (throwing himself at her feet). No! I will not venture to touch her. The old saying that the body of the slain bleeds at the touch of the murderer, frightens me. And who is her murderer? Am I not he, more than Marwood? (rises) She is dead now, Sir; she does not hear us any more. Curse me now. Vent your grief in well-deserved curses. May none of them miss their mark, and may the most terrible be fulfilled twofold! Why do you remain silent? She is dead! She is certainly dead. Now, again, I am nothing but Mellefont! I am no more the lover of a tender daughter, whom you would have reason to spare in him. What is that? I do not want your compassionate looks! This is your daughter! I am her seducer. Bethink yourself, Sir! In what way can I rouse your anger? This budding beauty, who was yours alone, became my prey! For my sake her innocent virtue was abandoned! For my sake she tore herself from the arms of a beloved father! For my sake she had to die! You make me impatient with your forbearance, Sir! Let me see that you are a father!

SIR WILLIAM.

I am a father, Mellefont, and am too much a father not to respect the last wish of my daughter. Let me embrace you, my son, for whom I could not have paid a higher price!

MELLEFONT.

Not so, Sir! This angel enjoined more than human nature is capable of! You cannot be my father. Behold, Sir (drawing the dagger from his bosom), this is the dagger which Marwood drew upon me to-day. To my misfortune, I disarmed her. Had I fallen a guilty victim of her jealousy, Sara would still be living. You would have your daughter still, and have her without Mellefont. It is not for me to undo what is done--but to punish myself for it is still in my power! (he stabs himself and sinks down at Sara's

side.)

SIR WILLIAM.

Hold him, Waitwell! What new blow upon my stricken head! Oh, would that my own might make the third dying heart here.

MELLEFONT (dying)

.

I feel it. I have not struck false. If now you will call me your son and press my hand as such, I shall die in peace. (Sir William

embraces him.) You have heard of an Arabella, for whom Sara pleaded; I should also plead for her; but she is Marwood's child as well as mine. What strange feeling seizes me? Mercy--O Creator, mercy!

SIR WILLIAM.

If the prayers of others are now of any avail, Waitwell, let us help him to pray for this mercy! He dies! Alas! He was more to pity than to blame.

Scene

XI.

Norton, The Others

.

NORTON.

Doctors, Sir!----

SIR WILLIAM.

If they can work miracles, they may come in! Let me no longer remain at this deadly spectacle! One grave shall enclose both. Come and make immediate preparations, and then let us think of Arabella. Be she who she may, she is a legacy of my daughter! (Exeunt.)

PHILOTAS.

A TRAGEDY IN ONE ACT.

Philotos was written at Berlin in the year 1759. It was never represented, and was probably not intended for the stage. It is here translated for the first time into English.

DRAMATIS PERSONÆ

Aridäus

, the King.

Strato

, a General of Aridäus

.

Philotas

, a prisoner.
Parmenio
, a soldier.
PHILOTAS.
Scene
I.
The scene is laid in a tent in the camp of Aridäus
.
PHILOTAS.

Am I really a prisoner? A prisoner? A worthy commencement this of my apprenticeship in war. O ye gods! O my father! How gladly would I persuade myself that all was but a dream! My earliest years have never dreamt of anything but arms and camps, battles and assaults. Could not the youth too be dreaming now of loss and defeat? Do not delude thyself thus, Philotas!--If I did not see, did not feel the wound through which the sword dropped from my palsied hand.--They have dressed it for me against my will! O cruel mercy of a cunning foe! "It is not mortal," said the surgeon, and thought to console me. Wretch, it should be mortal! And one wound only, only one! Did I know that I should make it mortal by tearing it open and dressing it and tearing it open again.--I rave, unhappy wretch. And with what a scornful face--I now recall it--that aged warrior looked at me--who snatched me from my horse! He called me--child! His king, too, must take me for a child, a pampered child. To what a tent he has had me brought! Adorned and provided with comforts of every sort! It must belong to one of his mistresses! A disgusting place for a soldier! And instead of being guarded, I am served. O mocking civility!

Scene
II.
Strato. Philotas
.
STRATO.
Prince--
PHILOTAS.
Another visitor already? Old man, I like to be alone!
STRATO.
Prince! I come by order of the king.
PHILOTAS.

I understand you! It is true, I am the king's prisoner, and it rests with him how he will have me treated. But listen: if you are the man whose features you bear,--if you are an old and honest warrior, have pity on me, and beg the king to have me treated as a soldier, not as a woman.

STRATO.
He will be with you directly; I come to announce his approach.
PHILOTAS.

The king with me? And you come to announce him? I do not wish that he should spare me one of the humiliations to which a prisoner must submit. Come, lead me to him! After the disgrace of having been disarmed, nothing is disgraceful to me now.

STRATO.

Prince! Your countenance, so full of youthful graces, bespeaks a softer heart!

PHILOTAS.

Mock not my countenance! Your visage, full of scars, is assuredly a more handsome face.

STRATO.

By the gods! A grand answer! I must admire and love you.

PHILOTAS.

I would not object if only you had feared me first.

STRATO.

More and more heroic! We have the most terrible of enemies before us, if there are many like Philotas amongst his youths.

PHILOTAS.

Do not flatter me! To become terrible to you, they must combine greater deeds with my thoughts. May I know your name?

STRATO.

Strato.

PHILOTAS.

Strato? The brave Strato, who defeated my father on the Lycus?

STRATO.

Do not recall that doubtful victory! And how bloodily did your father revenge himself in the plain of Methymna! Such a father must needs have such a son.

PHILOTAS.

To you, the worthiest of my father's enemies, I may bewail my fate! You only can fully understand me; you too, you too have been consumed in your youth by the ambition of the glory--the glory of bleeding for your native land. Would you otherwise be what you are? How have I not begged, implored, conjured him--my father these seven days--for only seven days has the manly toga covered me conjured him seven times on each of these seven days upon my knees to grant me that I should not in vain have outgrown my childhood,--to let me go with his warriors who had long cost me many a tear of jealousy. Yesterday I prevailed on him, the best of fathers, for Aristodem assisted my entreaties. You know Aristodem; he is my father's Strato.--"Give me this youth, my king, to go with me to-morrow," spoke Aristodem, "I am going to scour the mountains, in order to keep open the way to Cäsena." "Would I could accompany you!" sighed my father. He still lies sick from his wounds. "But be it so!" and with these words he embraced me. Ah, what did his happy son feel in that embrace! And the night which followed! I did not close my eyes; and yet dreams of glory and victory kept me on my couch until the second watch. Then I sprang up, threw on my new armour, pushed the uncurled hair beneath the helmet, chose from amongst my father's swords the one which matched my strength, mounted my horse and had tired out one already before the silver trumpet awakened the chosen band. They came, and I spoke with each of my companions, and many a brave warrior there pressed me to his scarred breast. Only with my father I did not speak; for I feared he might retract his word, if he should see me again. Then we marched. By the side of the immortal gods one cannot feel happier than did I by the side of Aristodem. At every encouraging glance from him I would have attacked a host alone, and thrown myself on the certain death of the enemy's swords. In quiet determination I rejoiced at every hill, from which I hoped to discern the enemy in the plain below, at every bend of the valley behind which I flattered myself that we should come upon them. And when at last I saw them rushing down upon us from the woody height,--showed them to my companions with the point of my sword,--flew up the mountain towards them, recall, O renowned warrior, the happiest of your youthful ecstasies, you could never have been happier. But now, now behold me, Strato; behold me ignominiously fallen from the summit of my lofty expectations! O how I shudder to repeat this fall again in thought! I had rushed too far in advance; I was wounded, and--imprisoned! Poor youth, thou hadst prepared thyself only for wounds, only for death,--and thou art made a prisoner! Thus always do the gods, in their severity, send only unforeseen evils to stultify our self-complacency. I weep--I must weep, although I fear to be despised for it by you. But despise me not! You turn away?

STRATO.

I am vexed: you should not move me thus. I become a child with you.

PHILOTAS.

No; hear why I weep! It is no childish weeping which you deign to accompany with your manly tears. What I thought my greatest happiness, the tender love with which my father loves me, will now become my greatest misery. I fear, I fear he loves me more than he loves his empire! What will he not sacrifice, what will not your king exact from him, to rescue me from prison! Through me, wretched youth, will he lose in one day more than he has gained in three long toilsome years with the blood of his noble warriors, with his own blood. With what face shall I appear again before him? I, his worst enemy! And my father's subjects--mine at some future day, if I had made myself worthy to rule them. How will they be able to endure the ransomed prince amongst them without contemptuous scorn. And when I die for shame, and creep unmourned to the shades below, how gloomy and proud will pass by the souls of those heroes who for their king had to purchase with their lives those gains, which, as a father, he renounces for an unworthy son! Oh, that is more than a feeling heart can endure!

STRATO.

Be comforted, dear prince! It is the fault of youth always to think itself more happy or less than it really is. Your fate is not so cruel yet;--the king approaches, you will hear more consolation from his lips.

Scene

III.

King Aridäus, Philotas, Strato

.

ARIDÄUS.

The wars which kings are forced to wage together are no personal quarrels. Let me embrace you, prince! Ah what happy days your blooming youth recalls to me! Thus bloomed your father's youth! This was his open, speaking eye; these his earnest, honest features; this his noble bearing! Let me embrace you again; in you I embrace your younger father. Have you never heard from him, prince, what good friends we were at your age? That was the blessed age, when we could still abandon ourselves to our feelings without restraint. But soon we were both called to the throne, and the anxious king, the jealous neighbour, stifled, alas, the willing friend.

PHILOTAS.

Pardon me, O king, if you find me too cold in my reply to such sweet words. My youth has been taught to think, but not to speak. What can it now aid me, that you and my father once were friends? Were! so you say yourself. The hatred which one grafts on an extinguished friendship bears the most deadly fruit of all; or I still know the human heart too little. Do not, therefore, O king, do not prolong my despair. You have spoken as the polished statesman: speak now as the monarch, who has the rival of his greatness completely in: his power.

STRATO.

O king, do not let him be tormented longer by the uncertainty of his fate!

PHILOTAS.

I thank you, Strato! Yes, let me hear at once, I beg you, how despicable you will render an unfortunate son in his father's eyes. With what disgraceful peace, with how many lands shall he redeem him? How small and contemptible shall he become, in order to regain his child? O my father!

ARIDÄUS.

This early, manly language too, prince, was your father's! I like to hear you speak thus. And would that my son, no less worthy of me, spoke thus before your father now.

PHILOTAS.

What mean you by that?

ARIDÄUS.

The gods--I am convinced of it--watch over our virtue, as they watch over our lives. To preserve both as long as possible is their secret and eternal work. Where is the mortal who knows how wicked he is at heart,--how viciously he would act, if they allowed free scope to each treacherous inducement to disgrace himself by little deeds! Yes, prince! Perhaps I might be he, whom you think me; perhaps I might not have sufficient nobleness of thought to use with modesty the strange fortune of war, which delivered you into my hands; perhaps I might have tried through you to exact that for which I would no longer venture to contend by arms; perhaps--but fear nothing; a higher power has forestalled this. Perhaps. I cannot let your father redeem his son more dearly than by--mine.

PHILOTAS.

I am astounded! You give me to understand that----

ARIDÄUS.

That my son is your father's prisoner, as you are mine.

PHILOTAS.

Your son my father's prisoner? Your Polytimet? Since when? How? Where?

ARIDÄUS.

Fate willed it thus! From equal scales it took equal weights at the same time, and the scales are balanced still.

STRATO.

You wish to know more details. Polytimet led the very squadron, towards which you rushed too rashly; and when your soldiers saw that you were lost, rage and despair gave them superhuman strength. They broke through the lines and all assailed the one in whom they saw the compensation for their loss. The end you know! Now accept a word of advice from an old soldier: The assault is not a race; not he who first, but he who most surely meets the enemy, approaches victory. Note this, too ardent prince! otherwise the future hero may be stifled in his earliest bud.

ARIDÄUS.

Strato, you vex the prince with your warning, though it be friendly. How gloomily he stands there!

PHILOTAS.

Not so. But do not mind me. In deep adoration of Providence--

ARIDÄUS.

The best adoration, prince, is grateful joy! Cheer up! We fathers will not long withhold our sons from one another. My herald is now ready; he shall go and hasten the exchange. But you know that joyful tidings, heard from the enemy alone, have the appearance of snares. They might suspect that you, perchance, had died from your wound. It will be necessary, therefore, for you to send a trustworthy messenger to your father with the herald. Come with me! Choose among the prisoners one whom you hold worthy of your confidence.

PHILOTAS.

You wish, then, that I shall detest myself a hundredfold? In each of the prisoners I shall behold myself! Spare me this embarrassment!

ARIDÄUS.

But----

PHILOTAS.

Parmenio must be among the prisoners. Send him to me! I will despatch him.

ARIDÄUS.

Well, be it so! Come, Strato! Prince, we shall see each other soon again!

Scene

IV.

PHILOTAS.

O God! the lightning could not have struck nearer without destroying me entirely. Wondrous gods! The flash returns! The vapour passes off, and I was only stunned. My whole misery then was seeing how miserable I might have become--how miserable my father through me!--Now I may appear again before you, my father! But still with eyes cast down; though shame alone will cast them down, and not the burning consciousness of having drawn you down with me to destruction. Now I need fear nothing from you but a smiling reprimand; no silent grief; no curses stifled by the stronger power of paternal love----

But--yes, by Heavens! I am too indulgent towards myself. May I forgive myself all the errors which Providence seems to pardon me? Shall I not judge myself more severely than Providence and my father judge me? All too indulgent judges! All other sad results of my imprisonment the gods could annihilate; one only they could not--the disgrace! It is true they could wipe out that fleeting shame, which falls from the lips of the vulgar crowd: but not the true and lasting disgrace, which the inner judge, my impartial self, pronounces over me!

And how easily I delude myself! Does my father then lose nothing through me?

The weight which the capture of Polytimet must throw into the scale if I were not a prisoner--is that nothing? Only through me does it become nothing! Fortune would have declared for him for whom it should declare;--the right of my father would triumph, if Polytimet was prisoner and not Philotas and Polytimet!

And now--but what was that which I thought just now? Nay, which a god thought within me--I must follow it up! Let me chain thee, fleeting thought! Now I have it again! How it spreads, farther and farther; and now it beams throughout my soul!

What did the king say? Why did he wish that I myself should send a trustworthy messenger to my father? In order that my father should not suspect--yes, thus ran his own words--that I had already died, perchance, from my wounds. He thinks, then, that the affair would take a different aspect, if I had died already from my wound. Would it do so? A thousand thanks for this intelligence. A thousand thanks! Of course it is so. For my father would then have a prince as his prisoner, for whom he could make any claim; and the king, his enemy, would have the body of a captured prince, for which he could demand nothing; which he must have buried or burned, if it should not become an object of disgust to him.

Good! I see that! Consequently, if I, I the wretched prisoner, will still turn the victory into my father's hands--on what does it depend? on death? On nothing more? O truly--the man is mightier than he thinks, the man who knows how to die!

But I? I, the germ, the bud of a man, do I know how to die? Not the man, the grown man alone, knows how to die; the youth also, the boy also; or he knows nothing at all. He who has lived ten years has had ten years time to learn to die; and what one does not learn in ten years, one neither learns in twenty, in thirty, nor in more. All that which I might have been, I must show by what I already am. And what could I, what would I be? A hero! Who is a hero? O my excellent, my absent father, be now wholly present in my soul! Have you not taught me that a hero is a man who knows higher goods than life? A man who has devoted his life to the welfare of the state; himself, the single one, to the welfare of the many? A hero is a man--a man? Then not a youth, my father? Curious question! It is good that my father did not hear it. He would have to think that I should be pleased, if he answered "No" to it. How old must the pine-tree be which has to serve as a mast? How old?--It must be tall enough, and must be strong enough.

Each thing, said the sage who taught me, is perfect if it can fulfil its end. I can fulfil my end, I can die for the welfare of the state; I am therefore perfect, I am a man. A man! although but a few days ago I was still a boy.

What fire rages in my veins? What inspiration falls on me? The breast becomes too narrow for the heart! Patience, my heart! Soon will I give thee space! Soon will I release thee from thy monotonous and tedious task! Soon shalt thou rest, and rest for long! Who comes? It is Parmenio! Quick! I must decide! What must I say to him? What message must I send my father through him?--Right! that I must say, that message I must send.

Scene

V.

Parmenio. Philotas

.

PHILOTAS.

Approach, Parmenio! Well? Why so shy--so full of shame? Of whom are you ashamed? Of yourself or of me?

PARMENIO.

Of both of us, prince!

PHILOTAS.

Speak always as you think! Truly, Parmenio, neither of us can be good for much, since we are here. Have you already heard my story?

PARMENIO.

Alas!

PHILOTAS.

And when you heard it?

PARMENIO.

I pitied you, I admired you, I cursed you; I do not know myself what I did.

PHILOTAS.

Yes, yes! But now that you have also learned, as I suppose, that the misfortune is not so great since Polytimet immediately afterwards was----

PARMENIO.

Yes, now; now I could almost laugh! I find that Fate often stretches its arm to terrible length to deal a trifling blow. One might think it wished to crush us, and it has after all done nothing but killed a fly upon our forehead.

PHILOTAS.

To the point. I am to send you to my father with the king's herald.

PARMENIO.

Good! Your imprisonment will then plead for mine. Without the good news which I shall bring him from you, and which is well worth a friendly look, I should have had to promise myself rather a frosty one from him.

PHILOTAS.

No, honest Parmenio; in earnest now! My father knows that the enemy carried you from the battle-field bleeding and half dead. Let him boast who will. He whom approaching death has already disarmed is easily taken captive. How many wounds have you now, old warrior?

PARMENIO.

O, I could cite a long list of them once. But now I have shortened it a good deal.

PHILOTAS.

How so?

PARMENIO.

Ha! I do not any more count the limbs on which I am wounded; to save time and breath I count those which still are whole. Trifles after all! For what else has one bones, but that the enemy's iron should notch itself upon them?

PHILOTAS.

That is bold! But now--what will you say to my father?

PARMENIO.

What I see: that you are well. For your wound, if I have heard the truth----

PHILOTAS.

Is as good as none.

PARMENIO.

A sweet little keepsake. Such as an ardent maid nips in our cheek. Is it not, prince?

PHILOTAS.

What do I know of that?

PARMENIO.

Well, well, time brings experience! Further I will tell your father what I believe you wish----

PHILOTAS.

And what is that?

PARMENIO.

To be with him again as soon as possible. Your childlike longing, your anxious impatience----

PHILOTAS.

Why not home-sickness at once! Knave! Wait and I will teach you to think differently.

PARMENIO.

By Heavens you must not! My dear youthful hero, let me tell you, you are still a child! Do not let the rough soldier so soon stifle in you the loving child! Or else one might not put the best construction on your heart; one might take your valour for inborn ferocity. I also am a father, father of an only son, who is but a little older than you, who with equal ardour--But you know him!

PHILOTAS.

I know him. He promises everything that his father has accomplished.

PARMENIO.

But if I knew that the young rogue did not long for his father at every moment when service leaves him free, and did not long for him as the lamb longs for its dam, I should wish--you see--that I had not begotten him. At present he must love more than respect me. I shall soon enough have to content myself with the respect, when nature guides the stream of his affection in another channel; when he himself becomes a father. Do not grow angry, prince!

PHILOTAS.

Who can grow angry with you? You are right! Tell my father everything which you think a loving son should say to him at such a time. Excuse my youthful rashness, which has almost brought him and his empire to destruction. Beg him to forgive my fault. Assure him that I shall never again remind him of it by a similar fault; that I will do everything that he too may be able to forget it. Entreat him----

PARMENIO.

Leave it to me! Such things we soldiers can say well. And better than a learned orator, for we say it more sincerely. Leave it to me! I know it all already. Farewell, prince! I hasten----

PHILOTAS.

Stop!

PARMENIO.

Well? What means this serious air which you suddenly assume?

PHILOTAS.

The son has done with you, but not yet the prince. The one had to feel; the other has to think! How willingly would the son be again with his father,--his beloved father--this very moment--sooner than were possible; but the prince, the prince cannot.--Listen!

PARMENIO.

The prince cannot?

PHILOTAS.

And will not!

PARMENIO.

Will not?

PHILOTAS.

Listen!

PARMENIO.

I am surprised!

PHILOTAS.

I say, you shall listen and not be surprised. Listen!

PARMENIO.

I am surprised, because I listen. It has lightened, and I expect the thunderbolt. Speak!--But, young prince, no second rashness!

PHILOTAS.

But, soldier, no subtilising! Listen! I have my reasons for wishing not to be redeemed before to-morrow. Not before to-morrow! Do you hear? Therefore tell our king that he shall not heed the haste of our enemy's herald! Tell him that a certain doubt, a certain plan compelled Philotas to this delay. Have you understood me?

PARMENIO.

No!

PHILOTAS.

Not? Traitor!

PARMENIO.

Softly, prince! A parrot does not understand, but he yet recollects what one says to him. Fear not! I will repeat everything to your father that I hear from you.

PHILOTAS.

Ha! I forbade you to subtilise; and that puts you out of humour. But how is it that you are so spoiled? Do all your generals inform you of their reasons?

PARMENIO.

All, prince!--Except the young ones.

PHILOTAS.

Excellent! Parmenio, if I were so sensitive as you----

PARMENIO.

And yet he only to whom experience has given twofold sight can command my blind obedience.

PHILOTAS.

Then I shall soon have to ask your pardon. Well, I ask your pardon, Parmenio! Do not grumble, old man! Be kind again, old father! You are indeed wiser than I am. But not the wisest only have the best ideas. Good ideas are gifts of fortune, and good fortune, as you well know, often gives to the youth rather than to the old man. For Fortune is blind.

Blind, Parmenio! Stone blind to all merit. If it were not so, would you not have been a general long ago?

PARMENIO.

How you know how to flatter, prince! But in confidence, beloved prince, do you not wish to bribe me--to bribe me with flatteries?

PHILOTAS.

I flatter? And bribe you? You are the man indeed whom one could bribe!

PARMENIO.

If you continue thus, I may become so. Already I no longer thoroughly trust myself.

PHILOTAS.

What was it I was saying? One of those good ideas, which fortune often throws into the silliest brain, I too have seized--merely seized, not the slightest portion of it is my own. For if my reason,--my invention had some part in it, should I not wish to consult with you about it? But this I cannot do; it vanishes, if I impart it; so tender, so delicate is it, that I do not venture to clothe it in words. I conceive it only, as the philosopher has taught me to conceive God, and at the most I could only tell you what it is not. It is possible enough that it is in reality a childish thought; a thought which I consider happy, because I have not yet had a happier. But let that be; if it can do no good, it can at least do no harm. That I know for certain; it is the most harmless idea in the world; as harmless as--as a prayer! Would you cease to pray because you are not quite certain whether the prayer will be of use to you? Do not then spoil my pleasure, Parmenio, honest Parmenio! I beg you, I embrace you. If you love me but a very little--will you? Can I rely on you? Will you manage that I am not exchanged before to-morrow? Will you?

PARMENIO.

Will? Must I not? Must I not? Listen, prince; when you shall one day be king, do not give commands. To command is an unsure means of being obeyed. If you have a heavy duty to impose on anyone, do with him as you have just now done with me; and if he then refuses his obedience--Impossible! He cannot refuse it to you. I too must know what a man can refuse.

PHILOTAS.

What obedience? What has the kindness which you show me to do with obedience? Will you, my friend----

PARMENIO.

Stop! Stop! You have won me quite already. Yes! I will do everything. I will, I will tell your father, that he shall not exchange you until to-morrow. But why only to-morrow? I do not know! That I need not know. That he need not know either. Enough that I know you wish it. And I wish everything that you wish. Do you wish nothing else? Is there nothing else that I shall do? Shall I run through the fire for you? Shall I cast myself from a rock for you? Command only, my dear young friend, command! I will do everything now for you. Even say a word and I will commit a crime, an act of villainy for you! My blood, it is true, curdles; but still, prince, if you wish, I will--I will----

PHILOTAS.

O my best, my fiery friend! O how shall I call you? You creator of my future fame! I swear to you by everything that is sacred to me, by my father's honour, by the fortune of his arms, by the welfare of his land--I swear to you never in my life to forget this your readiness, your zeal! Would that I also could reward it sufficiently! Hear, ye gods, my oath! And now, Parmenio, swear too! Swear to keep your promise faithfully!

PARMENIO.

I swear? I am too old for swearing.

PHILOTAS.

And I too young to trust you without an oath. Swear to me! I have sworn to you by my father, swear you by your son. You love your son? You love him from your heart?

PARMENIO.

From my heart, as I love you! You wish it, and I swear. I swear to you by my only son, by my blood which flows in his veins, by the blood which I would willingly have shed for your father's sake, and which he will also willingly shed some future day for yours--by this blood I swear to you to keep my word. And if I do not keep it, may my son fall in his first battle, and never live to see the glorious days of your reign! Hear, ye gods, my oath!

PHILOTAS.

Hear him not yet, ye gods! You will make fun of me, old man! To fall in the first battle--not to live to see my reign; is that a misfortune? Is it a misfortune to die early?

PARMENIO.

I do not say that. Yet only to see you on the throne, to serve you, I should like--what otherwise I should not wish at all--to become young again. Your father is good; but you will be better than he.

PHILOTAS.

No praise that slights my father! Alter your oath! Come, alter it like this. If you do not keep your word, let your son become a coward, a scoundrel; in the choice between death and disgrace, let him choose the latter; let him live ninety years the laughing-stock of women, and even die unwillingly in his ninetieth year.

PARMENIO.

I shudder, but I swear. Let him do so. Hear the most terrible of oaths, ye gods!

PHILOTAS.

Hear it! Well, you can go, Parmenio! We have detained each other long enough, and almost made too much ado about a trifle. For is it not a very trifle to tell my father--to persuade him not to exchange us until tomorrow? And if he should wish to know the reason--well, then invent a reason on your way!

PARMENIO.

That, too, I'll do. Yet I have never, though I am so old, devised a lie. But for your sake, prince--Leave it to me. Wickedness may still be learned even in old age. Farewell!

PHILOTAS.

Embrace me! Go!

Scene

VI.

PHILOTAS.

There are said to be so many rogues in the world, and yet deceiving is so hard, even when done with the best intentions. Had I not to turn and twist myself! Only see, good Parmenio, that my father does not exchange us before to-morrow, and he shall not need to exchange us at all. Now I have gained time enough! Time enough to strengthen myself in my purpose--time enough to choose the surest means. To strengthen myself in my purpose! Woe to me if I need that! Firmness of age, if thou art not mine, then obstinacy of youth, stand thou by me!

Yes, it is resolved! It is firmly resolved! I feel that I grow calm--I am calm! Thou who standest there, Philotas (surveying himself)--Ha! It must be a glorious, a grand sight; a youth stretched on the ground, the sword in his breast! The sword? Gods! O unhappy wretch that I am. And now only do I become aware of it! I have no sword; I have not anything! It became the booty of the warrior who made me prisoner. Perhaps he would have left it me, but the hilt was of gold. Accursed gold! art thou then always the ruin of virtue?

No sword? I no sword? Gods, merciful gods, grant me this one thing! Mighty gods, ye who have created heaven and earth, ye could not create a sword for me, if ye wished to do so? What is now my grand and glorious design? I become a bitter cause of laughter to myself.

And there the king comes back already! Stop! Suppose I played the child? This idea is promising. Yes, perhaps I may succeed.

Scene

VII.

Aridäus. Philotas

.

ARIDÄUS.

The messengers have now gone, my prince! They have started on their swiftest horses, and your father's camp is so near at hand, that we can receive a reply in a few hours.

PHILOTAS.

You are then very impatient, king, to embrace your son once more?

ARIDÄUS.

Will your father be less so to press you to his heart again? But let me enjoy your company, dearest prince! The time will speed more quickly in it, and perhaps in other respects it may also have good results, if we become more intimately acquainted with each other. Often already have loving children been the mediators of their angry fathers. Follow me therefore to my tent, where the greatest of my generals await you! They burn with the desire to see you, and offer you their admiration.

PHILOTAS.

Men must not admire a child, king! Leave me here, therefore, I pray! Shame and vexation would make me play a very foolish part. And as to your conversation with me, I do not see at all what good could come of it. I know nothing else, but that you and my father are involved in war; and the right--the right, I think, is on my father's side. This I believe, king! and will believe, even though you could prove the reverse indisputably. I am a son and a soldier, and have no other opinion than that of my father and my general.

ARIDÄUS.

Prince! it shows a great intelligence thus to deny one's intelligence. Yet I am sorry that I shall not ever be able to justify myself before you. Accursed war!

PHILOTAS.

Yes, truly, an accursed war! And woe to him who caused it.

ARIDÄUS.

Prince! prince! remember that it was your father who first drew the sword. I do not wish to join in your curses. He was rash, he was too suspicious.

PHILOTAS.

Well, my father drew the first sword. But does the conflagration only take its rise when the bright flame already breaks through the roof? Where is the patient, quiet creature, devoid of all feeling, which cannot be embittered through incessant irritations? Consider--for you compel me to speak of things of which I have no right to speak--consider what a proud and scornful answer you sent him when he--but you shall not compel me; I will not speak of it! Our guilt and our innocence are liable to endless misinterpretations, endless excuses. Only to the undeceived eye of the gods do we appear as we are; they alone can judge us. But the gods, you know it, king, speak their verdict through the sword of the bravest. Let us therefore wait to hear their bloody sentence. Why shall we turn in cowardice from this highest of judgments to a lower? Are our arms already so weary that the pliant tongue must take their place?

ARIDÄUS.

I hear with astonishment----

PHILOTAS.

Ah! a woman, too, may be listened to with astonishment.

ARIDÄUS.

With astonishment, prince, and not without grief. Fate has destined you for the throne! To you it will confide the welfare of a mighty and noble nation; to you! What dreadful future reveals itself to me! You will overwhelm your people with laurels,--and with misery. You will count more victories than happy subjects. Well for me, that my days will not reach into yours! But woe to my son, to my honest son! You will scarcely allow him to lay aside his armour----

PHILOTAS.

Comfort the father, O king! I shall allow your son far more!--far more!

ARIDÄUS.

Far more? Explain yourself.

PHILOTAS.

Have I spoken a riddle? O do not ask, king, that a youth, such as I am, shall always speak with caution and design. I only wished to say the fruit is often very different from what the blossom promises. An effeminate prince, history has taught me, has often proved a warlike king. Could not the reverse occur with me? Or perhaps the meaning of what I said was that I had still a long and dangerous way to the throne. Who knows if the gods will allow me to accomplish it? And do not let me accomplish it, father of gods and men, if in the future thou seest in me a waster of the most precious gift which thou hast entrusted to me,--the blood of my subjects!

ARIDÄUS.

Yes, prince; what is a king, if he be not a father? What is a hero void of human love? Now I recognise this also in you, and am your friend again! But come, come; we must not remain alone here! We are too serious for one another. Follow me!

PHILOTAS.

Pardon, king----

ARIDÄUS.

Do not refuse!
PHILOTAS.
Thus, as I am, shall I show myself to many eyes?
ARIDÄUS.
Why not?
PHILOTAS.
I cannot, king, I cannot!
ARIDÄUS.
And the reason?
PHILOTAS.
O, the reason! It would make you laugh.
ARIDÄUS.
So much the better,--let me hear it! I am a human being, and like to laugh and cry.
PHILOTAS.
Well, laugh then! See, king, I have no sword, and should not like to appear amongst soldiers without this mark of the soldier.
ARIDÄUS.
My laughing turns to joy! I have thought of that beforehand, and your wish will be gratified at once. Strato has the order to get your sword again for you.
PHILOTAS.
Let us then await him here!
ARIDÄUS.
And then you will accompany me?
PHILOTAS.
Then I will follow you immediately.
ARIDÄUS.
As we willed it! There he comes! Well, Strato!
Scene
VIII.
Strato
(with a sword in his hand), Aridäus, Philotas
.
STRATO.
King! I came to the soldier who had taken the prince and demanded the prince's sword from him in your name. But hear how nobly the soldier refused! "The king," he said, "must not take the sword from me! It is a good sword, and I shall use it in his service. I must also keep a remembrance of this deed. By the gods, it was none of my least! The prince is a young demon. But perhaps you wish only the precious hilt!" And on this, before I could prevent it, his strong hand had broken off the hilt, and throwing it contemptuously before my feet--"There it is," he continued, "what care I for your gold?"
ARIDÄUS.
O Strato, make good for me what this man has done!
STRATO.
I have done so. And here is one of your swords!
ARIDÄUS.

Give it me! Will you accept it, prince, instead of yours?

PHILOTAS.

Let me see! Ha! (aside.) Be thanked, ye gods! (eyeing it long and earnestly). A sword!

STRATO.

Have I not chosen well, prince?

ARIDÄUS.

What do you find in it so worthy of your deep attention?

PHILOTAS.

That it is a sword!--(recovering himself.) And a beautiful sword! I shall not lose anything by this exchange. A sword!

ARIDÄUS.

You tremble, prince!

PHILOTAS.

With joy! It seems, however, a trifle short for me. But why short? A step nearer to the enemy replaces what is wanting in the steel. Beloved sword! What a beautiful thing is a sword,--to play with and to use! I have never played with anything else.

ARIDÄUS (to Strato

)

.

O the wondrous combination of child and hero!

PHILOTAS (aside)

.

Beloved sword! Could I but be alone with thee! But, courage!

ARIDÄUS.

Now gird on the sword, prince, and follow me!

PHILOTAS.

Directly! Yet one must not know one's friend and one's sword only outwardly (he draws it, and Strato

steps between him and the king).

STRATO.

I understand the steel better than the workmanship. Believe me, prince, the steel is good. The king has cleft more than one helmet with it since his youth.

PHILOTAS.

I shall never grow so strong as that! But--Do not step so near, Strato!

STRATO.

Why not?

PHILOTAS.

So! (springing back and swinging the sword through the air). It has the right swing.

ARIDÄUS.

Prince, spare your wounded arm! You will excite yourself!

PHILOTAS.

Of what do you remind me, king? Of my misfortune--no, of my shame! I was wounded and made prisoner. Yes, but I shall never be so again! By this my sword, I shall never be so again! No, my father, no! To-day a wonder spares you the shameful ransom of your son; his death may spare it you in the future!--His certain death, when he shall see himself surrounded again! Surrounded again? Horrible! I am so! I am surrounded! What now? Companions! Friends! Brothers! Where are you? All dead? Enemies everywhere! Through here, Philotas! Ha! That is for you, rash fellow!--And that for you!--And that for you! (striking around him.)

STRATO.

Prince! what ails you? Calm yourself (approaches him.)

PHILOTAS (stepping away from him)

.

You too, Strato? You too? O, foe, be generous! Kill me! Do not make me captive! No, I do not deliver myself up! Were you all, who surround me, Stratos, yet I will defend myself against you all--against a world will I defend myself! Do your best, my foes! But you will not? You will not kill me, cruel men? You only wish to have me alive? I laugh at you! To take me prisoner alive? Me? Sooner shall this sword--this sword--shall piercc this breast--sooner--before--(he stabs himself.)

ARIDÄUS.

God! Strato!

STRATO.

King!

PHILOTAS.

I wished it thus! (sinking back.)

ARIDÄUS.

Hold him, Strato! Help! help for the prince! Prince, what raving anguish----

PHILOTAS.

Forgive me, king! I have dealt you a more deadly blow than myself! I die, and soon will peaceful lands enjoy the fruit of my death. Your son, king, is a prisoner, and the son of my father is free!

ARIDÄUS.

What do I hear?

STRATO.

Then it was your purpose, prince? But as our prisoner, you had no right ovcr yourself!

PHILOTAS.

Do not say that, Strato! Should a man be able to fetter another's liberty to die, the liberty which the gods have left in all vicissitudes of life?

STRATO.

O king! Terror has paralyzed him! King!

ARIDÄUS.

Who calls me?

STRATO.

King!

ARIDÄUS.

Be silent!

STRATO.

The war is over, king!

ARIDÄUS.

Over? You lie, Strato! The war is not over, prince! Die! yes, die! But carry with you this tormenting thought! You believed, as a true ignorant boy, that fathers were all of one and the same mould,--all of the soft, effeminate nature of your father. They are not all like him! I am not so! What do I care about my son? And do you think that he cannot die as well for his father as you did for yours? Let him die! Let his death too spare me the disgraceful ransom! Strato, I am bereft now, I poor man! You have a son;--he shall be mine. For a son one must have! Happy Strato!

PHILOTAS.

Your son too lives still, king! And will live! I hear it!

ARIDÄUS.

Does he live still? Then I must have him back. But you--die! I will have him back, let what will come of it. And in exchange for you! Or I will have such disgrace and dishonour shown to your body--I will have it----

PHILOTAS.

The dead body!--If you will revenge yourself, king, awaken it again!

ARIDÄUS.

Ah! What do I say?

PHILOTAS.

I pity you! Farewell, Strato! There, where all virtuous friends and all brave men are members of one blessed state--in Elysium we shall meet again! We also, king, shall meet again.

ARIDÄUS.

And reconciled! Prince!

PHILOTAS.

O then, ye gods, receive my triumphant soul; and thou, goddess of peace, thy offering!

ARIDÄUS.

Hear me, prince!

STRATO.

He dies! Am I traitor, king, if I weep over your enemy? I cannot restrain myself. A wondrous youth!

ARIDÄUS.

Weep over him, weep! And I too! Come! I must have my son again. But do not oppose me, if I pay too high a ransom for him! In vain have we shed our streams of blood, in vain have we conquered lands. There he departs with our booty, the greater victor!--Come! Get me my son! And when I have him, I will no more be king. Do ye believe, ye men, that one does not grow weary of it? (Exeunt.)

EMILIA GALOTTI.

A TRAGEDY IN FIVE ACTS.

(Translated by B. Dillon Boylan.)

'Emilia Galotti' was commenced in 1757, when Lessing was at Leipzig, but was thrown aside for some years, until in 1767, when at Hamburg, he again took it up, intending to have it represented on the Hamburg stage. But on the failure of the theatrical enterprise with which he was connected, he once more abandoned it until 1771, when he again turned his attention to it, and completed it in February of the following year. It was immediately represented on the Brunswick stage.

DRAMATIS PERSONÆ.
Emilia Galotti

.

Odoardo
and
Claudia Galotti

,

parents of Emilia

.

Hettore Gonzaga
, Prince of Guastalla.
Marinelli
, the Prince's Chamberlain.
Camillo Rota
, one of the Prince's Councillors.
Conti
, an artist.
Count Appiani

.

Angelo
, a bandit.
Pirro
and sundry servants.
EMILIA GALOTTI.
ACT I.
Scene
I.--The Prince's Cabinet

.

The Prince
, seated at a desk, which is covered with papers.
PRINCE.
Complaints; nothing but complaints! Petitions; nothing but petitions! Wretched employment! And yet we are envied! To be sure, if we could relieve every one, we might indeed be envied. Emilia? (opening a petition, and looking at the signature.) An Emilia? Yes--but an Emilia Bruneschi--not Galotti. Not Emilia Galotti. What does she want, this Emilia Bruneschi? (Reads) She asks much--too much. But her name is Emilia. It is granted (signs the paper, and rings).
Enter a Servant

.

PRINCE.
Are any of the Councillors in the antechamber?
SERVANT.
No, your Highness.
PRINCE.

I have begun the day too early. The morning is so beautiful, I will take a drive. The Marquis Marinelli shall accompany me. Let him be called. (Exit Servant

.) I can attend to nothing more. I was so happy--delightful thought! so happy--when all at once this wretched Bruneschi must be named Emilia. Now all my peace is fled.

Re-enter the Servant

, bringing a note.

SERVANT.

The Marquis has been sent for; and here is a letter from the Countess Orsina.

PRINCE.

The Countess Orsina? Put it down.

SERVANT.

Her courier waits.

PRINCE.

I will send an answer if necessary. Where is she, in town, or at her villa?

SERVANT.

She arrived in town yesterday.

PRINCE.

So much the worse--the better, I mean. There is less reason for the messenger to wait. (Exit Servant

.) My dear Countess! (with sarcasm, as he takes up the letter) as good as read (throwing it down again). Well, well, I fancied I loved her--one may fancy anything. It may be that I really did love her. But--I did.

Re-enter Servant

.

SERVANT.

The painter Conti requests the honour----

PRINCE.

Conti? Good! admit him. That will change the current of my thoughts (rising).

Scene

II.

Conti

, The Prince

.

PRINCE.

Good morning, Conti. How goes it with you? How does art thrive?

CONTI.

Art is starving, Prince.

PRINCE.

That must not--shall not be, within the limits of my small dominions. But the artist must be willing to work.

CONTI.

Work! that is his happiness. But too much work may rain his claim to the title of artist.

PRINCE.

I do not mean that his works should be many, but his labour much: a little, but well done. But you do not come empty-handed, Conti?

CONTI.

I have brought the portrait which your Highness ordered; and another which you did not order; but as it is worthy of inspection----

PRINCE.

That one, is it? And yet I do not well remember----

CONTI.

The Countess Orsina.

PRINCE.

True. The commission, however, was given rather long ago.

CONTI.

Our beauties are not every day at the artist's command. In three months, the Countess could only make up her mind to sit once.

PRINCE.

Where are the pictures?

CONTI.

In the antechamber. I will fetch them (exit).

Scene

III.

PRINCE.

Her portrait! Let it come; it is not herself. But perhaps I may see in the picture what I can no longer find in her person. But I have no wish to make such a discovery. The importunate painter! I almost believe that she has bribed him. But even were it so, if another picture which is pourtrayed in brighter colours and on a different canvas, could be obliterated to make room for her once more in my heart, I really think that I should be content. When I loved the Countess, I was ever gay, sprightly, and cheerful; now I am the reverse. But no, no, no; happy or unhappy, it is better as it is.

Scene

IV.

The Prince, Conti

, with the portraits; he places one with the face reversed against a chair, and prepares to show the other.

CONTI.

I beg your Highness will bear in mind the limits of our art; much of the highest perfection of beauty lies altogether beyond its limits. Look at it in this position.

PRINCE (after a brief inspection)

.

Excellent! Conti, most excellent! It does credit to your taste,--to your skill. But flattered, Conti--quite, infinitely flattered!

CONTI.

The original did not seem to be of your opinion. But, in truth, she is not more flattered than art is bound to flatter. It is the province of art to paint as plastic nature--if there is such a thing--intended her original design, without the defects which the unmanageable materials render inevitable, and free from the ravages which result from a conflict with time.

PRINCE.

The intelligent artist has therefore double merit. But the original, you say, notwithstanding all this----

CONTI.

Pardon me, Prince! The original is a person who commands my respect. I did not intend to insinuate anything to her disadvantage.

PRINCE.

As much as you please. But what said the original?

CONTI.

"I am satisfied," said the Countess, "if I am not plainer."

PRINCE.

Not plainer! The original herself!

CONTI.

And she uttered this with an expression of which the portrait affords no trace, no idea.

PRINCE.

That is just what I meant; therein lies your infinite flattery. Oh! I know well her proud, contemptuous look, which would disfigure the face of one of the Graces. I do not deny that a handsome mouth set off with a slight curl of scorn, sometimes acquires thereby additional beauty. But, observe, it must be only slight; the look must not amount to grimace, as it does with this Countess. The eyes, too, must keep control over the disdainful charmer; eyes which the worthy Countess decidedly does not possess. You do not even give them to her in the picture.

CONTI.

Your Highness, I am perfectly amazed.

PRINCE.

And wherefore? All that could be achieved by the resources of art out of the great prominent staring Medusa eyes of the Countess, you have honourably accomplished. Honourably, I say, but less honourably would have been more honest; for tell me yourself, Conti, is the character of the individual expressed by this picture? yet it should be. You have converted pride into dignity, disdain into a smile, and the gloom of discontent into soft melancholy.

CONTI (somewhat vexed)

.

Ah! Prince, we painters expect that a portrait when finished will find the lover as warm as when he ordered it. We paint with eyes of love, and the eyes of love alone must judge our works.

PRINCE.

'Tis true, Conti; but why did you not bring it a month sooner? Lay it aside. What is the other?

CONTI (taking it up and holding it still reversed)

.

It is also a female portrait.

PRINCE.

Then I had almost rather not see it; for the ideal depicted here (pointing to his forehead), or rather here (laying his hand upon his heart), it cannot equal. I should like, Conti, to admire your art in other subjects.

CONTI.

There may be more admirable examples of art, but a more admirable subject than this cannot exist.

PRINCE.

Then I'll lay a wager, Conti, that it is the portrait of the artist's own mistress. (Conti turns the picture.) What do I see? Your work, Conti, or the work of my fancy? Emilia Galotti!

CONTI.

How, Prince! do you know this angel?

PRINCE (endeavouring to compose himself, but unable to remove his eyes from the picture)

.

A little; just enough to recognise her. A few weeks ago I met her with her mother at an assembly; since then I have only seen her in sacred places, where staring is unseemly. I know her father also; he is not my friend. He it was who most violently opposed my pretensions to Sabionetta. He is a veteran, proud and unpolished, but upright and brave.

CONTI.

You speak of the father, this is the daughter.

PRINCE.

By Heavens! you must have stolen the resemblance from her mirror (with his eyes still rivetted on the picture). Oh, you well know, Conti, that we praise the artist most when we forget his merits in his works.

CONTI.

Yet I am extremely dissatisfied with this portrait, and nevertheless I am satisfied with being dissatisfied with myself. Alas! that we cannot paint directly with our eyes! On the long journey from the eye through the arm to the pencil, how much is lost! But, as I have already said, though I know what is lost, and how and why it is lost, I am as proud and prouder of this loss than of what I have preserved. For by the former I perceive more than by the latter, that I am a good painter, though my hand is not always so. Or do you hold, Prince, that Raffaelle would not have been the greatest of all artists even had he unfortunately been born without hands?

PRINCE (turning his eyes a moment from the picture)

.

What do you say, Conti? What was your enquiry?

CONTI.

Oh, nothing--nothing; mere idle observations! Your soul, I observe, was wholly in your eyes. I like such souls and such eyes.

PRINCE (affecting coldness)

.

And so, Conti, you really consider Emilia Galotti amongst the first beauties of our city.

CONTI.

Amongst them? Amongst the first? The first of our city? You jest, Prince, or your eyesight must have been all this time as insensible as your hearing.

PRINCE.

Dear Conti (again fixing his eyes on the picture), how can we uninitiated trust our eyes? In fact, none but an artist can judge of beauty.

CONTI.

And must the feeling of every person wait for the decision of a painter? To a cloister with him who would learn from us what is beautiful! But this much I must own to you, as a painter, Prince. It is one of the greatest delights of my life that Emilia Galotti has sat to me. This head, this countenance, this forehead, these eyes, this nose, this mouth, this chin, this neck, this bosom, this shape, this whole form, are from the present time forward my only model of female beauty. The original picture for which she sat, is in the possession of her absent father. But this copy----

PRINCE (turning to him quickly)

.

Well, Conti--is not surely bespoke already?

CONTI.

Is for you, Prince, if it affords you any pleasure.

PRINCE.

Pleasure! (smiling.) How can I do better than make your model of female beauty my own? There, take back that other portrait, and order a frame for it.

CONTI.

Good.

PRINCE.

As rich and splendid as the carver can possibly make it. It shall be placed in the gallery. But this must remain here. A study need not be treated with so much ceremony; one does not hang it up for display. It should always be at hand. I thank you, Conti, cordially. And as I said before, the arts shall never starve in my dominions, as long as I have bread. Send to my treasurer, Conti, and let him pay your own price for both pictures; as much as you please, Conti.

CONTI.

I must begin to fear, Prince, that you mean to reward me for something else besides my art?

PRINCE.

Oh the jealousy of an artist! No, no! But remember, Conti, as much as you please.

(Exit Conti

.)

Scene

V.

The Prince

.

PRINCE.

Yes, as much as he pleases. (Turning to the picture.) Thou art mine, too cheap at any price. Oh, thou enchanting work of art! Do I then possess thee? But who shall possess thyself, thou still more beautiful masterpiece of nature? Claim what you will, honest old mother; ask what you will, morose old father. Demand any price. Yet, dear enchantress, I should be far more happy to buy thee from thyself! This eye! how full of love and modesty! This mouth! when it speaks, when it smiles! This mouth!--Some one comes.-

-I am still too jealous of thee. (Turning the picture to the wall.) It is Marinelli. I wish I had not sent for him! What a morning might I have had!

Scene

VI.

Marinelli

, The Prince

.

MARINELLI.

Your Highness will pardon me; I was not prepared for so early a summons.

PRINCE.

I felt an inclination to drive out, the morning was so fine. But now it is almost over, and my inclination has subsided. (After a short pause). Any news, Marinelli?

MARINELLI.

Nothing of importance that I know. The Countess Orsina arrived in town yesterday.

PRINCE.

Yes, here lies her morning salutation (pointing to the letter), or whatever it may be. I am not inquisitive about it. Have you seen her?

MARINELLI.

Am I not unfortunately her confidant? But if ever I am so again with a lady who takes it into her head to love you desperately, Prince, may I----

PRINCE.

No rash vows, Marinelli.

MARINELLI.

Indeed, Prince! Is it possible? The Countess, then, is not so utterly mistaken.

PRINCE.

Quite mistaken, certainly. My approaching union with the Princess of Massa compels me in the first place to break off all such connections.

MARINELLI.

If that were all, the Countess would doubtless know as well how to submit to her fate, as the Prince to his.

PRINCE.

My fate is harder far than hers. My heart is sacrificed to a miserable political consideration. She has but to take back hers, and need not bestow it against her inclination.

MARINELLI.

Take it back! "Why take it back," asks the Countess, "for a wife, whom policy and not love attaches to the Prince?" With a wife of that kind the mistress may still hold her place. It is not, therefore, for a wife that she dreads being sacrificed, but----

PRINCE.

Perhaps another mistress. What then? would you make a crime of that, Marinelli?

MARINELLI.

I, Prince? Oh, confound me not with the foolish woman whose cause I advocate--from pity! For yesterday I own she greatly moved me. She wished not to mention her attachment to you, and strove to appear cold and tranquil. But in the midst of the most indifferent topics, some expression, some allusion, escaped her, which betrayed her tortured heart. With the most cheerful demeanour she said the most melancholy things, and on the other hand uttered the most laughable jests with an air of deep distress. She has taken to books for refuge, which I fear will be her ruin.

PRINCE.

Yes, for books gave the first blow to her poor understanding. And, Marinelli, you will scarcely employ for the purpose of renewing my attachment, that which was the chief cause of our separation. If love renders her foolish, she would sooner or later have become so, even without such influence. But enough of her! To something else. Is there nothing new in town?

MARINELLI.

Next to nothing; for that Count Appiani will be married to-day is little better than nothing.

PRINCE.

Count Appiani! To whom? I have not heard that he is engaged.

MARINELLI.

The affair has been kept a profound secret. And indeed, there was not much to create a sensation. You will smile, Prince; but it ever happens so with sentimental youths! Love always plays the worst of tricks. A girl without fortune or rank has managed to catch him in her snares, without any trouble, but with a little display of virtue, sensibility, wit, and so forth.

PRINCE.

The man who can wholly resign himself to the impressions which innocence and beauty make upon him is, in my opinion, rather to be envied than derided. And what is the name of the happy fair one? For though I well know, Marinelli, that you and Appiani dislike each other, he is nevertheless a very worthy young man, a handsome man, a rich man, and an honourable man. I should like to be able to attach him to myself.

MARINELLI.

If it be not too late; for, as far as I can learn, it is not his intention to seek his fortune at court. He will retire with his spouse to his native valleys of Piedmont, and indulge himself in hunting chamois or training marmots upon the Alps. What can he do better? Here his prospects are blighted by the connection he has formed. The first circles are closed against him.

PRINCE.

The first circles! What are they worth, mere resorts of ceremony, restraint, ennui, and poverty? But how call you the fair being who is the cause of all these wondrous sacrifices?

MARINELLI.

A certain--Emilia Galotti?

PRINCE.

What! Marinelli! a certain----

MARINELLI.

Emilia Calotti.

PRINCE.

Emilia Galotti? Never!----

MARINELLI.

Assuredly, your Highness.

PRINCE.

But no, I say. It is not, and it cannot be! You mistake the name. The family of Galotti is numerous. It may be a Galotti, but not Emilia Galotti!

MARINELLI.

Emilia--Emilia Galotti.

PRINCE.

There must be another who bears the same names. You said, however, a certain Emilia Galotti,--a certain one. Of the real Emilia, none but a fool could so speak.

MARINELLI.

Your Highness is excited. Do you know this Emilia?

PRINCE.

It is my place to question, not yours, Marinelli. Is she the daughter of Colonel Galotti, who resides at Sabionetta?

MARINELLI.

The same.

PRINCE.

Who lives here in Guastalla with her mother.

MARINELLI.

The same.

PRINCE.

Near the church of All-Saints.

MARINELLI.

The same.

PRINCE.

In a word (turning hastily to the portrait, and giving it to Marinelli

)--there! is it this Emilia Galotti? Pronounce again those damning words, "the same," and plunge a dagger in my heart.

MARINELLI.

The same.

PRINCE.

Traitor! This? this Emilia Galotti--will to-day be----

MARINELLI.

The Countess Appiani. (The Prince

seizes the portrait from the hands of Marinelli

, and flings it aside.)--The marriage will be celebrated privately at her father's villa, in Sabionetta. About noon the mother and daughter, the Count, and perhaps a few friends, will leave town together.

PRINCE (throwing himself in a state of desperation into a chair)

.

Then I am lost, and care no more for life.

MARINELLI.

What thus affects your Highness?

PRINCE (starting towards him again)

.

Traitor! what affects me thus? Yes, in truth, I love her! I adore her! You may, perhaps, know it, may even long have known it; all of you who desire that I should wear for ever the ignominious fetters of the proud Orsina. That you, Marinelli, who have so often assured me of your sincere friendship--but a Prince has no friend, can have no friend--that you should act so treacherously, so deceitfully, as to conceal till this moment the peril which threatened my love.--Oh, if ever I forgive you this, let no sin of mine be pardoned!

MARINELLI.

I could scarcely find words, Prince, to express my astonishment--even if you gave me the opportunity. You love Emilia Galotti? Hear, then, my oath in reply to yours. If I have ever known or suspected this attachment in the slightest degree, may the angels and saints abandon me! I repeat the same imprecation for Orsina. Her suspicions were directed to a wholly different quarter.

PRINCE.

Pardon me, then, Marinelli (throwing himself into his arms), and pity me.

MARINELLI.

Well, yes, Prince. There see the consequence of your reserve. "A prince has no friends." And why? Because he will have none. To-day you honour us with your confidence, entrust to us your most secret wishes, open your whole soul to us--and to-morrow we are as perfect strangers to you, as if you had never exchanged a word with us.

PRINCE.

Alas, Marinelli, how could I entrust a secret to you which I would scarcely confess to myself?

MARINELLI.

And, which you have, therefore, of course, not confessed to the author of your uneasiness?

PRINCE.

To her!--All my endeavours have been fruitless to speak with her a second time.

MARINELLI.

And the first time----

PRINCE.

I spoke to her;--Oh, my brain is turned, and must I continue this conversation longer? You behold me at the mercy of the waves, and why inquire how all this has happened? Save me if you can, and then question me.

MARINELLI.

Save you! Is there much to save? What your Highness has not confessed to Emilia Galotti, you will confess to the Countess Appiani. Goods which cannot be obtained in their primitive perfection, must be bought at second hand, and are often, on that account, bought at a cheaper rate.

PRINCE.

Be serious, Marinelli, or----

MARINELLI.

To be sure, such articles are generally so much the worse----

PRINCE.

For shame, Marinelli.

MARINELLI.

And the Count intends to leave this country too. Well, we must devise some scheme----

PRINCE.

And what scheme? My best and dearest Marinelli, contrive something for me. What would you do, were you in my situation?

MARINELLI.

Above all things, I should regard a trifle as a trifle--and say to myself that I would not be what I am for nothing--your Highness!

PRINCE.

Delude me not with a power of which I can, on this occasion, make no use. To-day, said you?--This very day?

MARINELLI.

To-day it is to take place;--but it is only things which have taken place that cannot be recalled. (After a short pause.) Prince, will you let me act as I please? Will you approve all I do?

PRINCE.

Anything, Marinelli, which can avert this blow.

MARINELLI.

Then let us lose no time. You must not remain in town, but go to your palace at Dosalo. The road to Sabionetta passes it. Should I not succeed in removing the Count, I think--yes, yes, he will be caught in that snare without doubt. You wish to send an ambassador to Massa respecting your marriage. Let the Count be ambassador, and order him to depart this very day.

PRINCE.

Excellent!--Bring him to my palace.--Haste, haste!--I will leave town instantly. (Exit Marinelli.)

Scene

VII.

PRINCE.

Instantly, instantly. Where is it? (Turns to the portrait) On the ground! That was too bad. (Takes it up) But look! And yet I will look at thee no more now. Why should I plunge the arrow deeper into the wound? (Lays it on the table). I have suffered and sighed long enough--longer than I ought, but done nothing, and my listless inactivity had nearly ruined all.--And may not all yet be lost? May not Marinelli fail? Why should I rely on him alone?--It occurs to me that at this hour (looks at his watch) at this very hour, the pious girl daily attends mass at the church of the Dominicans. How, if I attempted to address her there? But to-day--the day of her marriage--her heart will be occupied with other things than mass. Yet, who knows?--'tis but a step--(rings, and whilst he hastily arranges the papers on the table)--

Enter Servant

.

My carriage!--Have none of the council arrived?

SERVANT.

Camillo Rota waits without.

PRINCE.

Admit him. (Exit Servant

). But he must not attempt to detain me long. Not now--another time, I will attend to his scrupulous investigations----There was a petition of one Emilia Bruneschi--here it is--but, good Bruneschi, if your intercessor----

Scene

VIII.

Enter Camillo Rota

.

Come, Rota, come. There lie the papers which I have opened this morning--not very consoling--you will see what is to be done. Take them with you.

CAMILLO.

I will attend to them.

PRINCE.

Here is a petition from one Emilia Galot--I mean Bruneschi. I have already signed my consent to it--but yet the request is no trifle. You may defer the execution of it--or not--as you please.

CAMILLO.

Not as I please, your Highness.

PRINCE.

What more is there--anything to sign?

CAMILLO.

Sentence of death for your Highness's signature.

PRINCE.

With all my heart!--Where is it? Quick!

CAMILLO (starts and gazes at the Prince

)

.

I said a death--warrant.

PRINCE.

I understood you plain enough. It might have been done by this. I am in haste.

CAMILLO (looking at his papers)

.

I really believe I have not brought it. I beg your Highness's forgiveness. It can be deferred till to-morrow.

PRINCE.

Be it so. Just collect these papers together. I must away. The rest to-morrow, Rota.

CAMILLO (shaking his head, as he collects the papers)

.

"With all my heart!"--A death-warrant, with all my heart! I would not have let him sign at such a moment, had the criminal murdered my own son.--"With all my heart!" "With all my heart"--The cruel words pierce my very soul.

(Exit.)

ACT II.

Scene

I.--A room in Galotti's
house
.
Claudia Galotti, Pirro
.
CLAUDIA.
Who dismounted just now in the court-yard? Pirro.
PIRRO.
My master, madam.
CLAUDIA.
My husband? Is it possible?
PIRRO.
Here he comes.
CLAUDIA.
So unexpectedly? (hastens towards him). My dearest lord!
Scene
II.
Odoardo
, and the foregoing.
ODOARDO.
Good morning, my love. Does not my arrival surprise you?
CLAUDIA.
Most agreeably. But is it intended as no more than a surprise?
ODOARDO.
No more. Be not alarmed. The happiness of to-day awakened me early. The morning was so fine, and the ride so short, I fancied you would be so busy here to-day, and thought you might perhaps forget something: in a word, I am come to see you, and shall return immediately. Where is Emilia? Occupied with her dress, I have no doubt?
CLAUDIA.
With her soul. She is gone to hear mass. "I have need," she said, "to-day more than at any other time to implore a blessing from above;" then leaving all else she took her veil, and disappeared.
ODOARDO.
Alone!
CLAUDIA.
It is but a few steps----
ODOARDO.
One incautious step often leads to mischief.
CLAUDIA.
Be not angry; but come in and rest a moment, and, if you please, take some refreshment.
ODOARDO.
Well, well, as you like. But she ought not to have gone alone.
CLAUDIA.
Stay here, Pirro, in the antechamber, and excuse me to all visitors. (Exeunt Odoardo

and Claudia
.)
Scene
III.
Pirro
, and afterwards Angelo
.
PIRRO.
All inquisitive visitors. How I have been questioned! Who comes here? (Enter Angelo, in a short mantle, with which he conceals his face.)
ANGELO.
Pirro! Pirro!
PIRRO.
An acquaintance, it seems. (Angelo throws back the mantle). Heavens! Angelo. You!
ANGELO.
Yes, Angelo, as you perceive. I have been wandering long enough round the house, in order to speak to you. One word with you----
PIRRO.
And dare you again appear in public? Don't you know that, in consequence of your last murder, you are declared an outlaw, a price has been put upon your head?
ANGELO.
You don't intend to claim it, I presume?
PIRRO.
What do you want? I implore you not to involve me in misfortune.
ANGELO.
In this way, you mean? (Showing a purse). Take it; it belongs to you.
PIRRO.
To me?
ANGELO.
Have you forgotten? The German gentleman, your last master----
PIRRO.
Hush!
ANGELO.
----Whom you led into our clutches on the road to Pisa----
PIRRO.
If any one should overhear us!
ANGELO.
----Had the kindness, you know, to bequeath us a valuable ring. Do you not remember? It was so valuable that we could not immediately convert it into money without suspicion. At length, however, I succeeded. I received a hundred pistoles for it, and this is your share. Take it.
PIRRO.
No, no! You may keep it.
ANGELO.

Well, with all my heart! If you don't care at what price you put your head in the market.

PIRRO.

Give it me, then (takes it). And now, what do you want? for I suppose you did not come in search of me merely for that purpose.

ANGELO.

It seems to you not very credible. Rascal! what do you think of us? That we are capable of withholding any man's earnings? That may be the way with honest people; but we don't follow their fashions. Farewell! (Affects to be going, but turns at the door). One question I must ask. Old Galotti has just come hurriedly into town quite alone. What does he want?

PIRRO.

Nothing, merely a ride. His daughter is to be married this evening, at his country house, whence he has come to Count Appiani. He awaits the moment with impatience.

ANGELO.

Then he will return soon?

PIRRO.

So soon, that if you remain any longer he will discover you. But you surely have no thoughts of attacking him. Take care. He is a man----

ANGELO.

Don't I know him? Have I not served under him in the army; but nevertheless if one could only get much from him! At what time do the young people follow him?

PIRRO.

Towards noon.

ANGELO.

With many attendants?

PIRRO.

A single carriage will contain the party--the mother, the daughter, and the count. A few friends from Sabionetta attend as witnesses.

ANGELO.

And the servants?

PIRRO.

Only two besides myself. I shall ride before.

ANGELO.

Good. Another question. Is the carriage Galotti's or the Count's?

PIRRO.

The Count's.

ANGELO.

That is unlucky. There is another outrider, besides a courageous driver. However----

PIRRO.

I am amazed. What do you intend? The few ornaments which the bride has will scarcely reward your trouble.

ANGELO.

Then the bride herself shall be the reward.

PIRRO.

And you mean that I should be your accomplice in this crime?

ANGELO.

You ride before! Then ride, ride, and take no trouble about the matter.

PIRRO.

Never!

ANGELO.

What?--I believe the fellow means to play the conscientious--you rascal! I think you know me. If you utter a syllable--if every circumstance be not as you have described it----

PIRRO.

But, Angelo, for Heaven's sake----

ANGELO.

Do what you cannot avoid. (Exit.)

PIRRO.

Ha! let the devil hold thee by a single hair, and thou art his for ever! Wretch that I am!

Scene

IV.

Odoardo

and Claudia Galotti, Pirro

.

ODOARDO.

She stays too long.

CLAUDIA.

One moment more, Odoardo. It would distress her to miss seeing you.

ODOARDO.

I must wait upon the Count, too. How eager am I to call this worthy man my son! His conduct enchants me, and, above everything, his resolution to pass his days in his native valleys.

CLAUDIA.

My heart almost breaks when I think of it. Must we so entirely lose our dear and only child!

ODOARDO.

Can you think you have lost her, when you know she is in the arms of an affectionate husband? Does not her happiness make your delight? You almost make me again suspect that your motive for remaining with her in town, far from an affectionate husband and father, was the bustle and the dissipation of the world, and proximity of the court, rather than the necessity of giving our daughter a proper education.

CLAUDIA.

How unjust, Odoardo! But to-day, I may be allowed to speak somewhat in favour of town and court, though both are so hateful to your strict virtue; for here alone could love have united a couple formed for each other; here alone could the Count have found our Emilia, and he has found her.

ODOARDO.

That I allow. But were you right, good Claudia, because the result has been fortunate? It is well that this court education has ended so happily. Let us not affect to be wise, when we have only been fortunate. It is well that it has ended so happily. They who were destined for each other have found each other. Now let them go where peace and innocence invite them. Why should the Count remain here? To cringe--to fawn--to flatter--to supplant the Marinellis--to make a fortune which he does not want--to obtain a dignity, which he does not value?--Pirro!

PIRRO.

Sir!

ODOARDO.

Lead my horse to the Count's door. I'll follow you anon, and mount it there. (Exit Pirro

).--Why should the Count serve here, when he may command elsewhere? Besides, you do not consider, Claudia, that, by his union with my daughter, he is utterly ruined with the Prince? The Prince hates me----

CLAUDIA.

Less, perhaps, than you fear.

ODOARDO.

Fear! Should I fear anything so contemptible?

CLAUDIA.

Why, have I not already told you that the Prince has seen our daughter?

ODOARDO.

The Prince! Where?

CLAUDIA.

At the last assembly of the Chancellor Grimaldi, which he honoured with his presence. He conducted himself so graciously towards her----

ODOARDO.

Graciously?

CLAUDIA.

Yes. He conversed with her for some time.

ODOARDO.

Conversed with her?

CLAUDIA.

Appeared to be so delighted with her cheerfulness and good sense----

ODOARDO.

Delighted?

CLAUDIA.

Spoke of her elegance and beauty, in terms of such admiration----

ODOARDO.

Admiration? And all this you relate to me in a tone of rapture. Oh, Claudia! vain, foolish mother!

CLAUDIA.

Why so?

ODOARDO.

Well, well. This, too, has ended happily.--Ha! when I think----That were exactly the point where a wound would be to me most deadly.--A libertine, who admires, and seduces----Claudia! Claudia! The very thought rouses my fury. You ought to have mentioned this to me immediately.--But to-day I would not willingly say anything to vex you. And I should (as she takes him by the hand), were I to stay longer. Therefore, let me begone. God be with you, Claudia; follow me in safety. (Exit.)

Scene

V.

Claudia, Galotti

.

CLAUDIA.

What a man! What rigid virtue--if virtue that should be called, to which everything seems suspicious and culpable. If this be a knowledge of mankind, who would not wish to remain in ignorance? Why does Emilia stay so long?----He dislikes the father--consequently, if he admire the daughter, he must mean to bring disgrace upon him!

Scene

VI.

Emilia

and Claudia Galotti

.

EMILIA (rushing in, much alarmed.)

Heaven be praised! I am now in safety. Or has he even followed me hither? (Throwing back her veil and espying her mother). Has he, my mother, has he?--No, thank Heaven.

CLAUDIA.

What has happened to you, my daughter?

EMILIA.

Nothing--nothing.

CLAUDIA.

And yet you look wildly round, and tremble in every limb!

EMILIA.

What have I had to hear?--And where have I been forced to hear it?

CLAUDIA.

I thought you were at church.

EMILIA.

I was. But what are churches and altars to the vicious?--Oh, my mother! (Throws herself into Claudia's arms.)

CLAUDIA.

Speak, my daughter, and remove my fears. What evil can have happened to you in so holy a place?

EMILIA.

Never should my devotion have been more fervent and sincere than on this day. Never was it less what it ought to have been.

CLAUDIA.

Emilia we are all human. The faculty of praying fervently is not always in our power; but, in the eye of Heaven, the wish to pray is accepted as prayer.

EMILIA.

And our wish to sin as sin.

CLAUDIA.

That my Emilia never wished.

EMILIA.

No, my mother. The grace of Heaven has preserved me from falling so low. But, alas! that the vice of others should render us accomplices in vice against our will!

CLAUDIA.

Compose yourself.--Collect your thoughts as well as you can. Tell me at once what has happened to you.

EMILIA.

I had just sunk upon my knees, further from the altar than usual--for I arrived too late. I had just begun to raise my thoughts towards Heaven--when some person placed himself behind me--so close behind me! I could neither move forwards nor aside, however much I desired it, in my fear lest the devotion of my neighbour might interrupt my prayers. Devotion was the worst thing which I suspected. But it was not long before I heard a deep sigh close to my ear, and not the name of a saint;--no--the name--do not be angry, dear mother--the name of your daughter.--My own name! Oh, that a peal of thunder had at that moment made me deaf to the rest. The voice spoke of beauty and of love--complained that this day, which crowned my happiness (if such should prove the case) sealed his misery for ever. He conjured me--all this I was obliged to hear, but I did not look round. I wished to seem as if I was not listening. What more could I do? Nothing but pray that my guardian angel would strike me with deafness--even with eternal deafness. This was my prayer--the only prayer which I could utter. At length it was time to rise; the service came to an end. I trembled at the idea of being obliged to turn round--trembled at the idea of beholding him whose impiety had so much shocked me--and when I turned--when I beheld him----

CLAUDIA.

Whom, my daughter?

EMILIA.

Guess, dear mother, guess: I thought I should have sunk into the earth. Himself!

CLAUDIA.

Whom do you mean?

EMILIA.

The Prince!

CLAUDIA.

The Prince! Blest be your father's impatience! He was here just now, and would not stay till you returned.

EMILIA.

My father here--and not stay till I returned!

CLAUDIA.

If, in the midst of your confusion, you had told him too.

EMILIA.

Well, dear mother--could he have found anything in my conduct deserving of censure?

CLAUDIA.

No--as little as in mine. And yet, yet--you do not know your father. When enraged, he would have mistaken the innocent for the guilty--in his anger he would have fancied me the cause of what I could neither prevent nor foresee. But proceed, my daughter, proceed. When you recognised the Prince, I trust that you were sufficiently composed to convince him by your looks, of the contempt which he deserved.

EMILIA.

That I was not. After the glance by which I recognised him, I had not courage to cast a second. I fled.

CLAUDIA.

And the Prince followed you?

EMILIA.

I did not know it till I had reached the porch, where I felt my hand seized--by him. Shame compelled me to stop; as an effort to extricate myself would have attracted the attention of every one who was passing. This was the only reflection of which I was capable, or which I at present remember. He spoke, and I replied--but what he said, or what I replied, I know not.--Should I recollect it, my dear mother, you shall hear it. At present I remember nothing further. My senses had forsaken me.--In vain do I endeavour to recollect how I got away from him, and escaped from the porch. I found myself in the street--I heard his steps behind me--I heard him follow me into the house, and pursue me up the stairs----

CLAUDIA.

Fear has its peculiar faculty, my daughter. Never shall I forget the look with which you rushed into this room!--No. He dared not follow you so far.--Heavens! had your father known this!--How angry was he when I merely told him that the Prince had lately beheld you with admiration! Be at ease, however, my dear girl. Fancy what has happened to be a mere dream. The result will be less, even, than a dream. You will be assured to-day from all similar designs.

EMILIA.

No, mother! The Count must know it--to him I must relate it.

CLAUDIA.

Not for the world. Wherefore? Why? Do you wish to make him uneasy without a cause? And granting that he may not become so at present--know, my child, the poison which does not operate immediately, is not on that account less dangerous. That which has no effect upon the lover, may produce a serious one upon the husband. The lover might even be flattered at winning the prize from so great a rival; but when he has won it--alas, my dear Emilia, the lover often becomes quite another being. Heaven preserve you from such experience!

EMILIA.

You know, dear mother, how willingly I ever submit to your superior judgment. But should he learn from another that the Prince spoke to me to-day, would not my silence sooner or later increase his uneasiness?--I think it would be better not to conceal anything from him.

CLAUDIA.

Weakness--a fond weakness. No, on no account, my daughter! Tell him nothing. Let him observe nothing.

EMILIA.

I submit. I have no will, dear mother, opposed to yours. Ah! (sighing deeply), I shall soon be well again. What a silly, timid thing I am! am I not, mother? I might have conducted myself otherwise, and should, perhaps, have compromised myself just a little.

CLAUDIA.

I would not say this, my daughter, till your own good sense had spoken, which I was sure would be as soon as your alarm was at an end. The Prince is a gallant. You are too little used to the unmeaning language of gallantry. In your mind a civility becomes an emotion--a compliment, a declaration--an idea, a wish--a wish, a design. A mere nothing, in this language, sounds like everything, while everything is in reality nothing.

EMILIA.

Dear mother, my terror cannot but appear ridiculous to myself now. But my kind Appiani shall know nothing of it. He might, perhaps, think me more vain than virtuous----Ah! there he comes himself. That is his step.

Scene

VII.

Enter Appiani

, in deep meditation. His eyes are cast down, and he approaches without observing Claudia

and Emilia

, till the latter runs towards him.

APPIANI.

Ha! My dearest! I did not expect to find you in the ante-room.

EMILIA.

I wish you to be cheerful, even where you do not expect to see me. Why so grave and solemn? Should not this day inspire joyful emotions?

APPIANI.

It is of greater value to me than my whole life; but it teems with so much bliss for me--perhaps it is this very bliss which makes me so grave--so solemn, as you express it (espies Claudia

). Ha! You too here, dear madam. This day I hope to address you by a more familiar name.

CLAUDIA.

Which will be my greatest pride.--How happy you are, Emilia! Why would not your father share our delight?

APPIANI.

But a few minutes have elapsed since I tore myself from his arms--or rather he from mine.--What a man your father is, my Emilia! A pattern of every manly virtue! With what sentiments does his presence inspire my soul! Never is my resolution to continue just and good, so firm as when I see or think of him. And by what, but by fulfilling this resolution, can I make myself worthy of the honour to be called his son--to become your husband, dear Emilia?

EMILIA.

And he would not wait for me!

APPIANI.

Because, in my opinion, this brief interview with his Emilia would have distressed him too much, too deeply affected his soul.

CLAUDIA.

He expected to find you busy with your bridal ornaments, and heard----

APPIANI.

What I have learnt from him with the tenderest admiration. Right, my Emilia. I shall be blessed with a pious wife--and one who is not proud of her piety.

CLAUDIA.

But let us not, whilst we attend to one subject, forget another. It is high time, Emilia. Go!

APPIANI.

Go! Why?

CLAUDIA.

Surely, my lord, you would not lead her to the altar in her present attire.

APPIANI.

In truth, I was not, till you spoke, aware of that. Who can behold Emilia, and take heed of her dress? Yet why should I not lead her to the altar thus?

EMILIA.

No, dear Count, not exactly thus; yet in a dress not much more gay. In a moment I shall be ready. I do not mean to wear those costly jewels, which were the last present of your prodigal generosity, no, nor anything suited to such jewels. Oh, I could quarrel with those jewels were they not your present--for thrice I've dreamt----

CLAUDIA.

Indeed! I know nothing of that.

EMILIA.

That while I wore them, every diamond changed suddenly to a pearl--and pearls, you know, dear mother, signify tears.

CLAUDIA.

Child, the interpretation is more visionary than the dream. Were you not always more fond of pearls than diamonds?

EMILIA.

I assuredly, dear mother--assuredly----

APPIANI (thoughtful and melancholy)

.

Signify tears!

EMILIA.

How! Does that affect you? You?

APPIANI.

It does, though I ought to be ashamed that such is the case; yet when the fancy is once disposed to sad impressions----

EMILIA.

But why should yours be so? Guess the subject of my thoughts. What did I wear, and how did I look when I first attracted your attention? Do you remember?

APPIANI.

Remember! I never see you in idea but in that dress, and I see you so, even when you are not thus attired.

EMILIA.

I mean to wear one of the same colour and form--flowing and loose.

APPIANI.

Excellent!

EMILIA.

And my hair----

APPIANI.

In its own dark beauty, in curls formed by the hand of nature.

EMILIA.

Not forgetting the rose. Right! Have a little patience, and you shall see me thus. (Exit.)

Scene

VIII.

Count Appiani, Claudia Galotti

.

APPIANI (looks after her with a downcast mien)

.

"Pearls signify tears!"--a little patience! Yes! if we could but defy time! If a minute on the clock were not sometimes an age within us!

CLAUDIA.

Emilia's remark was no less just than quick, Count. You are to-day more grave than usual. And yet you are but a step from the object of your wishes. Do you repent that you have attained the wished-for goal?

APPIANI.

How could you, dear mother, suspect this of your son? But it is true. I am to-day unusually dejected and gloomy. All that I have seen, heard or dreamt, has preached since yesterday, and before yesterday this doctrine to me--to be but one step from the goal, and not to have attained it, is in reality the same. This one idea engrosses all my thoughts. What can it mean? I understand it not.

CLAUDIA.

You make me uneasy, Count.

APPIANI.

One thought succeeds another. I am vexed--angry with my friends and with myself.

CLAUDIA.

Why so?

APPIANI.

My friends absolutely require, that, before I solemnize my marriage, I should acquaint the Prince with my intentions. They allow I am not bound to do this, but maintain that respect towards him demands it; and I have been weak enough to consent. I have already ordered my carriage for the purpose.

CLAUDIA (starts)

.

To wait upon the Prince!

Scene

IX.
Pirro
, afterwards Marinelli, Count Appiani, Claudia
.
Enter Pirro
.
PIRRO.
My lady, the Marquis Marinelli is at the door, and inquires for the Count.
APPIANI.
For me!
PIRRO.
Here his lordship comes. (Opens the door and exit.)
Enter Marinelli
.
MARINELLI.
I ask pardon, madam. My lord Count, I called at your house, and was informed that I should find you here. I have important business with you. Once more pardon, madam. It will occupy but a few minutes.
CLAUDIA.
I will not impede it. (Curtseys and exit.)
Scene
X.
Marinelli, Appiani
.
APPIANI.
Now, my lord?
MARINELLI.
I come from his Highness.
APPIANI.
What are his commands?
MARINELLI.
I am proud to be the bearer of this distinguished favour; and if Count Appiani will not wilfully misunderstand one of his most devoted friends----
APPIANI.
Proceed, I pray, without more ceremony.
MARINELLI.
I will. The Prince is obliged to send an ambassador immediately to the Duke of Massa respecting his marriage with the Princess his daughter. He was long undetermined whom to appoint, till his choice at last has fallen upon you, my lord.
APPIANI.
Upon me?
MARINELLI.
Yes--and if friendship may be allowed to boast, I was instrumental----
APPIANI.

Truly I am at a loss for thanks. I had long renounced the hope of being noticed by the Prince.

MARINELLI.

I am sure he only waited for a proper opportunity, and if the present mission be not sufficiently worthy of Count Appiani, I own my friendship has been too precipitate.

APPIANI.

Friendship, friendship! every third word. With whom am I speaking? The Marquis Marinelli's friendship I never dreamt of gaining.

MARINELLI.

I acknowledge my fault, Count Appiani, my unpardonable fault in wishing to be your friend without your permission. But what of that? The favour of his Highness, and the dignity he offers, remain the same. I do not doubt you will accept them with pleasure.

APPIANI (after some consideration)

.

Undoubtedly.

MARINELLI.

Come, then, with me.

APPIANI.

Whither?

MARINELLI.

To the Prince's palace at Dosalo. All is ready. You must depart to-day.

APPIANI.

What say you? To-day?

MARINELLI.

Yes. Rather now than an hour hence. The business presses.

APPIANI.

Indeed! Then I am sorry I must decline the honour which the Prince intended to confer upon me.

MARINELLI.

How?

APPIANI.

I cannot depart to-day,--nor to-morrow--nor the next day.

MARINELLI.

You are jesting, Count.

APPIANI.

With you?

MARINELLI.

Incomparable! If with the Prince, the joke is so much the merrier.--You cannot?

APPIANI.

No, my lord, no--and I trust that the Prince himself will think my excuse sufficient.

MARINELLI.

I am eager to hear it.

APPIANI.

Oh, it is a mere trifle. I mean to be married to-day.

MARINELLI.

Indeed!--and what then?
APPIANI.
And what then?--Your question shows a cursed simplicity!
MARINELLI.
There are examples, Count, of marriages having been deferred. I do not mean to infer that the delay was pleasant to the bride and bridegroom. To them it was, no doubt, a trial, yet the sovereign's command----
APPIANI.
Sovereign's command? A sovereign of my own option, I am not so strictly bound to obey. I admit that you owe the Prince absolute obedience, but not I. I came to his court a volunteer. I wished to enjoy the honour of serving him, but not of being his slave. I am the vassal of a greater sovereign.
MARINELLI.
Greater or smaller, a monarch is a monarch.
APPIANI.
Idle controversy! Enough! Tell the Prince what you have heard. Tell him I am sorry I cannot accept the honour, as I to-day intend to solemnize an union which will consummate my happiness.
MARINELLI.
Will you not at the same time inform him with whom?
APPIANI.
With Emilia Galotti.
MARINELLI.
The daughter of this family?
APPIANI.
Yes.
MARINELLI.
Humph!
APPIANI.
What do you mean?
MARINELLI.
I mean that there would be the less difficulty in deferring the ceremony till your return.
APPIANI.
The ceremony?
MARINELLI.
Yes. The worthy parents will not think much about it.
APPIANI.
The worthy parents?
MARINELLI.
And Emilia will remain faithful to you, of course.
APPIANI.
Of course?----You are an impertinent ape, with your "of course."
MARINELLI.
This to me, Count?
APPIANI.

Why not?

MARINELLI.

Heaven and hell! You shall hear from me.

APPIANI.

Pshaw! The ape is malicious, but----

MARINELLI.

Death and damnation!--Count, I demand satisfaction.

APPIANI.

You shall have it.

MARINELLI.

----And would insist upon it instantly--but that I should not like to spoil the day for the loving bridegroom.

APPIANI.

Good--natured creature!--(seizes his arm). I own an embassy to Massa does not suit me, but still I have time enough to take a walk with you. Come.

MARINELLI (extricates himself from the Count's

grasp)

.

Patience, my lord, patience! (Exit.)

Scene

XI.

Appiani, Claudia

.

APPIANI.

Go, worthless wretch----Ha! that does me good. My blood circulates----I feel different and all the better.

CLAUDIA (hastily and alarmed)

.

Heavens! My lord--I overheard an angry altercation. Your cheek is flushed. What has happened?

APPIANI.

Nothing, Madam, nothing. The chamberlain Marinelli has conferred a favour on me. He has saved me a visit to the Prince.

CLAUDIA.

Indeed!

APPIANI.

We can therefore leave town earlier. I go to give orders to my people, and shall return immediately. Emilia will, in the meantime, get ready.

CLAUDIA.

May I feel quite at ease, my lord?

APPIANI.

Perfectly so, dear Madam. (Exeunt severally.)

ACT III.

Scene

, an apartment in the Prince's

country palace.
Scene
I.
Enter Prince
and Marinelli
.
MARINELLI.
In vain. He refused the proffered honour with the greatest contempt.
PRINCE.
This ends all hope, then. Things take their course,
MARINELLI.
According to all appearances.
PRINCE.
I relied so firmly on your project--but who knows how ridiculously you acted? I ought to have recollected that though a blockhead's counsel may be good, it requires a clever man to execute it.
MARINELLI.
A pretty reward, this!
PRINCE.
Why should you be rewarded?
MARINELLI.
For having risked my life on the venture. Finding that neither raillery nor reason could induce the Count to sacrifice his love to honour, I tried to rouse his anger. I said things to him which made him forget himself. He used insulting expressions, and I demanded satisfaction--yes, satisfaction on the spot. One of us must fall, thought I. Should it be his fate, the field is ours--should it be mine--why, he must fly, and the Prince will at least gain time.
PRINCE.
Did you act thus, Marinelli?
MARINELLI.
Yes; he, who is ready to sacrifice his life for princes, ought to learn beforehand how grateful they are likely to be.
PRINCE.
And the Count? Report says that he is not the man to wait till satisfaction is a second time demanded.
MARINELLI.
No doubt, in ordinary cases. Who can blame him? He said that he had then something of greater consequence than a duel to occupy his thoughts, and put me off till a week after his marriage.
PRINCE.
With Emilia Galotti. The idea drives me to distraction----Thus, then, the affair ended, and now you come hither to boast that you risked your life in my behalf--sacrificed yourself for me.
MARINELLI.
What more, my lord, would you have had me do?

PRINCE.

More? As if you had done anything!

MARINELLI.

May I be allowed to ask what your Highness has done for yourself? You were so fortunate as to see her at church. What is the result of your conference?

PRINCE (with a sneer)

.

You have curiosity enough--but I will satisfy it. All happened as I wished. You need take no further trouble, my most serviceable friend. She met my proposal more than half way. I ought to have taken her with me instantly. (In a cold and commanding tone.) Now you have heard what you wished to know, and may depart.

MARINELLI.

And may depart! Yes, yes. Thus the song ends, and so 'twould be were I to attempt the impossible. The impossible, did I say? No. Impossible it is not--only a daring attempt. Had we the girl in our power, I would answer for it that no marriage should take place.

PRINCE.

Ay--you would answer for anything. I suppose, for instance, you would like to take a troop of my guards, lie in ambush by the highway, fall to the number of fifty upon one carriage, and bear the girl in triumph to me.

MARINELLI.

A girl has been carried off before now by force, though there has been no appearance of force in the transaction.----

PRINCE.

If you were able to do this, you would not talk so much about it.

MARINELLI.

----But I cannot be answerable for the consequences. Unforeseen accidents may happen.

PRINCE.

Is it my custom to make people answerable for what they cannot help?

MARINELLI.

Therefore your Highness will--(a pistol is fired at a distance). Ha! What was that? Did not my ears deceive me? Did not your Highness also hear a shot. And hark! Another!

PRINCE.

What means this? What is the matter?

MARINELLI.

How if I were more active than you deemed me?

PRINCE.

More active! Explain, then----

MARINELLI.

In short, what I mentioned is now taking place.

PRINCE.

Is it possible?

MARINELLI.

But forget not, Prince, what you just now promised. You pledge your word that----

PRINCE.

The necessary precautions I hope have been taken.

MARINELLI.

Yes, as carefully as possible. The execution of my plan is entrusted to people on whom I can rely. The road, as you know, runs close by your park fence. There the carriage will be attacked by a party, apparently to rob the travellers. Another band (one of whom is my trusty servant) will rush from the park as if to assist those who are attacked. During the sham battle between the two parties, my servant will seize Emilia, as if to rescue her, and bring her through the park into the palace. This is the plan. What says your Highness now?

PRINCE.

You surprise me beyond measure. A fearful anxiety comes o'er me. (Marinelli walks to the window.) What are you looking at?

MARINELLI.

That must be the scene of action--yes, and see, some one in a mask has just leapt over the fence--doubtless to acquaint me with the result. Withdraw awhile, your Highness.

PRINCE.

Ah, Marinelli----

MARINELLI.

Well--now, doubtless, I have done too much--as I before had done too little.

PRINCE.

Not so--not so--yet I cannot perceive----

MARINELLI.

Perceive?--It is best done at one blow. Withdraw quickly. You must not be seen here. (Exit Prince

.)

Scene

II.

Marinelli

and presently Angelo

.

MARINELLI (goes again to the window)

.

The carriage is returning slowly to town. So slowly? and at each door a servant? These appearances do not please me; they show the plot has only half succeeded. They are driving some wounded person carefully, and he is not dead. The fellow in the mask comes nearer. 'Tis Angelo himself--foolhardy! But he knows the windings of this place. He beckons to me--he must know that he has succeeded.--Ha! ha! Count Appiani. You, who refused an embassy to Massa, have been obliged to go a longer journey. Who taught you to recognize apes so well? 'Tis true, they are malicious (walks towards the door). Well, Angelo?

Enter Angelo

, with his mash in his hand.

ANGELO.

Be ready, my lord. She will be here directly.

MARINELLI.

How did you succeed in other respects?
ANGELO.
As you wished, I have no doubt.
MARINELLI.
How is it with the Count?
ANGELO.
So, so. But he must have had some suspicions, for he was not quite unprepared.
MARINELLI.
Quick, tell me--is he dead?
ANGELO.
I am sorry for him, poor man.
MARINELLI.
There! Take that for thy compassion (gives him a purse).
ANGELO.
And our poor Nicolo too, he has shared the same luck.
MARINELLI.
What! Loss on both sides?
ANGELO.
Yes. I could cry for the honest lad's fate; though I come in for another quarter of this purse by it; for I am his heir, since I avenged him. This is a law among us, and as good a law, methinks, as ever was made for the support of friendship and fidelity. This Nicolo, my lord----
MARINELLI.
No more of your Nicolo! The Count----
ANGELO.
Zounds! The Count finished him, and I finished the Count. He fell, and though he might be alive when they put him into the coach, I'll answer for it that he will never come alive out of it.
MARINELLI.
Were you but sure of this, Angelo----
ANGELO.
I'll forfeit your custom, if it be not true. Have you any further commands? For I have a long journey. We must be across the frontier before sunset.
MARINELLI.
Go, then.
ANGELO.
Should anything else occur in my way, you know where to inquire for me. What any other can venture to do will be no magic for me, and my terms are lower than any other's. (Exit.)
MARINELLI.
'Tis well--yet not so well as it might have been. Shame on thee, Angelo, to be such a niggard! Surely the Count was worthy of a second shot. Now, he may die in agony; poor Count! Shame, Angelo! It was a cruel and bungling piece of work. The Prince must not know what has happened. He himself must discover how advantageous this death is to him. Death! What would I not give to be certain of it!

Scene
III.
The Prince, Marinelli
.

PRINCE.
Here she comes up the avenue. She flies before the servants. Fear gives wings to her feet. She must not suspect our design. She thinks she is escaping from robbers. How long will her mistake last?
MARINELLI.
At least we have her here.
PRINCE.
But will not her mother come in search of her? Will not the Count follow her? What can we do then? How can I keep her from them?
MARINELLI.
To all this I confess I can make no reply. But we must see. Compose yourself, Prince. This first step was, at all events, necessary.
PRINCE.
How so, if we are obliged to recede?
MARINELLI.
But perhaps we need not. There are a thousand things on which we may make further steps. Have you forgotten the chief one?
PRINCE.
How can I have forgotten that of which I never thought? What mean you by the chief one?
MARINELLI.
The art of pleasing and persuading--which in a prince who loves can never fail.
PRINCE.
Can never fail! True, except when it is most needed. I have already made a poor attempt in this art to-day. All my flattery, all my entreaties could not extract one word from her. Mute, trembling, and abashed, she stood before me like a criminal who fears the judge's fatal sentence. Her terror was infectious. I trembled also and concluded by imploring her forgiveness. Scarcely dare I speak to her again--and, at all events, I dare not be present when she arrives. You, Marinelli, must receive her. I will listen to your conversation, and join you when I am more collected.
Scene
IV.
Marinelli
, presently his servant Battista
, and Emilia
.

MARINELLI.
If she did not see him fall--and of course she could not, as she fled instantly But she comes, and I too do not wish to be the first to meet her eye (withdraws to a corner of the apartment).
Enter Battista

and Emilia

.

BATTISTA.

This way--this way--dear lady.

EMILIA (out of breath)

.

Oh! I thank you, my friend--I thank you. But, Heavens! Where am I? Quite alone, too! Where are my mother, and the Count? They are surely coming? Are they not close behind me?

BATTISTA.

I suppose so.

EMILIA.

You suppose so? Are you not certain? Have you not seen them? Were not pistols fired behind us?

BATTISTA.

Pistols? Was it so?

EMILIA.

Surely. Oh, Heavens! and the Count or my mother is shot.

BATTISTA.

I'll go in search of them instantly.

EMILIA.

Not without me! I'll go with you! I must go with you. Come, my friend.

MARINELLI (approaches as if he had just entered)

.

Ha! fair lady! What misfortune, or rather what good fortune--what fortunate misfortune has procured us the honour----

EMILIA (astonished)

.

How!--You here, my lord!--This then is doubtless your house. Pardon my intrusion. We have been attacked by robbers. Some good people came to our assistance,--and this honest man took me out of the carriage and conducted me hither. But I am alarmed to find that I alone am rescued. My mother must be still in danger. I heard pistols fired behind us. Perhaps she is dead,--and yet I live. Pardon me. I must away, I must return to the place, which I ought not to have left.

MARINELLI.

Compose yourself, dear lady. All is well. The beloved persons, for whom you feel this tender anxiety, will soon be here.--Run, Battista; they may perhaps not know where the lady is. See whether you can find them in any of the lodges, and conduct them hither instantly.

(Exit Battista

.)

EMILIA.

Are you sure they are all safe? Has nothing happened to them?--Oh, what a day of terrors has this been to me! But I ought not to remain here; I should hasten to meet them.

MARINELLI.

Why so, dear lady? You are already breathless and exhausted. Compose yourself, and condescend to step into this room, where you will find better accommodation than here. I feel certain that the Prince has already found your gracious mother, and is escorting her hither.

EMILIA.

Who do you say?

MARINELLI.

Our gracious Prince himself.

EMILIA (extremely terrified)

.

The Prince!

MARINELLI.

He flew to your assistance at the first intelligence. He is highly incensed that such a crime should have been committed so near to his villa, nay, almost before his eyes. He has sent in search of the villains, and if they be seized, their punishment will be most severe.

EMILIA.

The Prince!--Where am I then?

MARINELLI.

At Dosalo, the Prince's villa.

EMILIA.

How strange!--And you think he will soon arrive?--But with my mother too?

MARINELLI.

Here he is, already.

Scene

V.

The Prince, Emilia

, and Marinellies

.

PRINCE.

Where is she? Where is she?--We have sought you everywhere, dear lady.--You are well, I hope? Now, all is well. The Count and your mother----

EMILIA.

Oh, your Highness! Where are they? Where is my mother?

PRINCE.

Not far off, close at hand.

EMILIA.

Heavens! In what a situation shall I perhaps find one or other of them! For your Highness conceals from me--I perceive----

PRINCE.

I conceal nothing, be assured. Lean on my arm, and accompany me to them without fear.

EMILIA (irresolute)

.

But--if they be not wounded--if my suspicions be not true--why are they not already here?

PRINCE.

Hasten then, that all these sad apprehensions may at once be banished.

EMILIA.

What shall I do? (wrings her hands).

PRINCE.

How, dear lady! Can you harbour any suspicion against me?

EMILIA (falls at his feet)

.

On my knees I entreat you----

PRINCE (raising her)

.

I am quite ashamed.--Yes, Emilia, I deserve this mute reproach. My conduct this morning cannot be justified, or even excused. Pardon my weakness: I ought not to have made you uneasy by an avowal, from which I could expect no advantage. I was amply punished by the speechless agitation with which you listened to it, or rather did not listen to it. And if I might be allowed to think this accident the signal of more favourable fortune--the most wondrous respite of my final sentence--this accident, which allows me to behold and speak to you again before my hopes for ever vanish--this accident, which gives me an opportunity of imploring your forgiveness--yet will I--do not tremble--yet will I rely only and entirely on your looks. Not a sigh, not a syllable shall offend you. Only wound me not with suspicions--do not for a moment doubt the unbounded influence which you possess over me--only imagine not that you need any protection against me. And now come--come where delights more in harmony with your feelings, await you. (Leads her away, not without opposition.) Follow us, Marinelli.

(Exeunt Prince

and Emilia

.)

MARINELLI.

Follow us! That means of course--Follow us not. And why should I follow them? He will now find how far he can proceed with her, without witnesses. All that I have to do is to prevent intrusion. From the Count I no longer expect it--but from her mother. Wonderful, indeed, would it be, were she to have departed quietly, leaving her daughter unprotected. Well, Battista, what now?

Scene

VI.

Battista

and Marinelli

.

BATTISTA (in haste)

.

The mother, my lord chamberlain----

MARINELLI.

As I suspected. Where is she?

BATTISTA.

She will be here immediately, unless you prevent it. When you ordered me to pretend to look for her, I felt little inclination to do so. But in the distance I heard her shrieks. She is in search of her daughter, and will discover the whole plot. All the people who inhabit this retired spot have gathered round her, and each vies with his neighbour to show her the way. Whether she has been told that you are here, or that the Prince is here, I know not. What is to be done?

MARINELLI.

Let us see (considering). Refuse her admittance when she knows that her daughter is here? That will not do. She will certainly open her eyes when she finds her lambkin in the clutches of the wolf. Eyes! They would be of little consequence; but Heaven have mercy on our ears! Well, well. A woman's lungs are not inexhaustible. She will be silent, when she can shriek no longer. Besides, the mother it is whom we should gain over to our side--and if I be a judge of mothers--to be a sort of prince's step--mother would flatter most of them. Let her come, Battista, let her come.

BATTISTA.

Hark, my lord!

CLAUDIA (within)

.

Emilia! Emilia! My child! Where are you?

MARINELLI.

Go, Battista, and use your endeavours to dismiss her inquisitive companions.

Scene

VII.

Claudia, Battista, Marinelli

.

As Battista

is going, Claudia

meets him.

CLAUDIA.

Ha! You took her out of the carriage. You led her away. I know you again. Where is she? Speak, wretch.

BATTISTA.

Are these your thanks?

CLAUDIA.

Oh, if you merit thanks (in a mild tone), forgive me, worthy man. Where is she? Let me no longer be deprived of her. Where is she?

BATTISTA.

She could not be more safe, were she in heaven.--My master, here, will conduct you to her. (Observes that some people are beginning to follow Claudia

.) Back there! Begone! (Exit, driving them away.)

Scene

VIII.

Claudia, Marinelli

.

CLAUDIA.

Your master? (espies Marinelli

, and starts). Ha! Is this your master? You here, Sir--and my daughter here--and you--you will conduct me to her?

MARINELLI.

With great pleasure, madam.

CLAUDIA.

Hold! It just occurs to me. It was you, I think, who visited Count Appiani this morning at my house,--whom I left alone with him,--and with whom he afterwards had a quarrel?

MARINELLI.

A quarrel? That I did not know. We had a trifling dispute respecting affairs of state.

CLAUDIA.

And your name is Marinelli?

MARINELLI.

The Marquis Marinelli.

CLAUDIA.

True. Hear, then, Marquis Marinelli. Your name, accompanied with a curse----but no--I will not wrong the noble man--the curse was inferred by myself--your name was the last word uttered by the dying Count.

MARINELLI.

The dying Count? Count Appiani?----You hear, Madam, what most surprises me in this your strange address--the dying Count?--What else you mean to imply, I know not.

CLAUDIA (with asperity, and in a deliberate tone)

.

Marinelli was the last word uttered by the dying Count.--Do you understand me now? I myself did not at first understand it, though it was spoken in a tone--a tone which I still hear. Where were my senses that I could not understand it instantly?

MARINELLI.

Well, Madam, I was always the Count's friend--his intimate friend. If, therefore, he pronounced my name at the hour of death----

CLAUDIA.

In that tone!--I cannot imitate--I cannot describe it--but it signified----everything. What! Were we attacked by robbers? No--by assassins--by hired assassins: and Marinelli was the last word uttered by the dying Count, in such a tone----

MARINELLI.

In such a tone? Did any one ever hear that a tone of voice used in a moment of terror could be a ground of accusation against an honest man?

CLAUDIA.

Oh that I could appear before a tribunal of justice, and imitate that tone? Yet, wretch that I am! I forget my daughter. Where is she--dead too? Was it my daughter's fault that Appiani was thy enemy?

MARINELLI.

I revere the mother's fears, and therefore pardon you.--Come, Madam. Your daughter is in an adjoining room, and I hope her alarms are by this time at an end. With the tenderest solicitude is the Prince himself employed in comforting her.

CLAUDIA.
Who?
MARINELLI.
The Prince.
CLAUDIA.
The Prince! Do you really say the Prince--our Prince?
MARINELLI.
Who else should it be?
CLAUDIA.
Wretched mother that I am!--And her father, her father! He will curse the day of her birth. He will curse me.
MARINELLI.
For Heaven's sake, Madam, what possesses you?
CLAUDIA.
It is clear. To-day--at church--before the eyes of the All-pure--in the presence of the Eternal, this scheme of villainy began. (To Marinelli
.) Murderer! Mean, cowardly murderer! Thou wast not bold enough to meet him face to face, but base enough to bribe assassins that another might be gratified. Thou scum of murderers! honourable murderers would not endure thee in their company. Why may I not spit all my gall, all my rancour into thy face, thou panderer?
MARINELLI.
You rave, good woman. Moderate your voice, at any rate, and remember where you are.
CLAUDIA.
Where I am! Remember where I am! What cares the lioness, when robbed of her young, in whose forest she roars?
EMILIA (within).
Ha! My mother! I hear my mother's voice.
CLAUDIA.
Her voice? 'Tis she! She has heard me. Where are you, my child?--I come, I come (rushes into the room, followed by Marinelli
).
ACT IV.
Scene
I.--The same

.
The Prince
and Marinelli

.
PRINCE.
Come, Marinelli, I must collect myself--I look to you for explanation.
MARINELLI.
Oh! maternal anger! Ha! ha! ha!
PRINCE.
You laugh?

MARINELLI.

Had you, Prince, but seen her frantic conduct in this room! You heard how she screamed; yet how tame she became as soon as she beheld you! Ha! ha! Yes--I never yet knew the mother who scratched a prince's eyes out, because he thought her daughter handsome.

PRINCE.

You are a poor observer. The daughter fell senseless into her mother's arms. This made the mother forget her rage. It was her daughter, not me, whom she spared, when, in a low voice, she uttered--what I myself had rather not have heard--had rather not have understood.

MARINELLI.

What means your Highness?

PRINCE.

Why this dissimulation? Answer me. Is it true or false?

MARINELLI.

And if it were true!

PRINCE.

If it were! It is, then--he is dead (in a threatening tone). Marinelli! Marinelli!

MARINELLI.

Well?

PRINCE.

By the God of justice I swear that I am innocent of this blood. Had you previously told me that the Count's life must be sacrificed--God is my witness I would as soon have consented to lose my own.

MARINELLI.

Had I previously told you! As if the Count's death was part of my plan! I charged Angelo that on his soul he should take care that no person suffered injury; and this, too, would have been the case, had not the Count begun the fray, and shot the first assailant on the spot.

PRINCE.

Indeed! he ought to have understood the joke better.

MARINELLI.

So that Angelo was enraged, and instantly avenged his comrade's death----

PRINCE.

Well, that is certainly very natural.

MARINELLI.

I have reproved him for it.

PRINCE.

Reproved him! How good--natured! Advise him never to appear again in my dominions; for my reproof might not be found so good-natured.

MARINELLI.

Just as I foresaw! I and Angelo.--Design and accident; all the same.--It was, however, agreed, and indeed promised, that I should not be answerable for any accidents which might happen.

PRINCE.

Might happen, say you, or must?

MARINELLI.

Still better! Yet one word, your Highness, before you say in harsh phrase what you think of me. The Count's death was far from being a matter of indifference to me. I had challenged him. He left the world without giving me satisfaction, and my honour, consequently, remains tarnished. Allowing, therefore, what under other circumstances I deserved the suspicion you allude to, can I in this? (with assumed anger.) He who can so suspect me----

PRINCE (yielding)

.

Well, well!

MARINELLI.

Oh that he were still alive! I would give all that I possess--(with bitterness)--even the favour of my Prince--even that treasure, invaluable and never to be trifled with, would I give.

PRINCE.

Well, well! I understand you. His death was accidental, merely accidental--you assure me that it was so, and I believe it. But will any one else believe it? Will Emilia--her mother--the world?

MARINELLI (coldly)

.

Scarcely.

PRINCE.

What, then, will they believe? You shrug your shoulders. They will suppose Angelo the tool and me the prime mover.

MARINELLI (still more coldly)

.

Probable enough!

PRINCE.

Me! me, myself!--or from this hour I must resign all hopes of Emilia.

MARINELLI (in a tone of perfect indifference)

.

Which you must also have done, had the Count lived.

PRINCE (violently)

.

Marinelli!--(checking his warmth)--But you shall not rouse my anger. Be it so. It is so. You mean to imply that the Count's death is fortunate for me;--the best thing which could have happened--the only circumstance which could bring my passion to a happy issue--and, therefore, no matter how it happened. A Count more or less in the world is of little consequence. Am I right?--I am not alarmed at a little crime; but it must be a secret little crime, a serviceable little crime. But ours has not been either secret or serviceable. It has opened a passage only to close it again. Every one will lay it to our door. And, after all, we have not perpetrated it at all. This can only be the result of your wise and wonderful management.

MARINELLI.

If your Highness have it so----

PRINCE.

Why not?--I want an explanation----

MARINELLI.

I am accused of more than I deserve.

PRINCE.

I want an explanation.

MARINELLI.

Well then, what error in my plans has attached such obvious suspicion to the Prince? The fault lies in the master-stroke which your Highness so graciously put to my plans----

PRINCE.

I?

MARINELLI.

Allow me to say that the step which you took at church this morning--with whatever circumspection it was done, or however inevitable it might be--was not part of my programme.

PRINCE.

How did that injure it?

MARINELLI.

Not indeed the whole plan, but its opportuneness.

PRINCE.

Do I understand you?

MARINELLI.

To speak more intelligibly. When I undertook the business, Emilia knew nothing of the Prince's attachment. Her mother just as little. How if I formed my foundation upon this circumstance, and in the meantime the Prince was undermining my edifice?

PRINCE (striking his forehead)

.

Damnation!

MARINELLI.

How, if he himself betrayed his intentions?

PRINCE.

Cursed interposition!

MARINELLI.

For had he not so behaved himself I should like to know what part of my plan could have raised the least suspicion in the mind of the mother or the daughter?

PRINCE.

You are right.

MARINELLI.

And therein I certainly am very wrong.--Pardon me.

Scene

II.

Battista, The Prince, Marinelli

.

Enter BATTISTA

(hastily).
The Countess is arrived.
PRINCE.
The Countess? What Countess?
BATTISTA.
Orsina!
PRINCE.
Orsina? Marinelli!
MARINELLI.
I am as much astonished as yourself.
PRINCE (to Battista
)
.

Go--run--Battista. She must not alight. I am not here--not here to her. She must return this instant. Go, go. (Exit Battista
). What does the silly woman want? How dares she take this liberty? How could she know that we were here? Is she come as a spy? Can she have heard anything? Oh, Marinelli, speak, answer me. Is the man offended, who vows he is my friend--offended by a paltry altercation? Shall I beg pardon?
MARINELLI.
Prince, as soon as you recover yourself, I am yours again, with my whole soul. The arrival of Orsina is as much an enigma to me as to you. But she will not be denied. What will you do?
PRINCE.
I will not speak to her. I will withdraw.
MARINELLI.
Right! Do so instantly; I will receive her.
PRINCE.
But merely to dismiss her. No more. We have other business to perform.
MARINELLI.
Not so, not so. Our other things are done. Summon up resolution and all deficiencies will be supplied. But do I not hear her? Hasten, Prince. In that room (pointing to an adjoining apartment, to which the Prince
retires)--you may, if you please, listen to our conversation. She comes, I fear, at an unpropitious moment for her.
Scene
III.
The Countess Orsina, Marinelli
.
ORSINA (without perceiving Marinelli
)
.

What means this? No one comes to meet me, but a shameless servant, who endeavours to obstruct my entrance. Surely I am at Dosalo, where, on former occasions, an army of attendants rushed to receive me--where love and ecstasy awaited me. Yes. The place is the same, but----Ha! you here, Marinelli? I am glad the Prince has brought you with him. Yet, no. My business with his Highness must be transacted with himself only. Where is he?

MARINELLI.

The Prince, Countess?

ORSINA.

Who else?

MARINELLI.

You suppose that he is here, then,--or know it, perhaps. He, however, does not expect a visit from your ladyship.

ORSINA.

Indeed! He has not then received my letter this morning.

MARINELLI.

Your letter? But--yes. I remember he mentioned that he had received one.

ORSINA.

Well? Did I not in that letter request he would meet me here to-day? I own he did not think proper to return a written answer; but I learnt that an hour afterwards he drove from town to Dosalo. This I thought a sufficient answer, and therefore I have come.

MARINELLI.

A strange accident!

ORSINA.

Accident! It was an agreement--at least as good as an agreement. On my part, the letter--on his, the deed. How you stand staring, Marquis! What surprises you?

MARINELLI.

You seemed resolved yesterday never to appear before the Prince again.

ORSINA.

Night is a good councillor. Where is he? Where is he? Doubtless in the chamber, whence sighs and sobs were issuing as I passed. I wished to enter, but the impertinent servant would not let me pass.

MARINELLI.

Dearest Countess----

ORSINA.

I heard a woman's shriek. What means this, Marinelli? Tell me--if I be your dearest Countess--tell me. A curse on these court slaves! Their tales! their lies! But what matters it whether you choose to tell me or not? I will see for myself.

MARINELLI (holding her back)

.

Whither would you go?

ORSINA.

Where I ought to have gone long since. Is it proper, think you, that I should waste any time in idle conversation with you in the ante-chamber, when the Prince expects me in the saloon?

MARINELLI.

You are mistaken, Countess. The Prince does not expect you here. He cannot--will not see you.

ORSINA.

And yet is here, in consequence of my letter.

MARINELLI.

Not in consequence of your letter.

ORSINA.

He received it, you say.

MARINELLI.

Yes, but he did not read it.

ORSINA (violently)

.

Not read it! (Less violently.) Not read it! (Sorrowfully, and wiping away a tear.) Not even read it!

MARINELLI.

From preoccupation, I am certain, not contempt.

ORSINA (with pride)

.

Contempt! Who thought of such a thing? To whom do you use the term? Marinelli, your comfort is impertinent. Contempt! Contempt! To me! (In a milder tone.) It is true that he no longer loves me. That is certain. And in place of love something else has filled his soul. It is natural. But why should this be contempt? Indifference would be enough. Would it not, Marinelli?

MARINELLI.

Certainly, certainly.

ORSINA (with a scornful look)

.

Certainly! What an oracle, who can be made to say what one pleases! Indifference in the place of love!--That means nothing in the place of something. For learn, thou mimicking court-parrot, learn from a woman, that indifference is but an empty word, a mere sound which means nothing. The mind can only be indifferent to objects of which it does not think; to things which for itself have no existence. Only indifferent for a thing that is nothing--that is as much as saying not indifferent. Is that meaning beyond thee, man?

MARINELLI (aside)

.

Alas! how prophetic were my fears?

ORSINA.

What do you mutter?

MARINELLI.

Mere admiration! Who does not know, Countess, that you are a philosopher?

ORSINA.

Am I not? True; I am a philosopher. But have I now shown it; ah, shame! If I have shown it, and have often done so, it were no wonder if the Prince despised me. How can man love a creature which, in spite of him, will think? A woman who thinks is as silly as a man who uses paint. She ought to laugh--do nothing but laugh, that the mighty lords of the creation may be kept in good humour--What makes me laugh now, Marinelli? Why, the accidental circumstance that I should have written to the Prince to come hither--that he should not have read my letter and nevertheless have come. Ha! ha! ha! 'Tis an odd accident, very pleasant and amusing. Why don't you laugh, Marinelli? The mighty lords of the creation may laugh, though we poor creatures dare not think. (In a serious and commanding tone.) Then laugh, you!

MARINELLI.

Presently, Countess, presently.

ORSINA.

Blockhead! while you speak the proper moment is for ever past. No. Do not laugh--for mark me, Marinelli, (with emotion) that which makes me laugh, has, like every thing in the world, its serious side. Accident! Could it be accidental that the Prince, who little thought that he would see me here, must see me?--Accident! Believe me, Marinelli, the word accident is blasphemy. Nothing under the sun is accidental, and least of all this, of which the purpose is so evident.--Almighty and all--bounteous Providence, pardon me that I joined this poor weak sinner in giving the name of accident to what so plainly is Thy work--yes, Thy immediate work. (In a hasty tone to Marinelli

.) Dare not again to lead me thus astray from truth.

MARINELLI.

This is going too far (aside)--But, Countess----

ORSINA.

Peace with your but--that word demands reflection, and--my head, my head!--(Puts her hand to her forehead)--Contrive that I may speak to the Prince immediately, or I shall soon want strength to do so. You see, Marinelli, that I must speak to him--that I am resolved to speak to him.

Scene

IV.

The Prince, Orsina, Marinelli

.

PRINCE (aside, as he advances)

.

I must come to his assistance.

ORSINA (espies him, but remains irresolute whether to approach him or not)

.

Ha! There he is.

PRINCE (walks straight across the room towards the other apartments)

.

Ha! The fair Countess, as I live. How sorry I am, Madam, that I can to-day so ill avail myself of the honour of your visit. I am engaged. I am not alone. Another time, dear Countess, another time. At present stay no longer--no longer, I beg. And you, Marinelli--I want you. (Exit.)

Scene

V.

Orsina, Marinelli

.

MARINELLI.

Your ladyship has now heard, from himself, what you would not believe from my lips, have you not?

ORSINA (as if petrified)

.

Have I? Have, I indeed?

MARINELLI.

Most certainly.

ORSINA (deeply affected).

"I am engaged, I am not alone." Is this all the excuse I am worth? For whose dismissal would not these words serve? For every importunate, for every beggar. Could he not frame one little falsehood for me? Engaged! With what? Not alone! Who can be with him? Marinelli, dear Marinelli, be compassionate--tell me a falsehood on your own account. What can a falsehood cost you? What has he to do? Who is with him? Tell me, tell me. Say anything which first occurs to you, and I will go.

MARINELLI (aside)

.

On this condition, I may tell her part of the truth.

ORSINA.

Quick, Marinelli, and I will go. He said, "Another time, dear Countess!" Did he not? That he may keep his promise--that he may have no prbook to break it--quick, then, Marinelli,--tell me a falsehood, and I will go.

MARINELLI.

The Prince, dear Countess, is really not alone. There are persons with him, whom he cannot leave for a moment--persons, who have just escaped imminent danger. Count Appiani----

ORSINA.

Is with him! What a pity that I know this to be false! Quick, another! for Count Appiani, if you do not know it, has just been assassinated by robbers. I met the carriage, with his body in it, as I came from town. Or did I not? Was it a dream?

MARINELLI.

Alas, it was not a dream. But they who accompanied the Count were fortunately rescued, and are now in this palace; namely, a lady to whom he was betrothed, and whom, with her mother, he was conducting to Sabionetta, to celebrate his nuptials.

ORSINA.

They are with the Prince! A lady and her mother! Is the lady handsome?

MARINELLI.

The Prince is extremely sorry for her situation.

ORSINA.

That he would be, I hope, even if she were hideous--for her fate is dreadful. Poor girl! at the moment he was to become thine for ever, he was torn for ever from thee. Who is she? Do I know her? I have of late been so much out of town, that I am ignorant of every thing.

MARINELLI.

It is Emilia Galotti.

ORSINA.

What? Emilia Galotti? Oh, Marinelli, let me not mistake this lie for truth.
MARINELLI.
Why?
ORSINA.
Emilia Galotti?
MARINELLI.
Yes. Whom you can scarcely know.
ORSINA.
I do know her--though our acquaintance only began to-day. Emilia Galotti! Answer me seriously. Is Emilia Galotti the unfortunate lady whom the Prince is consoling?
MARINELLI (aside)

.

Can I have disclosed too much?
ORSINA.
And Count Appiani was her destined bridegroom--Count Appiani, who was shot to-day?
MARINELLI.
Exactly.
ORSINA (clapping her hands)

.

Bravo! Bravo! Bravo!
MARINELLI.
What now?
ORSINA.
I could kiss the devil that tempted him to do it.
MARINELLI.
Whom? Tempted? To do what?
ORSINA.
Yes, I could kiss--him--even wert thou that devil, Marinelli.
MARINELLI.
Countess!
ORSINA.
Come hither. Look at me--steadfastly--eye to eye.
MARINELLI.
Well?
ORSINA.
Know you not my thoughts?
MARINELLI.
How can I?
ORSINA.
Have you no concern in it?
MARINELLI.
In what?
ORSINA.

Swear. No, do not swear, for that might be another crime. But yes--swear. One sin more or less is of no consequence to a man who is already damned. Have you no concern in it?

MARINELLI.

You alarm me, Countess.

ORSINA.

Indeed! Now, Marinelli--has your good heart no suspicion?

MARINELLI.

Suspicion? Of what?

ORSINA.

'Tis well. Then I will entrust you with a secret--a secret, which will make each hair upon your head stand on end. But here, so near the door, some one might overhear us. Come here--(puts her finger to her mouth)--mark me, it is a secret--a profound secret. (Places her mouth to his ear, as if about to whisper, and shouts as loudly as she can) The Prince is a murderer!

MARINELLI.

Countess! Countess! Have you lost your senses?

ORSINA.

Senses? Ha! ha! ha! (laughing loudly). I have very seldom, if ever, been so satisfied with my understanding as I am at this moment. Depend upon it, Marinelli--but it is between ourselves--(in a low voice)--the Prince is a murderer--the murderer of Count Appiani. The Count was assassinated, not by robbers, but by the Prince's myrmidons, by the Prince himself.

MARINELLI.

How can so horrid a suspicion fall from your lips, or enter your imagination?

ORSINA.

How? Very naturally. This Emilia Galotti, who is now in the palace, and whose bridegroom--was thus trundled head over heels out of the world--this Emilia Galotti did the Prince to-day accost in the Church of the Dominicans, and held a lengthy conversation with her. That I know, for my spies not only saw it, but heard what he said. Now, sir, have I lost my senses? Methinks I connect the attendant circumstances very tolerably together. Or has all this happened, too, by accident? If so, Marinelli, you have as little idea of the wickedness of man as you have of prevision.

MARINELLI.

Countess, you would talk your life into danger----

ORSINA.

Were I to mention this to others? So much the better! So much the better! To-morrow I will repeat it aloud in the market-place--and, if any one contradict me--if any one contradict me, he was the murderer's accomplice. Farewell. (As she is going, she meets Odoardo

entering hastily.)

Scene

VI.

Odoardo, Orsina, Marinelli

.

ODOARDO.
Pardon me, gracious lady----
ORSINA.
I can grant no pardon here, for I can take no offence. You must apply to this gentleman (pointing to Marinelli
).
MARINELLI (aside)
.
The father! This completes the business.
ODOARDO.
Pardon a father, sir, who is in the greatest embarrassment, for entering unannounced.
ORSINA.
Father!--(turning round again)--Of Emilia, no doubt! Ha! Thou art welcome.
ODOARDO.
A servant came in haste to tell me that my family was in danger near here. I flew hither, he mentioned, and found that Count Appiani has been wounded--and carried back to town--and that my wife and daughter have found refuge in the palace. Where are they, sir, where are they?
MARINELLI.
Be calm, Colonel. Your wife and daughter have sustained no injury save from terror. They are both well. The Prince is with them. I will immediately announce you.
ODOARDO.
Why announce? merely announce me?
MARINELLI.
For reasons--on account of--on account of--you know, sir, that you are not upon the most friendly terms with the Prince. Gracious as may be his conduct towards your wife and daughter--they are ladies--will your unexpected appearance be welcome to him?
ODOARDO.
You are right, my lord, you are right.
MARINELLI.
But, Countess, may I not first have the honour of handing you to your carriage?
ORSINA.
By no means.
MARINELLI (taking her hand, not in the most gentle way)
.
Allow me to perform my duty.
ORSINA.
Softly!--I excuse you, Marquis. Why do such as you ever consider mere politeness a duty, and neglect as unimportant what is really an essential duty? To announce this worthy man immediately is your duty.
MARINELLI.
Have you forgotten what the Prince himself commanded?
ORSINA.
Let him come, and repeat his commands. I shall expect him.
MARINELLI (draws Odoardo

aside)

.

I am obliged to leave you, Colonel, with a lady whose intellect--you understand me, I mention this that you may know in what way to treat her remarks, which are sometimes singular. It were better not to enter into conversation with her.

ODOARDO.

Very well. Only make haste, my lord.

(Exit Marinelli

.)

Scene

VII.

Orsina, Odoardo

.

ORSINA (after a pause, during which she has surveyed Odoardo

with a look of compassion, while he has cast towards her a glance of curiosity).

Alas! What did he say to you, unfortunate man?

ODOARDO (half aside)

.

Unfortunate!

ORSINA.

Truth it certainly was not--at least, not one of those sad truths which await you.

ODOARDO.

Which await me? Do I, then, not know enough? Madam--but proceed, proceed.

ORSINA.

You know nothing?

ODOARDO.

Nothing.

ORSINA.

Worthy father! What would I give that you were my father! Pardon me. The unfortunate so willingly associate together. I would faithfully share your sorrows--and your anger.

ODOARDO.

Sorrows and anger? Madam--but I forget--go on.

ORSINA.

Should she even be your only daughter--your only child--but it matters not. An unfortunate child is ever an only one.

ODOARDO.

Unfortunate?--Madam! But why do I attend to her? And yet, by Heaven, no lunatic speaks thus.

ORSINA.

Lunatic? That, then, was the secret which he told you of me. Well, well. It is perhaps not one of his greatest falsehoods. I feel that I am something like one; and believe me, sir, they who, under certain circumstances, do not lose their intellect, have none to lose.

ODOARDO.

What must I think?

ORSINA.

Treat me not with contempt, old man. You possess strong sense. I know it by your resolute and reverend mien. You also possess sound judgment, yet I need but speak one word, and both these qualities are fled for ever.

ODOARDO.

Oh, Madam, they will have fled before you speak that word, unless you pronounce it soon. Speak, I conjure you; or it is not true that you are one of that good class of lunatics who claim our pity and respect; you are naught else than a common fool. You cannot have what you never possessed.

ORSINA.

Mark my words, then. What do you know, who fancy that you know enough? That Appiani is wounded? Wounded only? He is dead.

ODOARDO.

Dead? Dead? Woman, you abide not by your promise. You said you would rob me of my reason, but you break my heart.

ORSINA.

Thus much by the way. Now, let me proceed. The bridegroom is dead, and the bride, your daughter, worse than dead.

ODOARDO.

Worse? Worse than dead? Say that she too is dead--for I know but one thing worse.

ORSINA.

She is not dead; no, good father, she is alive, and will now just begin to live indeed; the finest, merriest fool's paradise of a life--as long as it lasts.

ODOARDO.

Say the word, Madam! The single word, which is to deprive me of my reason! Out with it! Distil not thus your poison drop by drop. That single word at once!

ORSINA.

You yourself shall put the letters of it together. This morning the Prince spoke to your daughter at church; this afternoon he has her at his----his summer-palace.

ODOARDO.

Spoke to her at church? The Prince to my daughter?

ORSINA.

With such familiarity and such fervour. Their agreement was about no trifling matter; and if they did agree, all the better: all the better if your daughter made this her voluntary asylum. You understand--and in that case this is no forcible seduction, but only a trifling--trifling assassination.

ODOARDO.

Calumny! Infamous calumny! I know my daughter. If there be murder here, there is seduction also, (Looks wildly round, stamping and foaming.) Now, Claudia! Now, fond mother! Have we not lived to see a day of joy? Oh, the gracious Prince! Oh, the mighty honour!

ORSINA (aside)

.

Have I roused thee, old man?

ODOARDO.

Here I stand before the robber's cave. (Throws his coat back on both sides, and perceives he has no weapon.) 'Tis a marvel that, in my haste, I have not forgotten my hands too. (Feeling in all his pockets.) Nothing, nothing.

ORSINA.

Ha! I understand, and can assist you. I have brought one. (Produces a dagger.) There! Take it, take it quickly, ere any one observes us. I have something else, too--poison--but that is for women, not for men. Take this (forcing the dagger upon him), take it.

ODOARDO.

I thank thee. Dear child, whosoever again asserts thou art a lunatic, he shall answer it to me.

ORSINA.

Conceal it, instantly. (Odoardo

hides the dagger.) The opportunity for using it is denied to me. You will not fail to find one, and you will seize the first that comes, if you are a man. I am but a woman, yet I came hither resolute. We, old man, can trust each other, for we are both injured, and by the same seducer. Oh, if you knew how preposterously, how inexpressibly, how incomprehensibly, I have been injured by him, you would almost forget his conduct towards yourself. Do you know me? I am Orsina, the deluded, forsaken Orsina--perhaps forsaken only for your daughter. But how is she to blame? Soon she also will be forsaken; then another, another, and another. Ha! (As if in rapture) What a celestial thought! When all who have been victims of his arts shall form a band, and we shall be converted into Mænads, into furies; what transport will it be to tear him piecemeal, limb from limb, to wallow through his entrails, and wrench from its seat the traitor's heart--that heart which he promised to bestow on each, and gave to none. Ha! that indeed will be a glorious revelry!

Scene

VIII.

Claudia, Odoardo, Orsina

.

Enter Claudia

.

CLAUDIA (looks round, and as soon as she espies her husband, runs towards him.)

I was right. Our protector, our deliverer! Are you really here? Do I indeed behold you, Odoardo? From their whisper and their manner I knew it was the case. What shall I say to you, if you are still ignorant? What shall I say to you if you already know everything? But we are innocent. I am innocent. Your daughter is innocent. Innocent; wholly innocent.

ODOARDO (who, on seeing his wife, has endeavoured to compose himself)

.

'Tis well. Be calm, and answer me.--(To Orsina

)--Not that I doubt your information, Madam. Is the Count dead?

CLAUDIA.

He is.

ODOARDO.

Is it true that the Prince spoke this morning to Emilia, at the church?

CLAUDIA.

It is; but if you knew how much she was alarmed--with what terror she rushed home.
ORSINA.
Now, was my information false?
ODOARDO (with a bitter laugh)

.

I would not that it were! For worlds I would not that it were!
ORSINA.
Am I a lunatic?
ODOARDO (wildly pacing the apartment)

.

Oh!--nor as yet am I.
CLAUDIA.
You commanded me to be calm, and I obeyed--My dear husband, may I--may I entreat----
ODOARDO.
What do you mean? Am I not calm? Who can be calmer than I? (Putting restraint upon himself.) Does Emilia know that Appiani is dead?
CLAUDIA.
She cannot know it, but I fear that she suspects it, because he does not appear.
ODOARDO.
And she weeps and sobs.
CLAUDIA.
No more. That is over, like her nature, which you know. She is the most timid, yet the most resolute of her sex; incapable of governing her first emotions, but upon the least reflection calm and prepared for all. She keeps the Prince at a distance--she speaks to him in a tone----Let us, dear Odoardo, depart immediately.
ODOARDO.
I came on horseback hither. What is to be done? You, Madam, will probably return to town?
ORSINA.
Immediately.
ODOARDO.
May I request you to take my wife with you.
ORSINA.
With pleasure.
ODOARDO.
Claudia, this is the Countess Orsina, a lady of sound sense, my friend and benefactress. Accompany her to town, and send our carriage hither instantly. Emilia must not return to Guastalla. She shall go with me.
CLAUDIA.
But--if only--I am unwilling to part from the child.
ODOARDO.
Is not her father here? I shall be admitted at last. Do not delay! Come, my lady. (Apart to her.) You shall hear from me.--Come, Claudia. (Exeunt.)
ACT V.

Scene
I.--As before

.

The Prince, Marinelli

.

MARINELLI.

From this window your Highness may observe him. He is walking to and fro under the arcade. Now he turns this way. He comes; no, he turns again. He has not yet altogether made up his mind; but is much calmer, or at least appears so. To us this is unimportant. He will scarcely dare utter the suspicions which these women have expressed! Battista says that he desired his wife to send the carriage hither as soon as she should reach the town, for he came hither on horseback. Mark my words. When he appears before your Highness, he will humbly return thanks for the gracious protection which you were pleased to afford to his family, will recommend himself and his daughter to your further favour, quietly take her to town, and with perfect submission await the further interest which your Highness may think proper to take in the welfare of his child.

PRINCE.

But should he not be so resigned--and I scarcely think he will, I know him too well to expect it--he may, perhaps, conceal his suspicions, and suppress his indignation; but instead of conducting Emilia to town, he may take her away and keep her with himself, or place her in some cloister beyond my dominions. What then?

MARINELLI.

Love's fears are farsighted. But he will not.

PRINCE.

But, if he were to do it, what would the death of the unfortunate Count avail us?

MARINELLI.

Why this gloomy supposition? "Forward!" shouts the victor, and asks not who falls near him--friend or foe. Yet if the old churl should act as you fear, prince--(After some consideration) I have it. His wish shall prove the end of his success. I'll mar his plan. But we must not lose sight of him. (Walks again to the window.) He had almost surprised us. He comes. Let us withdraw awhile, and in the meanwhile, Prince, you shall hear how we can elude the evil you apprehend.

PRINCE (in a threatening tone)

.

But, Marinelli----

MARINELLI.

The most innocent thing in the world. (Exeunt.)

Scene

II.

ODOARDO.

Still no one here? 'Tis well. They allow me time to get still cooler. A lucky chance. Nothing is more unseemly than a hoary-headed man transported with the rage of youth. So I have often thought, yet I have suffered myself to be aroused----by whom? By a woman whom jealousy had driven to distraction. What has injured virtue to do with the revenge of vice? I have but to save the former. And thy cause, my son--my son----I could never weep, and will not learn the lesson now. There is another, who will avenge thy cause. Sufficient for me that thy murderer shall not enjoy the fruit of his crime. May this torment him more than even the crime itself; and when at length loathsome satiety shall drive him from one excess to another, may the recollection of having failed in this poison the enjoyment of all! In every dream may the bride appear to him, led to his bedside by the murdered bridegroom; and when, in spite of this, he stretches forth his sinful arms to seize the prize, may he suddenly hear the derisive laughter of hell echo in his ears, and so awake.

Scene
III.
Marinelli, Odoardo
.

MARINELLI.
We have been looking for you, Sir.
ODOARDO.
Has my daughter been here?
MARINELLI.
No; the Prince.
ODOARDO.
I beg his pardon. I have been conducting the Countess to her carriage.
MARINELLI.
Indeed.
ODOARDO.
A good lady!
MARINELLI.
And where is your lady?
ODOARDO.
She accompanied the Countess that she might send my carriage hither. I would request the Prince to let me stay with my daughter till it arrives.
MARINELLI.
Why this ceremony? The Prince would have felt pleasure in conducting your daughter and her mother to town.
ODOARDO.
My daughter at least would have been obliged to decline that honour.
MARINELLI.
Why so?
ODOARDO.
She will not go to Guastalla again.
MARINELLI.
Indeed! Why not?
ODOARDO.
Count Appiani is dead.
MARINELLI.
For that very reason----
ODOARDO.

She must go with me.

MARINELLI.

With you?

ODOARDO.

With me.--I tell you the Count is dead--though she may not know it. What therefore has she to do in Guastalla? She must go with me.

MARINELLI.

The future residence of the lady must certainly depend upon her father--but at present----

ODOARDO.

Well? What?

MARINELLI.

At present, sir, you will, I hope, allow her to be conveyed to Guastalla.

ODOARDO.

My daughter, conveyed to Guastalla? Why so?

MARINELLI.

Why! Consider----

ODOARDO (incensed)

.

Consider! consider! consider that there is nothing to consider. She must and shall go with me.

MARINELLI.

We need have no contention on the subject, sir. I may be mistaken. What I think necessary may not be so. The Prince is the best judge--he, therefore, will decide. I go to bring him to you.

Scene

IV.

Odoardo

.

ODOARDO.

How? Never! Prescribe to me whether she shall go! Withhold her from me! Who will do this?--Who dares attempt it?--He, who dares here do anything he pleases?----'Tis well, 'tis well. Then shall he see how much I, too, dare, and whether I have not already dared. Short-sighted voluptuary! I defy thee.--He who regards no law is as independent as he who is subject to no law. Knowest thou not this? Come on, come on----But what am I saying? My temper once more overpowers my reason. What do I want? I should first know why I rave. What will not a courtier assert? Better had I allowed him to proceed. I should have heard his prbook for conveying my daughter to Guastalla, and I could have prepared a proper reply. But can I need a reply!--Should one fail me--should----I hear footsteps. I will be calm.

Scene

V.

The Prince, Marinelli, Odoardo

.

PRINCE.

My dear worthy Galotti.--Was such an accident necessary to bring you to your Prince? Nothing less would have sufficed--but I do not mean to reproach you.

ODOARDO.

Your Highness, I have ever thought it unbecoming to press into the presence of my Prince. He will send for those whom he wants. Even now I ask your pardon----

PRINCE.

Would that many, whom I know, possessed this modest pride!--But to the subject. You are, doubtless, anxious to see your daughter. She is again alarmed on account of her dear mother's sudden departure. And why should she have departed? I only waited till the terrors of the lovely Emilia were completely removed, and then I should have conveyed both the ladies in triumph to town. Your arrival has diminished by half the pleasure of this triumph; but I will not entirely resign it.

ODOARDO.

Your Highness honours me too much. Allow me to spare my unfortunate child the various mortifications, which friendship and enmity, compassion and malicious pleasure, prepare for her in town.

PRINCE.

Of the sweet comforts, which the friendly and compassionate bestow, it would be cruelty to deprive her; but against all the mortifications of enmity and malice, believe me, I will guard her, dear Galotti.

ODOARDO.

Prince, paternal love is jealous of its duties. I think I know what alone suits my daughter in her present situation. Retirement from the world--a cloister as soon as possible.

PRINCE.

A cloister?

ODOARDO.

Till then, let her weep under the protection of her father.

PRINCE.

Shall so much beauty wither in a cloister?----Should one disappointed hope embitter one against the world?--But as you please. No one has a right to dictate to a parent. Take your daughter wherever you think proper, Galotti.

ODOARDO (to Marinelli

)

.

Do you hear, my lord?

MARINELLI.

Nay, if you call upon me to speak----

ODOARDO.

By no means, by no means.

PRINCE.

What has happened between you two?

ODOARDO.

Nothing, your Highness, nothing. We were only settling which of us had been deceived in your Highness.

PRINCE.

How so?--Speak, Marinelli.
MARINELLI.
I am sorry to interfere with the condescension of my Prince, but friendship commands that I should make an appeal to him as judge.
PRINCE.
What friendship?
MARINELLI.
Your Highness knows how sincerely I was attached to Count Appiani--how our souls were interwoven----
ODOARDO.
Does his Highness know that? Then you are indeed the only one who does know it.
MARINELLI.
Appointed his avenger by himself----
ODOARDO.
You?
MARINELLI.
Ask your wife. The name of Marinelli was the last word of the dying Count, and was uttered in such a tone----Oh may that dreadful tone sound in my ears for ever, if I do not strain every nerve to discover and to punish his murderers!
PRINCE.
Rely upon my utmost aid.
ODOARDO.
And upon my most fervent wishes. All this is well. But what further?
PRINCE.
That I, too, want to know, Marinelli.
MARINELLI.
It is suspected that the Count was not attacked by robbers----
ODOARDO (with a sneer)

.
Indeed!
MARINELLI.
But that a rival hired assassins to despatch him.
ODOARDO (bitterly)

.
Indeed! A rival?
MARINELLI.
Exactly.
ODOARDO.
Well then--May damnation overtake the vile assassin!
MARINELLI.
A rival--a favoured rival too.
ODOARDO.
How? Favoured? What say you?
MARINELLI.
Nothing but what fame reports.

ODOARDO.

Favoured? favoured by my daughter?

MARINELLI.

Certainly not. That cannot be. Were you to say it I would contradict it. But, on this account, your Highness, though no prejudice, however well-grounded, can be of any weight in the scale of justice, it will, nevertheless, be absolutely necessary that the unfortunate lady should be examined.

PRINCE.

True--undoubtedly.

MARINELLI.

And where can this be done but in Guastalla?

PRINCE.

There you are right, Marinelli, there you are right.--This alters the affair, dear Galotti. Is it not so. You yourself must see----

ODOARDO.

Yes! I see----what I see. O God! O God!

PRINCE.

What now? What is the matter?

ODOARDO.

I am only angry with myself for not having foreseen what I now perceive. Well, then--she shall return to Guastalla. I will take her to her mother, and till she has been acquitted, after the most rigid examination, I myself will not leave Guastalla. For who knows--(with a bitter smile of irony)--who knows whether the court of justice may not think it necessary to examine me?

MARINELLI.

It is very possible. In such cases justice rather does too much than too little. I therefore even fear----

PRINCE.

What? What do you fear?

MARINELLI.

That the mother and daughter will not, at present, be suffered to confer together.

ODOARDO.

Not confer together?

MARINELLI.

It will be necessary to keep mother and daughter apart.

ODOARDO.

To keep mother and daughter apart?

MARINELLI.

The mother, the daughter, and the father. The forms of the court absolutely enjoin this caution; and I assure your Highness that it pains me that I must enforce the necessity of at least placing Emilia in strict security.

ODOARDO.

In strict security!--Oh, Prince, Prince!--Butyes--right!--of course, of course! In strict security! Is it not so, Prince? Oh! justice! oh justice is a fine thing! Excellent! (Hastily puts his hand into the pocket in which he had concealed the dagger.)

PRINCE (in a soothing tone)

.

Compose yourself, dear Galotti.

ODOARDO (aside, drawing his hand, without the dagger, from his pocket)

.

There spoke his guardian angel.

PRINCE.

You are mistaken. You do not understand him. You think, perhaps, by security is meant a prison and a dungeon.

ODOARDO.

Let me think so, and I shall be at ease.

PRINCE.

Not a word of imprisonment, Marinelli. The rigour of the law may easily be combined with the respect due to unblemished virtue. If Emilia must be placed in proper custody, I know the most proper situation for her--my chancellor's house. No opposition, Marinelli. Thither I will myself convey her, and place her under the protection of one of the worthiest of ladies, who shall be answerable for her safety. You go too far, Marinelli, you go too far, if you require more. Of course, Galotti, you know my chancellor Grimaldi and his wife?

ODOARDO.

Undoubtedly I do. I also know the amiable daughters of this noble pair. Who does not know them? (To Marinelli

).--No, my lord--do not agree to this. If my daughter must be confined, she ought to be confined in the deepest dungeon. Insist upon it, I beseech you. Fool that I was to make any request. Yes, the good Sybil was right. "They, who under certain circumstances, do not lose their intellect, have none to lose."

PRINCE.

I do not understand you. Dear Galotti, what can I do more? Be satisfied, I beseech you. She shall be conveyed to the chancellor's house. I myself will convey her thither; and if she be not there treated with the utmost respect, my word is of no value. But fear nothing; it is settled. You, Galotti, may do as you think proper. You may follow us to Guastalla, or return to Sabionetta, as you please. It would be ridiculous to dictate any conduct to you. And now, farewell for the present, dear Galotti.--Come, Marinelli. It grows late.

ODOARDO (who has been standing in deep meditation)

.

--How! May I not even see my daughter, then? May I not even see her here? I submit to everything--I approve of everything. A chancellor's house is, of course, a sanctuary of virtue. Take my daughter thither, I beseech your Highness--nowhere but thither. Yet I would willingly have some previous conversation with her. She is still ignorant of the Count's death, and will be unable to understand why she is separated from her parents. That I may apprise her gently of the one, and console her for this parting----I must see her, Prince, I must see her.

PRINCE.

Come, then, with us.

ODOARDO.
Surely the daughter can come to her father. Let us have a short conversation here, without witnesses. Send her hither, I beg your Highness.
PRINCE.
That, too, shall be done. Oh, Galotti, if you would be my friend, my guide, my father! (Exeunt Prince
and Marinelli
).
Scene
VI.
Odoardo
.
ODOARDO (after a pause, during which his eyes follow the Prince
)
.
Why not? Most willingly. Ha! ha! ha! (Looks wildly around.) Who laughed? By Heaven I believe it was myself. 'Tis well. I will be merry. The game is near an end. Thus must it be, or thus. But--(pauses)--how if she were in league with him? How if this were the usual deception? How if she were not worthy of what I am about to do for her? (Pauses again.) And what am I about to do for her? Have I a heart to name it even to myself? A thought comes to me--a thought which can be but a thought. Horrible!--I will go. I will not wait until she comes. (Raises his eyes towards Heaven.) If she be innocent, let Him who plunged her into this abyss, extricate her from it. He needs not my hand. I will away. (As he is going he espies Emilia
.) Ha! 'Tis too late. My hand is required--He requires it.
Scene
VII.
Emilia, Odoardo
.
Enter Emilia
.
EMILIA.
How! Ton here, my father? And you alone--without the Count--without my mother? So uneasy, too, my father?
ODOARDO.
And you so much at ease, my daughter?
EMILIA.
Why should I not be so, my father? Either all is lost, or nothing. To be able to be at ease, and to be obliged to be at ease, do they not come to the same thing!
ODOARDO.
But what do you suppose to be the case?
EMILIA.
That all is lost--therefore that we must be at ease, my father.
ODOARDO.

And you are at ease, because necessity requires it? Who are you? A girl; my daughter? Then should the man and the father be ashamed of you. But let me hear. What mean you when you say that all is lost?--that Count Appiani is dead?

EMILIA.

And why is he dead? Why? Ha! It is, then, true, my father--the horrible tale is true which I read in my mother's tearful and wild looks. Where is my mother? Where has she gone?

ODOARDO.

She is gone before us--if we could but follow her.

EMILIA.

Oh, the sooner the better. For if the Count be dead--if he was doomed to die on that account--Ha! Why do we stay here? Let us fly, my father.

ODOARDO.

Fly! Where is the necessity? You are in the hands of your ravisher, and will there remain.

EMILIA.

I remain in his hands?

ODOARDO.

And alone--without your mother--without me.

EMILIA.

I remain alone in his hands? Never, my father--or you are not my father. I remain alone in his hands? 'Tis well. Leave me, leave me. I will see who can detain me--who can compel me. What human being can compel another?

ODOARDO.

I thought, my child, you were tranquil.

EMILIA.

I am so. But what do you call tranquillity?--To lay my hands in my lap, and patiently bear what cannot be borne, and suffer what should be suffered.

ODOARDO.

Ha! If such be thy thoughts, come to my arms, my daughter. I have ever said, that Nature, when forming woman, wished to form her master-piece. She erred in that the clay she chose was too plastic. In every other respect man is inferior to woman. Ha! If this be thy composure, I recognize my daughter again. Come to my arms. Now, mark me. Under the pretence of legal examination, the Prince--tears thee (the hellish fool's play!) tears thee from our arms, and places thee under the protection of Grimaldi.

EMILIA.

Tears me from your arms? Takes me--would tear me--take me--would--would----As if we ourselves had no will, father.

ODOARDO.

So incensed was I, that I was on the point of drawing forth this dagger (produces it), and plunging it into the hearts of both the villains.

EMILIA.

Heaven forbid it! my father. This life is all the wicked can enjoy. Give me, give me the dagger.

ODOARDO.

Child, it is no bodkin.

EMILIA.

If it were, it would serve as a dagger. 'Twere the same.

ODOARDO.

What! Is it come to that? Not yet, not yet. Reflect. You have but one life to lose, Emilia.

EMILIA.

And but one innocence.

ODOARDO.

Which is proof against all force.

EMILIA.

But not against all seduction. Force! Force! What is that? Who may not defy force? What you call force is nothing. Seduction is the only real force. I have blood, my father, as youthful and as warm as that of others. I have senses too. I cannot pledge myself: I guarantee nothing. I know the house of Grimaldi. It is a house of revelry--a single hour spent in that society, under the protection of my mother, created such a tumult in my soul, that all the rigid exercises of religion could scarcely quell it in whole weeks. Religion! And what religion? To avoid no worse snares thousands have leapt into the waves, and now are saints. Give me the dagger, then, my father, give it to me.

ODOARDO.

And didst thou but know who armed me with this dagger----

EMILIA.

That matters not. An unknown friend is not the less a friend. Give me the dagger, father, I beseech you.

ODOARDO.

And if I were to give it you?--what then? There! (He presents it)

EMILIA.

And there! (She seizes it with ardour, and is about to stab herself when Odoardo wrests it from her.)

ODOARDO.

See how rash----No; it is not for thy hand.

EMILIA.

Tis true; then with this bodkin will I! (she searches for one in her hair, and feels the rose in her head). Art thou still there? Down, down! thou shouldst not deck the head of one, such as my father wishes me to be!

ODOARDO.

Oh! my daughter!

EMILIA.

Oh, my father! if I understand you. But no, you will not do it, or why so long delayed. (In a bitter tone, while she plucks the leaves of the rose.) In former days there was a father, who, to save his daughter from disgrace plunged the first deadly weapon which he saw, into his daughter's heart--and thereby gave her life, a second time. But those were deeds of ancient times. Such fathers exist not now.

ODOARDO.

They do, they do, my daughter (stabs her). God of heaven! What have I done? (supports her in his arms as she sinks.)

EMILIA.

Broken a rose before the storm had robbed it of its bloom. Oh, let me kiss this kind parental hand.

Scene

VIII.

The Prince, Marinelli, Odoardo, Emilia

.

PRINCE (entering)

.

What means this? Is Emilia not well?

ODOARDO.

Very well, very well.

PRINCE (approaching her.)

What do I see? Oh, horror!

MARINELLI.

I am lost!

PRINCE.

Cruel father, what hast thou done.

ODOARDO.

Broken a rose before the storm had robbed it of its bloom. Said you not so, my daughter?

EMILIA.

Not you, my father. I, I myself----

ODOARDO.

Not thou my daughter--not thou! Quit not this world with falsehood on thy lips. Not thou, my daughter--thy father, thy unfortunate father.

EMILIA.

Ah!--My father----(Dies in his arms. He lays her gently on the floor.)

ODOARDO.

Ascend on high! There, Prince! Does she still charm you? Does she still rouse your appetites?--here, weltering in her blood--which cries for vengeance against you. (After a pause.) Doubtless you wait to see the end of this. You expect, perhaps, that I shall turn the steel against myself, and finish the deed like some wretched tragedy. You are mistaken. There! (Throws the dagger at his feet.) There lies the blood-stained witness of my crime. I go to deliver myself into the hands of justice. I go to meet you as my judge: then I shall meet you in another world, before the Judge of all. (Exit.)

PRINCE (after a pause, during which he surveys the body with a look of horror and despair, turns to Marinelli

)

.

Here! Raise her. How! Dost thou hesitate? Wretch! Villain! (Tears the dagger from his grasp.) No. Thy blood shall not be mixed with such as this. Go: hide thyself for ever.

Begone, I say. Oh God! Oh God! Is it not enough for the misery of many that monarchs are men? Must devils in disguise become their friends?

NATHAN THE WISE.

A DRAMATIC POEM IN FIVE ACTS.

(Translated by R. Dillon Boylan.)

The well-known Goetze Controversy is to be thanked for the appearance of this, the longest, and in many respects the most important of Lessing's dramatic works. It was written in 1778-9, in reply to some of the theological censures of the Hamburg pastor. In 1783, it was first acted at Berlin, but it met with little success there or elsewhere, until in 1801, when it was introduced on the Weimar stage, by Schiller and Goethe.

DRAMATIS PERSONÆ

Sultan Saladin

.

Sittah

, his Sister.

Nathan

, a rich Jew of Jerusalem.

Recha

, his adopted Daughter.

Daja

, a Christian woman living in the Jew's house as Recha's
companion.

A young Knight Templar

.

A Dervise

.

The Patriarch of Jerusalem

.

A Friar.

An Emir

and several of Saladin's Mamelukes

.

The scene is in Jerusalem.

NATHAN THE WISE.

"Introite, nam et heic Dii sunt."

Apud Gellium

.

ACT I.

Scene

I.--A Hall in Nathan's House.

Nathan

, returning from a journey; Daja

, meeting him.

DAJA.

'Tis he! 'Tis Nathan! endless thanks to Heaven

That you at last are happily returned.
NATHAN.
Yes, Daja! thanks to Heaven! But why at last?
Was it my purpose--was it in my power
To come back sooner? Babylon from here,
As I was forced to take my devious way,
Is a long journey of two hundred leagues;
And gathering in one's debts is not--at best,
A task that expedites a traveller's steps.
DAJA.
O Nathan! what a dire calamity
Had, in your absence, nigh befallen us!
Your house----
NATHAN.
Took fire. I have already heard.
God grant I may have learnt the whole that chanced!
DAJA.
Chance saved it, or it had been burnt to ashes.
NATHAN.
Then, Daja! we had built another house,
And a far better----
DAJA.
True--ay, true! but Recha
Was on the point of perishing amid
The flames----
NATHAN.
Of perishing? Who saidst thou? Recha?
I had not heard of that. I should not then
Have needed any house. What! on the point
Of perishing? Nay, nay; perchance she's dead--
Is burnt alive. Speak, speak the dreadful truth.
Kill me, but do not agonize me thus.
Tell me at once she's dead.
DAJA.
And if she were
Could you expect to hear it from these lips?
NATHAN.
Why then alarm me? Recha! O my Recha!
DAJA.
Your Recha? Yours?
NATHAN.
And can it ever be
That I shall cease to call this child my own?
DAJA.
Is all you have yours by an equal title?

NATHAN.
Nought by a better. What I else enjoy
Are Fortune's gifts, or Nature's. This alone--
This treasure do I owe to virtue.
DAJA.
Nathan!
How dearly must I pay for all your goodness!
If goodness practised for an end like yours
Deserves the name.
NATHAN.
An end like mine! What mean you?
DAJA.
My conscience----
NATHAN.
Daja, let me tell you first----
DAJA.
I say my conscience----
NATHAN.
Oh, the gorgeous robe
That I have bought for you in Babylon!
Costly it is and rare. For Recha's self
I have not bought a richer.
DAJA.
What of that?
My conscience can be silent now no more.
NATHAN.
I long to witness your delight, to see
The bracelets, earrings, and the golden chain
Which I selected at Damascus for you.
DAJA.
'Tis always so, you surfeit me with gifts.
NATHAN.
Accept them freely, as they are bestowed,
And silence!
DAJA.
Silence! Yes. But who can doubt
That you are generosity itself?
And yet----
NATHAN.
I'm but a Jew! Daja, confess
That I have guessed your thought.
DAJA.
You know my thoughts
Far better.
NATHAN.

Well, be silent!
DAJA.
I am dumb.
And henceforth all the evil that may spring
From this, which I cannot avert, nor change,
Fall on your head.
NATHAN.
Let it all fall on me!
But where is Recha? What detains her thus?
Are you deceiving me? Can she have heard
That I am here?
DAJA.
Yourself must answer that.
Terror still palpitates through every nerve,
And fancy mingles fire with all her thoughts.
In sleep her soul's awake; but when awake,
Is wrapt in slumber. Less than mortal now,
And now far more than angel, she appears.
NATHAN.
Poor child! how frail a thing is human nature!
DAJA.
She lay this morning with her eyelids closed--
One would have thought her dead--when suddenly
She started from her couch, and cried, "Hark, hark!
Here come my father's camels, and I hear
His own sweet voice again!" With that, her eyes
Once more she opened, and her arms' support
Withdrawn, her head droop'd softly on her pillow.
Quickly I hastened forth, and now behold,
I find you here. But marvel not at this.
Has not her every thought been long engrossed
With dreams of you and him?
NATHAN.
Of him! What him?
DAJA.
Of him who from the flames preserved her life.
NATHAN.
And who was he? Where is he? Name the man
Who saved my Recha?
DAJA.
A young Templar he!
Brought hither captive lately, and restored
To freedom by the Sultan.
NATHAN.
How? A Templar?

A captive, too, and pardoned by the Sultan?
Could not my Recha's life have been preserved
By some less wondrous miracle? O God!
DAJA.
But for this stranger's help, who risked afresh
The life so unexpectedly restored,
Recha had surely perished.
NATHAN.
Where is he?
Where is this noble youth? Where is he, Daja?
Oh, lead me to his feet! But you already
Have surely lavished on him all the wealth
That I had left behind; have given him all--
And promised more, much more.
DAJA.
How could we, Nathan?
NATHAN.
Why not?
DAJA.
He came we know not whence, he went
We know not whither. To the house a stranger,
And guided by his ear alone, he rushed
With fearless daring through the smoke and flame,
His mantle spread before him, till he reached
The spot whence issued piercing screams for help.
We thought him lost; when, bursting through the fire,
He stood before us, bearing in his arms
Her almost lifeless form. Unmoved and cold,
Deaf to our cries of thanks, he left his prize,
Passed through the wondering crowd, and disappeared.
NATHAN.
But not for ever, Daja, I would hope.
DAJA.
For some days after, 'neath yon spreading palms,
Which wave above our blest Redeemer's grave,
We saw him pacing thoughtful to and fro.
With transport I approached to speak my thanks.
I pleaded, begged, entreated that for once,
Once only, he would see the grateful maid,
Who longed to shed at her preserver's feet
Her tears of gratitude.
NATHAN.
Well?
DAJA.
All in vain!

Deaf to my warmest prayers, he poured on me
Such bitter taunts----
NATHAN.
That you withdrew dismayed.
DAJA.
Far otherwise. I sought to meet him daily,
And daily heard his harsh insulting words.
Much have I borne, and would have borne still more;
But lately he has ceased his lonely walk
Beneath the spreading palms that shade the grave
Of Him who rose from death; and no man knows
Where he may now be found. You seem surprised.
NATHAN.
I was considering how such a scene
Must work upon a mind like Recha's. Scorned
By one whom she can never cease to prize;
Repelled by one who still attracts her to him.
Her head and heart at strife! And long, full long
The contest may endure, without the power
To say if anger or regret shall triumph.
Should neither prove the victor, Fancy then
May mingle in the fray, and turn her brain.
Then Passion will assume fair Reason's garb,
And Reason act like Passion. Fatal change!
Such, doubtless, if I know my Recha well,
Must be her fate; her mind is now unhinged.
DAJA.
But her illusions are so sweet and holy.
NATHAN.
But yet she raves!
DAJA.
The thought she clings to most,
Is that the Templar was no earthly form,
But her blest guardian angel, such as she
From childhood fancied hovering o'er her path;
Who from his veiling cloud, amid the fire
Rushed to her aid in her preserver's form.
You smile incredulous. Who knows the truth?
Permit her to indulge the fond deceit,
Which Christian, Jew, and Mussulman alike
Agree to own. The illusion is so sweet!
NATHAN.
I love it too. But go, good Daja! go,
See what she does--if I can speak with her.
This guardian angel, wilful and untamed,

I'll then seek out--and if he still is pleased
To sojourn here a while with us--or still
Is pleased to play the knight so boorishly,
I'll doubtless find him out and bring him here.
DAJA.
You are too daring, Nathan.
NATHAN.
Trust me, Daja!
If fond delusion yield to sweeter truth--
For human beings ever to their kind
Are dearer after all than angels are--
You will not censure me, when you perceive
Our lov'd enthusiast's mind again restored.
DAJA.
You are so good, and so discerning, Nathan!
But see, behold! Yes, here she comes herself.
Scene
II.
Recha
, Nathan
, and Daja
.
RECHA.
And is it you! your very self, my father?
I thought you had but sent your voice before you,
Where are you lingering still? What mountains, streams,
Or deserts now divide us? Here we are
Once more together, face to face, and yet
You do not hasten to embrace your Recha!
Poor Recha! she was almost burnt alive!
Yet she escaped----But do not, do not shudder.
It were a dreadful death to die by fire!
NATHAN.
My child! my darling child!
RECHA.
Your journey lay
Across the Tigris, Jordan, and Euphrates,
And many other rivers. 'Till that fire
I trembled for your safety, but since then
Methinks it were a blessed, happy thing
To die by water. But you are not drowned,
Nor am I burnt alive. We will rejoice,
And thank our God, who bore you on the wings
Of unseen angels o'er the treacherous streams,
And bade my angel bear me visibly

On his white pinion through the raging flames.
NATHAN (aside)

.

On his white pinion! Ha! I see; she means
The broad white fluttering mantle of the Templar.
RECHA.
Yes, visibly he bore me through the flames,
O'ershadowed by his wings. Thus, face to face,
I have beheld an angel--my own angel.
NATHAN.
Recha were worthy of so blest a sight.
And would not see in him a fairer form
Than he would see in her.
RECHA (smiling)

.

Whom would you flatter--
The angel, dearest father, or yourself?
NATHAN.
And yet methinks, dear Recha, if a man--
Just such a man as Nature daily fashions--
Had rendered you this service, he had been
A very angel to you.
RECHA.
But he was
No angel of that stamp, but true and real.
And have I not full often heard you say
'Tis possible that angels may exist?
And how God still works miracles for those
Who love Him? And I love Him dearly, father.
NATHAN.
And He loves you; and 'tis for such as you
That He from all eternity has wrought
Such ceaseless wonders daily.
RECHA.
How I love
To hear you thus discourse!
NATHAN.
Well, though it sound
A thing but natural and common-place
That you should by a Templar have been saved,
Is it the less a miracle for that?
The greatest of all miracles seems this:
That real wonders, genuine miracles,
Can seem and grow so commonplace to us.
Without this universal miracle,

Those others would scarce strike a thinking man,
Awaking wonder but in children's minds,
Who love to stare at strange, unusual things,
And hunt for novelty.
DAJA.
Why will you thus
With airy subtleties perplex her mind,
Already overheated?
NATHAN.
Silence, Daja!
And was it then no miracle that Recha
Should be indebted for her life to one
Whom no small miracle preserved himself?
Who ever heard before, that Saladin
Pardoned a Templar? that a Templar asked it--
Hoped it--or for his ransom offered more
Than his own sword--belt, or at most his dagger?
RECHA.
That argues for me, father! All this proves
That my preserver was no Templar knight,
But only seemed so. If no captive Templar
Has e'er come hither but to meet his death,
And through Jerus'lem cannot wander free,
How could I find one, in the night, to save me?
NATHAN.
Ingenious, truly! Daja, you must speak.
Doubtless, you know still more about this knight;
For 'twas from you I learnt he was a prisoner.
DAJA.
'Tis but report indeed, but it is said
That Saladin gave freedom to the knight,
Moved by the likeness which his features bore
To a lost brother whom he dearly loved,
Though since his disappearance twenty years
Have now elapsed. He fell I know not where,
And e'en his very name's a mystery.
But the whole tale sounds so incredible,
It may be mere invention, pure romance.
NATHAN.
And why incredible? Would you reject
This story, Daja, as so oft is done,
To fix on something more incredible,
And credit that? Why should not Saladin,
To whom his race are all so dear, have loved
In early youth a brother now no more?

Since when have features ceased to be alike?
Is an impression lost because 'tis old?
Will the same cause not work a like effect?
What, then, is so incredible? My Daja,
This can to you be no great miracle;
Or does a wonder only claim belief
When it proceeds from you?
DAJA.
You mock me, Nathan!
NATHAN.
Nay, 'tis the very tone you use yourself.
And yet, dear Recha, your escape from death
Remains no less a miracle
Of Him who turns the proud resolves of kings
To mockery, or guides them to their end
By the most slender threads.
RECHA.
O father, father!
My error is not wilful, if I err.
NATHAN.
No, I have ever found you glad to learn.
See, then, a forehead vaulted thus or thus,
A nose of such a shape, and brows that shade
The eye with straighter or with sharper curve,
A spot, a mole, a wrinkle, or a line--
A nothing--in an European's face,
And you are saved in Asia from the flames!
Is that no wonder, wonder-seeking folk?
What need to summon angels to your aid?
DAJA.
But, Nathan, where's the harm,--if I may speak--
In thinking one was rescued by an angel
Rather than by a man? Are we not brought
Thus nearer to the first mysterious cause
Of our life's preservation?
NATHAN.
Pride, rank pride!
The iron pot would with a silver tongs
Be lifted from the furnace, to believe
Itself a silver vase! Well! where's the harm?
And "where's the good?" I well may ask in turn.
Your phrase, "It brings you nearer to the first
Mysterious cause!" is nonsense--if 'tis not
Rank blasphemy:--it works a certain harm.
Attend to me. To him who saved your life,

Whether he be an angel or a man,
You both--and you especially--should pay
Substantial services in just return.
Is not this true? Now, what great services
Have you the power to render to an angel!
To sing his praise--to pour forth sighs and prayers--
Dissolve in transports of devotion o'er him--
Fast on his vigil, and distribute alms?
Mere nothings! for 'tis clear your neighbour gains
Far more than he by all this piety.
Not by your abstinence will he grow fat,
Nor by your alms will he be rendered rich;
Nor by your transports is his glory raised,
Nor by your faith in him his power increased.
Say, is not all this true? But to a man----
DAJA.
No doubt a man had furnished us with more
Occasions to be useful to himself;
God knows how willingly we had seized them!
But he who saved her life demanded nought;
He needed nothing--in himself complete
And self--sufficient--as the angels are;
RECHA.
And when at last he vanished----
NATHAN.
How was that?
Did he then vanish? 'Neath yon spreading palms
Has he not since been seen? Or have you sought
Elsewhere to find him?
DAJA.
No, in truth we've not.
NATHAN.
Not sought him, Daja? Cold enthusiasts!
See now the harm: suppose your angel stretched
Upon a bed of sickness!
DAJA.
Sickness, what!
RECHA.
A chill creeps over me. I shudder, Daja!
My forehead, which till now was warm, becomes
As cold as very ice; come, feel it, Daja.
NATHAN.
He is a Frank, unused to this hot clime,
Young and unpractised in his order's rules,
In fastings and in watchings quite untrained.

RECHA.
Sick! sick!
DAJA.
Your father means 'twere possible.
NATHAN.
Friendless and penniless, he may be lying
Without the means to purchase aid.
RECHA.
Alas!
NATHAN.
Without advice, or hope, or sympathy,
May lie a prey to agony and death.
RECHA.
Where, where?
NATHAN.
And yet for one he never knew--
Enough for him it was a human being--
He plunged amid the flames and----
DAJA.
Spare her, Nathan!
NATHAN.
He sought no more to know the being whom
He rescued thus--he shunned her very thanks----
RECHA.
Oh, spare her!
NATHAN.
Did not wish to see her more,
Unless to save her for the second time--
Enough for him that she was human!
DAJA.
Hold!
NATHAN.
He may have nothing to console him dying,
Save the remembrance of his deed.
DAJA.
You kill her!
NATHAN.
And you kill him, or might have done at least.
'Tis med'cine that I give, not poison, Recha!
But be of better cheer: he lives--perhaps
He is not ill.
RECHA.
Indeed? not dead--not ill?
NATHAN.
Assuredly not dead--for God rewards

Good deeds done here below--rewards them hero.
Then go, but ne'er forget how easier far
Devout enthusiasm is, than good deeds.
How soon our indolence contents itself
With pious raptures, ignorant, perhaps,
Of their ulterior end, that we may be
Exempted from the toil of doing good.
RECHA.
O father! leave your child no more alone.--
But may he not have only gone a journey?
NATHAN.
Perhaps. But who is yonder Mussulman,
Numbering with curious eye my laden camels?
Say, do you know him?
DAJA.
Surely your own Dervise.
NATHAN.
Who?
DAJA.
Your Dervise--your old chess companion.
NATHAN.
Al-Hafi do you mean? What!--that Al-Hafi?
DAJA.
No other: now the Sultan's treasurer.
NATHAN.
What, old Al-Hafi? Do you dream again?
And yet 'tis he himself--he's coming hither.
Quick, in with you! What am I now to hear?
Scene
III.
Nathan
and the Dervise

.
DERVISE.
Ay, lift your eyes and wonder.
NATHAN.
Is it you?
A Dervise so magnificent!
DERVISE.
Why not?
Can you make nothing of a Dervise, Nathan?
NATHAN.
Ay, surely, but I've still been wont to think
A Dervise--I would say a thorough Dervise--
Will ne'er let anything be made of him.

DERVISE.
Well, by the Prophet! though it may be true
That I'm no thorough Dervise, yet one must----
NATHAN.
Must, Hafi! You a Dervise! No man must----
And least of all a Dervise.
DERVISE.
Nay, he must,
When he is much implored and deems it right.
NATHAN.
Well spoken, Hafi! Let us now embrace.
You're still, I trust, my friend.
DERVISE.
Why not ask first
What has been made of me?
NATHAN.
I take my chance,
In spite of all that has been made of you.
DERVISE.
May I not be a servant of the state
Whose friendship is no longer good for you?
NATHAN.
If you but still possess your Dervise heart
I'll run the risk of that. The stately robe
Is but your cloak.
DERVISE.
And yet it claims some honour.
But, tell me truly, at a court of yours
What had been Hafi's rank?
NATHAN.
A Dervise only--
Or, if aught else--perhaps my cook.
DERVISE.
Why yes!
That I might thus unlearn my native trade,
Your cook! why not your butler? But the Sultan--
He knows me better--I'm his treasurer.
NATHAN.
What, you?--his treasurer?
DERVISE.
Mistake me not,
I only bear his lesser purse; his father
Still manages the greater, and I am
The treasurer of his house.
NATHAN.

His house is large!
DERVISE.
Far larger than you think--all needy men
Are of his house.
NATHAN.
Yet Saladin is such
A foe to beggars!
DERVISE.
That he'd root them out,
Though he turned beggar in the enterprise.
NATHAN.
Bravo! I meant as much.
DERVISE.
He's one already.
His treasury at sunset every day
Is worse than empty; and although the tide
Flowed high at morn, 'tis ebb before the noon.
NATHAN.
Because it flows through channels such as we
Can neither stop nor fill.
DERVISE.
You hit the truth.
NATHAN.
I know it well.
DERVISE.
Ah! 'tis an evil case
When kings are vultures amid carcases,
But ten times worse when they're the carcases
Amid the vultures.
NATHAN.
Dervise, 'tis not so.
DERVISE.
Is that your thought? But, come, what will you give
If I resign my office in your favour?
NATHAN.
What are your profits?
DERVISE.
Mine? not much; but you
Would soon grow rich; for when, as oft occurs,
The Sultan's treasury is at an ebb,
You might unlock your sluices, pour in gold,
And take in form of interest what you please.
NATHAN.
And interest on the interest of the interest.
DERVISE.

Of course.
NATHAN.
Until my capital becomes
All interest.
DERVISE.
Well! is not the offer tempting?
Farewell for ever to our friendship then,
For I had counted on you.
NATHAN.
How so, Hafi?
DERVISE.
I thought you would have helped me to discharge
My task with credit; that I should have found
Your treasury ready. Ha! you shake your head.
NATHAN.
Let us explain. We must distinguish here.
To you, Dervise Al-Hafi, all I have
Is welcome; but to you, the Defterdar
Of Saladin--to that Al-Hafi, who----
DERVISE.
I guessed as much. You ever are as good
As you are wise and prudent. Only wait.
The two Al-Hafis you distinguish thus
Will soon be parted. See, this robe of honour,
Which Saladin bestowed, before 'tis worn
To rags, and suited to a Dervise back,
Will in Jerusalem hang from a nail;
Whilst I, upon the Ganges' scorching strand,
Barefoot amid my teachers will be found.
NATHAN.
That's like yourself!
DERVISE.
Or playing chess with them.
NATHAN.
Your greatest bliss!
DERVISE.
What do you think seduced me?
Hopes of escaping future penury,
The pride of acting the rich man to beggars,
Would this have metamorphosed all at once
The richest beggar to a poor rich man?
NATHAN.
No.
DERVISE.
But I yielded to a sillier whim.

For the first time I felt myself allured
By Saladin's kind-hearted, flattering words.
NATHAN.
And what were they?
DERVISE.
He said a beggar's wants
Are known but to the poor alone; that they
Alone can tell how want should be relieved.
"Thy predecessor was too cold," he said,
"Too harsh, and when he gave, 'twas with a frown.
He searched each case too strictly, not content
To find out want, he would explore the cause,
And thus he measured out his niggard alms.
Not so wilt thou bestow, and Saladin
Will not appear so harshly kind in thee.
Thou art not like that choked-up conduit-pipe,
Whence in unequal streams the water flows,
Which it receives in pure and copious stores.
Al-Hafi thinks, Al-Hafi feels like me."
The fowler whistled, and at last the quail
Ran to his net. Cheated, and by a cheat?
NATHAN.
Hush, Dervise, hush!
DERVISE.
What! is it not a cheat
To grind mankind by hundred thousands thus!
Oppress them, plunder, butcher, and torment,
And singly play the philanthropic part?
Not cheating, to pretend to imitate
That heavenly bounty, which in even course
Descends alike on desert and on plain,
On good and bad, in sunshine and in shower,
And not possess the never empty hand
Of the Most High! Not cheating----
NATHAN.
Dervise, cease!
DERVISE.
Nay, let me speak of cheating of my own,
How now? Were it not cheating to seek out
The bright side of impostures such as these,
That under colour of this brighter side
I might take part in them? What say you now?
NATHAN.
Fly to your desert quickly. Amongst men
I fear you'll soon unlearn to be a man.

DERVISE.
I fear so too. Farewell!
NATHAN.
What, so abrupt?
Stay, stay, Al-Hafi! Has the desert wings?
It will not fly away. Here, stay, Al-Hafi!
He's gone; he's gone. I would that I had asked
About that Templar; he must know the man.
Scene
IV.
Daja
(rushing in), Nathan
.
DAJA.
O Nathan, Nathan!
NATHAN.
Well! what now?
DAJA.
He's there.
He shows himself once more.
NATHAN.
Who, Daja--who?
DAJA.
He--he!
NATHAN.
Where cannot he be found? But he
You mean, is, I suppose, the only He.
That should not be, were he an angel's self.
DAJA.
Beneath the palms he wanders up and down,
And gathers dates.
NATHAN.
And eats them, I suppose,
Just as a Templar would.
DAJA.
You mock me, sir!
Her eager eye espied him long ago,
When scarcely seen amid the distant trees.
She watches him intently, and implores
That you will go to him without delay.
Then go, and from the window she will mark
Which way his paces tend. Go, go; make haste!
NATHAN.
What! thus, as I alighted from my camel?
Would that be seemly? But do you accost him;

Tell him of my return. I do not doubt
You'll find the honest man forbore our house
Because the host was absent. He'll accept
A father's invitation. Say I ask him,
I heartily request him.
DAJA.
All in vain!
In short, he will not visit any Jew.
NATHAN.
Then use your best endeavours to detain him,
Or, with unerring eye, observe his steps,
And mark him well. Go, I shall not be long.
(Nathan
enters the house. Daja
retires.)
Scene
V.
A Place of Palms. The Templar
, walking to and fro; a Friar
, following him at some distance, as if desirous of addressing him.
TEMPLAR.
It cannot be for pastime that this man
Follows me thus. See how he eyes my hands!
Good brother--or, perhaps I should say, father!
FRIAR.
No, brother; a lay brother, at your service.
TEMPLAR.
Well, brother, then, if I had anything--
But truly I have nothing----
FRIAR.
Thanks the same!
God will reward your purpose thousandfold.
The will and not the deed perfects the giver.
Nor was I sent to follow you for alms.
TEMPLAR.
Sent?
FRIAR.
From the convent.
TEMPLAR.
Where I even now
Was hoping to partake a pilgrim's fare.
FRIAR.
'Tis meal--time now, the tables all are full;
But if it please you, we will turn together.
TEMPLAR.

No matter, though I have not tasted meat
For many days; these dates, you see, are ripe.
FRIAR.
Be sparing of that fruit, sir, for too much
Is hurtful, sours the blood, and makes one sad.
TEMPLAR.
And what if sadness suits me? Though, methinks,
'Twas not to give this warning that you came.
FRIAR.
Oh, no! my mission was to question you--
To feel your pulse a little.
TEMPLAR.
And you tell
This tale yourself?
FRIAR.
Why not?
TEMPLAR.
An artful soul! (aside).
And has the convent many more like you?
FRIAR.
I know not. Mere obedience is my duty.
TEMPLAR.
And you obey without much questioning.
FRIAR.
Could it be rightly termed obedience else?
TEMPLAR.
The simple mind is ever in the right.--(aside).
But will you not inform me who it is
That wishes to know more of me? Not you,
I dare be sworn.
FRIAR.
Would such a wish become
Or profit me?
TEMPLAR.
Whom would it then become
Or profit to be thus inquisitive?
FRIAR.
Perhaps the Patriarch--'twas he that sent.
TEMPLAR.
The Patriarch? and does he know my badge
So ill?--The red cross on the snow-white robe.
FRIAR.
Why? I know that.
TEMPLAR.
Well, brother, hear me out.

I am a Templar--and a prisoner now.
Made captive with some others at Tebnin,
Whose fortress we had almost ta'en by storm
Just as the truce expired. Our hopes had been
To threaten Sidon next. Of twenty knights
Made prisoners there together, I alone
Was pardoned by command of Saladin.
The Patriarch now knows what he requires,
And more than he requires.
FRIAR.
And yet no more
Than he had learned already. He would ask
Why you, of all the captives doomed to die,
Alone were spared?
TEMPLAR.
Can I myself tell that?
Already with bare neck I had knelt down
Upon my mantle, to await the stroke,
When Saladin with steadfast eye surveys me.
Nearer he draws--he makes a sign--they raise me--
I am unbound--I would express my thanks--
I mark the tear-drop glisten in his eye--
We both stand mute--he turns and leaves the spot--
I stay. And now, how all this hangs together,
The Patriarch must explain.
FRIAR.
The Patriarch thinks
That Heaven preserved you for some mighty deed.
TEMPLAR.
Some mighty deed? To rescue from the flames
A Jewish maid! To lead to Sinai's mount
Bands of inquiring pilgrims--and the like!
FRIAR.
The time may come for more important tasks:
Perhaps the Patriarch has already planned
Some mighty business for you.
TEMPLAR.
Think you so?
Has he already given you a hint?
FRIAR.
Yes--but my task is first to sift a little,
To see if you are one to undertake----
TEMPLAR.
Well--sift away? (We'll see how this man sifts).
FRIAR.

The better course will be to name at once
What is the Patriarch's desire.
TEMPLAR.
It is----?
FRIAR.
To make you bearer of a letter.
TEMPLAR.
Me?
I am no carrier. Is that the office
More meritorious than to save from death
A Jewish maid?
FRIAR.
So, truly, it would seem.
The Patriarch says that this little note
Involves the general weal of Christendom,
And that to bear it to its destined hand,
Safely, will merit a peculiar crown
From Heaven--and of that crown, the Patriarch
Says none can worthier be than you.
TEMPLAR.
Than I!
FRIAR.
You have your liberty--can look around;
You understand how cities may be stormed,
And how defended, says the Patriarch;
You know the strength and weakness of the towers,
And of the inner rampart lately reared
By Saladin, and you could point out all
To the Lord's champions fully.
TEMPLAR.
May I know
Exactly the contents of this same letter?
FRIAR.
Of that I am not quite informed myself.
'Tis to King Philip; and our Patriarch--
I often wonder how that holy man,
Whose every thought would seem absorbed by Heaven,
Can stoop to earthly things, and how his mind
Can be so deeply skilled in human lore----
TEMPLAR.
Well, then, your Patriarch----
FRIAR.
Exactly knows
From secret sources, how, and with what force,
And in what quarter, should the war break out,

The foe and Saladin will take the field.
TEMPLAR.
Knows he so much?
FRIAR.
Ay, truly! and he longs
To send the urgent tidings to King Philip,
That he may better calculate if now
The danger be so great, as to demand
At every hazard that he should renew
The truce so boldly broken by the Templars.
TEMPLAR.
The noble Patriarch! He seeks in me
No common herald, but the meanest spy.
Therefore, good brother, tell your Patriarch,
That I am not--as far as you can sift--
The man to suit his ends. I hold myself
A captive still. I know a Templar's duty:
Ready to die, not live to play the spy.
FRIAR.
I thought as much. Nor can I censure you
For your resolve. The best has still to come.
Our Patriarch has learnt the very fort,
Its name, its strength, its site on Lebanon,
Wherein those countless treasures are concealed,
Wherewith the Sultan's prudent father pays
His troops, and all the heavy costs of war.
He knows that Saladin, from time to time,
Visits this fortress, by some secret way,
With but a few attendants.
TEMPLAR.
Well! what then?
FRIAR.
'Twould be an easy task, methinks, to seize
The Sultan thus defenceless--and to end him.
You shudder, knight! Two monks who fear the Lord,
Are ready now to undertake the task,
And wait a leader.
TEMPLAR.
And the Patriarch
Has pitched on me to do this noble deed?
FRIAR.
He thinks King Philip might from Ptolemais
Give aid in the design.
TEMPLAR.
Has pitched on me!

On me!--Say, brother, have you never heard
The boundless debt I owe to Saladin?
FRIAR.
Truly I have.
TEMPLAR.
And yet----
FRIAR.
The Patriarch
Says that is very well; but yet your order,
And vows to God----
TEMPLAR.
Change nothing; they command
No villainy.
FRIAR.
No. But the Patriarch
Says what seems villainy to human eyes,
May not appear so in the sight of God.
TEMPLAR.
Brother, I owe my life to Saladin,
And his shall my hand take?
FRIAR.
Oh, no!--But yet
The Patriarch maintains that Saladin,
Who is the common foe of Christendom,
Can never have a claim to be your friend.
TEMPLAR.
My friend? forsooth! because I will not be
A thankless wretch to him!
FRIAR.
'Tis so!--But yet
The Patriarch thinks gratitude is not
Before the eyes of God or man, a debt,
Unless, for our own sakes, some benefit
Has been conferred; and, says the Patriarch,
It is affirmed the Sultan spared your life
Merely because your voice, your look, your air,
Awoke a recollection of his brother----
TEMPLAR.
He knows all this, and yet?----Ah, were it true!
And, Saladin, could Nature form in me
A single feature in thy brother's likeness,
With nothing in my soul to answer it?
Or what does correspond, shall I belie
To please a Patriarch? No, surely Nature
Could never lie so basely! Nor, kind God,

Couldst thou so contradict Thyself! Go, brother,
And do not rouse my anger.
FRIAR.
I withdraw
More gladly than I came. And, pardon me:
A monk's first duty, sir, is to obey.
Scene
VI.--The Templar
and Daja
.
(She has been watching him from afar and now approaches.)
DAJA.
Methinks the monk left him in no good mood,
But, spite of that, I must my errand risk.
TEMPLAR.
This hits exactly. As the proverb goes,
Women and monks are ever Satan's tools,
And I to-day am subject to them both.
DAJA.
Whom do I see? Thank God, our noble knight.
Where have you been so long? Not ill, I hope?
TEMPLAR.
No.
DAJA.
In good health?
TEMPLAR.
Yes.
DAJA.
We have all been grieved
Lest something should have ailed you. Have you been
Upon a journey?
TEMPLAR.
Fairly guessed.
DAJA.
Since when
Have you returned to us?
TEMPLAR.
Since yesterday.
DAJA.
Our Recha's father, too, is just returned,
And now may Recha hope at last.
TEMPLAR.
For what?
DAJA.
For what she has so often asked in vain.

Her father pressingly invites you too.
He lately has arrived from Babylon
With twenty camels, bearing precious stones,
And stuffs and fragrant spices, which he sought
In India, Persia, Syria, and China.
TEMPLAR.
I am no merchant.
DAJA.
He is much esteemed
By all his nation--honoured as a prince--
And yet to hear how he is named by all
Nathan the Wise, and not the Rich, seems strange.
It often makes me wonder.
TEMPLAR.
But to them
It may be, wise and rich--both mean the same.
DAJA.
It seems to me he should be called the Good,
So rich a store of goodness dwells in him.
Since he has learned the weighty debt he owes
For service done to Recha there is nought
He would withhold from you.
TEMPLAR.
Well?
DAJA.
Try him, sir!
TEMPLAR.
What then? A moment passes soon away.
DAJA.
I had not dwelt with him so many years
Were he less kind. I know a Christian's worth,
And it was never o'er my cradle sung
That I to Palestine should wend my way,
Following a husband's steps, to educate
A Jewish maid. My husband was a page,
A noble page, in Emperor Frederick's court----
TEMPLAR.
By birth a Swiss, who earned the sorry fame
Of drowning in one river with his lord.
Woman! how often have you told this tale?
When will you cease to persecute me thus?
DAJA.
To persecute you!
TEMPLAR.
Ay, to persecute!

Now mark me. I will never see you more,
Hear you, nor be reminded of a deed
Performed at random. When I think of it,
I wonder somewhat, though I ne'er repent.
But hear me still. Should such a fatal chance
Again occur, you have yourself to blame
If I proceed more calmly, question first.
And let what's burning, burn.
DAJA.
Great God forbid!
TEMPLAR.
And now I have a favour to implore.
Know me henceforth no more. Grant me this grace,
And save me from her father; for with me
A Jew's a Jew; a Swabian blunt am I.
The image of the maid is now erased
Out of my soul--if it was ever there.
DAJA.
But yours remains with her.
TEMPLAR.
Well, and what then?
DAJA.
Who knows? Men are not always what they seem.
TEMPLAR.
They're seldom better.
(Going.)
DAJA.
Stay a little while.
What need of haste?
TEMPLAR.
Woman! forbear to make
These palm--trees odious: I have loved their shade.
DAJA.
Then go, thou German bear! Yet I must follow him.
(She follow him at a distance.)
ACT II.
Scene
I.--The Sultan's Palace

.

Saladin
and Sittah
(playing at chess).
SITTAH.
Where are your thoughts? How ill you play, dear brother!
SALADIN.

Not well in truth--and yet I thought----
SITTAH.
Oh, yes!
You're playing well for me; take back that move.
SALADIN.
Why?
SITTAH.
Don't you see you leave your knight exposed?
SALADIN.
Ay, true!--then so.
SITTAH.
And now I take your pawn.
SALADIN.
That's true again, dear Sittah! Well, then, check!
SITTAH.
That will not help you--I protect my king,
And all is safe again.
SALADIN.
Well, out of this
Dilemma 'tis not easy to escape.
I cannot save the knight.
SITTAH.
I pass him by;
I will not take him.
SALADIN.
Well, I owe you nothing;
The place you gain is better than the piece.
SITTAH.
Perhaps.
SALADIN.
But reckon not without your host;
You did not see that move.
SITTAH.
Not I, indeed;
I did not think you weary of your queen.
SALADIN.
My queen!
SITTAH.
Well, well! I see that I to-day
Shall win my thousand dinars and no more.
SALADIN.
Why so?
SITTAH.
Why so? Because designedly
You lose the game! You vex me, Saladin!

I find no pleasure in a game like this.
And even when I lose, I come off well;
For, to console me for the games you win,
You force me to accept a double stake.
SALADIN.
In that case, then, it may be by design
That you have sometimes lost. Is that the truth?
SITTAH.
At least your generosity's to blame
That I improve so little in my play.
SALADIN.
But we forget the game; come, finish it.
SITTAH.
Well, 'tis my move; now, check to king and queen!
SALADIN.
Indeed! I did not see the double check.
I lose my queen.
SITTAH.
Let's see! Can it be helped?
SALADIN.
No, take the queen--I have no luck with her.
SITTAH.
Only with her?
SALADIN.
Remove her from the board,
I shall not miss her. Now I am right again.
SITTAH.
I know from lessons which yourself have taught
How courteously we should behave to queens.
(Offering to restore the piece.)
SALADIN.
Take her or not, I shall not move her more.
SITTAH.
Why need I take her? Check, and check!
SALADIN.
Go on.
SITTAH.
Check, check, and check again!
SALADIN.
'Tis checkmate now.
SITTAH.
Hold!--no, not yet. You may advance the knight,
And ward the danger. But 'twill be the same.
SALADIN.
You are the winner, and Al-Hafi pays.

Let him be called, Sittah! You were not wrong.
My thoughts were wandering--were not in the game,
But who gives us so oft these shapeless bits
Of wood? which speak of naught--suggest no thought.
Was it with Iman that I've played--Well, well,
Ill-luck is ever wont to seek excuse.
Not the unmeaning squares or shapeless men
Have made me heedless; your dexterity,
Your calm, sharp eye, dear Sittah!
SITTAH.
What of that?
Is that to blunt the sting of your defeat?
Enough--your thoughts were wandering more than mine.
SALADIN.
Than yours? What subject could engage your thoughts?
SITTAH.
Far different cares than those which trouble you.
But, Saladin, say, when shall we again
Resume this pleasant pastime?
SALADIN.
Dearest Sittah,
This interruption will but whet our zeal.
Your thoughts are on the war: well, let it come--
'Twas not my arm that first unsheathed the sword;
I would have willingly prolonged the truce,
And willingly have knit a tender bond,
For Sittah's sake, with Richard's noble brother.
SITTAH.
How pleased you are, can you but praise your Richard.
SALADIN.
If Richard's sister had but been bestowed
Upon our brother Melek, what a house
Had then been ours! the best, the happiest
The earth could boast. You know I am not slow
To praise myself: I'm worthy of my friends.
What men these unions would have given us!
SITTAH.
Did I not smile at once at your fine dreams?
You do not, will not, know the Christian race.
It is their pride not to be men, but Christians.
The virtue which their founder felt and taught,
The charity He mingled with their creed,
Is valued, not because it is humane,
And good, and lovely, but for this alone,
That it was Christ who taught it, Christ who did it.

'Tis well for them He was so good a man,
Well that they take His goodness all on trust,
And in His virtues put their faith. His virtues!
'Tis not His virtues, but His name alone
They wish to thrust upon us--His mere name,
Which they desire should overspread the world,
Should swallow up the name of all good men,
And put the rest to shame. 'Tis for His name
Alone they care.
SALADIN.
Else, Sittah, as you say,
They would not have required that you and Melek
Should be called Christians, ere they suffered you
To feel for Christians the pure flame of love.
SITTAH.
As if from Christians, and from them alone,
That love can be expected, which the hand
Of our Creator gives to man and wife.
SALADIN.
Christians believe such vain absurdities,
That this may be among them. And yet, Sittah,
The Templars, not the Christians, are in this
To blame. 'Tis they alone who thwart my plans;
'Tis they who still hold Acca, pledged to us
By treaty as the dower of Richard's sister.
And, to maintain their order's interests,
They use this cant--the nonsense of the monk.
Scarce would they wait until the truce expired
To fall upon us. But, go on, good sirs!
Would that all else may thrive as well as this!
SITTAH.
Why, what else troubles you? What other care
Have you to struggle with?
SALADIN.
That constant grief--
I've been to Lebanon, and seen our father.
He's full of care.
SITTAH.
Alas!
SALADIN.
He must give way.
Straitened on every side, no aid, no help,
Nothing comes in.
SITTAH.
What ails him, Saladin?

SALADIN.
The only thing that I am loth to name,
Which, when I have it, so superfluous seems,
And, when I have it not, so necessary.
Where is Al-Hafi? Have they gone for him?
Will no one go? Oh, fatal, cursed money!
Welcome, Al-Hafi! You are come at last.
Scene
II.
The Dervise Al-Hafi
, Saladin
, and Sittah
.

AL-HAFI.
The gold from Egypt, I suppose, is come.
Say, is it much?
SALADIN.
What! have you heard of it?
AL-HAFI.
Not I. I thought I should receive it here.
SALADIN (pacing thoughtfully to and fro)
.
Sittah has won a thousand dinars, pay them.
AL-HAFI.
Pay without getting. That is worse than nothing!
And still to Sittah--once again for chess!
But let us see the board; how stands the game?
SITTAH.
You grudge me my good fortune?
AL-HAFI (examining the board)
.
Grudge you? When--
You know too well----
SITTAH (making signs to him)
.
Oh, hush! Al-Hafi, hush!
AL-HAFI (still examining the board)
.
Don't grudge it to yourself.
SITTAH.
Al-Hafi, hush!
AL-HAFI.
And were the white men yours?
You gave the check?
SITTAH.

'Tis well he does not hear.
AL-HAFI.
The move is his.
SITTAH (approaching nearer)
.
Then promise me that I shall have the money.
AL-HAFI (still intent upon the board)
.
You shall receive it as you've always done.
SITTAH.
How! are you mad?
AL-HAFI.
The game's not over yet.
You have not lost it, Saladin.
SALADIN (paying no attention)
.
Oh, yes;
Pay down the money.
AL-HAFI.
Pay! here stands the queen.
SALADIN (still heedless)
.
She's of no use; she's lost.
SITTAH.
Do say that I
May send and fetch the gold.
AL-HAFI (still studying the game)
.
Oh, yes! of course.
But though the queen be lost, you are not mate.
SALADIN (dashing down the board)
.
I say I am. I will be mate.
AL-HAFI.
If so,
Small pains, small gains, say I. So got, so spent.
SALADIN.
What is he muttering there?
SITTAH (to Saladin, making a sign meanwhile to Al-Hafi)
.
You know him well.
He likes entreaties--loves to be implored.
Who knows if he be not a little jealous?
SALADIN.
Well, not of thee--not of my sister, surely.

What do I hear? Al-Hafi, are you jealous?
AL-HAFI.
Perhaps I am. I wish I had her head,
Or that I were as good as she.
SITTAH.
My brother,
He always pays me fairly, and to-day
He'll do the same. Let him alone. Now go!
Al-Hafi! go! I'll have the money----
AL-HAFI.
No, not I.
I'll act this farce no more. He must know soon.
SALADIN.
Who? what?
SITTAH.
Al-Hafi! say, is this your promise?
Is't thus you keep your word?
AL-HAFI.
Could I foresee
That it would come to this?
SALADIN.
Well, tell me all.
SITTAH.
Al-Hafi! I implore you, be discreet.
SALADIN.
'Tis very strange; and what can Sittah have
So earnestly to sue for, from a stranger--
A Dervise--rather than from me, her brother?
Al-Hafi, I command you. Dervise, speak.
SITTAH.
Let not a trifle touch my brother nearer
Than is becoming, for you know that I
Have often won as much from you at chess.
But as I stand in little need of gold,
I've left the money in Al-Hafi's chest,
Which is not over full; but never fear,
It is not my intention to bestow
My wealth on either of you.
AL-HAFI.
Were this all!
SITTAH.
Some more such trifles are perhaps unclaimed:
My own allowance, which you set apart
Has lain some months untouched.
AL-HAFI.

Nor is this all.
SALADIN.
Then tell the whole.
AL-HAFI.
Whilst we've been waiting for
The gold from Egypt, she----
SITTAH.
Nay, hear him not.
AL-HAFI.
Not only has had nothing,----
SALADIN.
Dearest sister I--
But also has been lending it to you?
AL-HAFI.
Ay! at her sole expense maintained your state.
SALADIN (embracing her)

.

So like my sister!
SITTAH.
Who but you, my brother,
Could make me rich enough to have the power?
AL-HAFI.
And soon he'll make her once again as poor
As he is now.
SALADIN.
I poor! her brother poor!
When had I more--when had I less than now?
A cloak, a horse, a sabre, and my God!
What need I else? and these ne'er can I lack.
And yet, Al-Hafi, I could scold you now.
SITTAH.
Nay, brother, do not scold. I would that I
Could thus also relieve our father's cares!
SALADIN.
Ah! now my joy has vanished all at once.
We can want nothing; but he's destitute.
And whilst he wants, we all are poor indeed.
What shall I do? From Egypt we can hope
For nothing--though God only knows the cause.
'Tis general peace around, and as for me,
I could live sparingly, reduce, retrench,
If none else suffered; but 'twould not avail.
A cloak, a horse, a sword I ne'er can want.
As to my God, He is not to be bought.
He asks but little, only asks my heart.

I had relied, Al-Hafi, on your chest,
Upon the surplus there.
AL-HAFI.
A surplus there!
Say, should I not have been impaled or hanged,
If I had been detected hoarding up
A surplus? Deficits I might have ventured.
SALADIN.
Well, but what next? Could you have found out none
To borrow from, but Sittah?
SITTAH.
And would I
Have borne it, had another been preferred?
I claim that privilege. I am not yet
Quite beggared.
SALADIN.
No, not quite. Dear Sittah, this
Alone was wanting. But, Al-Hafi, go,
Inquire about, take where and what you can;
Borrow on promise, contract, anyhow;
But, mark me, not from those I have enriched.
'Twould seem as if I wished to have it back.
Go to the covetous. They gladliest lend.
They know how well their money thrives with me.
AL-HAFI.
I know of none.
SITTAH.
I recollect just now,
I heard, Al-Hafi, of your friend's return.
AL-HAFI (starting)

.
Friend! friend of mine! and who can that be, pray?
SITTAH.
Your boasted Jew.
AL-HAFI.
A Jew! and praised by me!
SITTAH.
On whom his God--I think I recollect
The very words you used, as touching him--
On whom his God, of all the choicest goods
Of earth, in full abundance, has bestowed
The greatest and the least.
AL-HAFI.
What could I mean
When I said so?

SITTAH.
The least of good things--wealth.
The greatest--wisdom!
AL-HAFI.
How! and of a Jew
Did I say that?
SITTAH.
Ay, that you did--of Nathan.
AL-HAFI.
Oh, true! of Nathan--yes! He did not now
Occur to me. But he's returned at last,
Then do not doubt that he's well off. He's called
The Wise, the Rich, by all the Jewish folk.
SITTAH.
Now more than ever is he named the Rich.
The town resounds with news of costly stuffs
And priceless treasures he has brought with him.
AL-HAFI.
Is he the Rich once more? Then, do not fear,
He'll be the Wise again.
SITTAH.
What think you? Will
You visit him, Al-Hafi?
AL-HAFI.
What, to borrow?
You know him, surely! Think you he will lend?
His very wisdom lies in this--that he
Will lend to no one.
SITTAH.
Formerly you gave
A picture very different of him.
AL-HAFI.
In case of need he'll lend you merchandise;
But money--money--never! He's a Jew,
Who has not many equals 'mongst his tribe.
He's wise, knows how to live, can play at chess;
Excels in evil, too, as well as good.
Rely not on him. To the poor, indeed,
He vies with Saladin himself in gifts;
And if not quite so much, he gives as freely,
To Jew, and Christian, and Mahometan--
To all alike.
SITTAH.
And such a man as this----
SALADIN.

How comes it, then, I never heard of him?
SITTAH.
Can he refuse to lend to Saladin,
Who wants for others--never for himself.
AL-HAFI.
Ay, there peeps out the Jew--the vulgar Jew:
Believe me, he is jealous, envious
Of generosity. It seems as though
To earn God's favour were his special mission.
And that he may possess wherewith to give,
He never lends. The law he serves, commands
That he show mercy, but not complaisance.
Thus him has mercy made the rudest churl
In all the world. 'Tis true I have not been
This long time past on friendly terms with him,
But do not think that I would do him wrong,
He's good in all things else, but not in that;
Therefore I'll go and knock at other doors.
I recollect this instant an old Moor,
Who's rich and covetous: I'll go to him. (Exit.)
SITTAH.
Why in such haste, Al-Hafi?
SALADIN.
Let him go.
Scene
III.
Sittah
, Saladin
.
SITTAH.
He speeds away, as though he would escape.
Why so? Is he indeed himself deceived,
Or would he now mislead me?
SALADIN.
Can I guess?
I scarcely know the man of whom you speak,
And, for the first time, hear to-day of him.
SITTAH.
Can it be possible you know him not
Who, it is said, has visited the
Of Solomon and David; knows the spell
To ope their marble lids, and thence obtain
The boundless stores that claim no lesser source.
SALADIN.
Were this man's wealth by miracle procured,

'Tis not at Solomon's or David's tomb
That it is found. Mere mortal fools lie there.
SITTAH.
Or knaves!--But still his source of opulence
Is more productive, more exhaustless than
A cave of Mammon.
SALADIN.
For he trades, I'm told.
SITTAH.
His caravans through every desert toil,
His laden camels throng the public roads,
His ships in every harbour furl their sails.
Al-Hafi long ago has told me this,
Adding, with pride, how Nathan gives away,
What he esteems it noble to have earned
By patient industry, for others' wants;
How free from bias is his lofty soul,
His heart to every virtue how unlocked,
To every lovely feeling how allied!
SALADIN.
And yet Al-Hafi spoke with coldness of him.
SITTAH.
Not coldness, but unwillingness, as if
He deemed it dangerous to praise too much,
Yet knew not how to blame without a cause.
Or can it be, in truth, that e'en the best
Amongst a tribe can never quite escape
The foibles of their race, and that, in fact,
Al-Hafi has in this to blush for Nathan?
But come what may, let him be Jew or not,
If he be rich, that is enough for me.
SALADIN.
You would not, sister, take his--wealth by force?
SITTAH.
By force? What mean you? Fire and sword? Oh, no!
What force is necessary with the weak
But their own weakness? Come awhile with me,
Into my harem. I have bought a songstress
You have not heard--she came but yesterday.
Meanwhile I'll think upon a subtle plan
For this same Nathan. Follow, Saladin!
Scene
IV.
The Place of Palms, near Nathan's
house, from which Recha

and Nathan
are coming; Daja
, meeting them.
RECHA.
Dear father! you have been so slow, that you
Will scarcely meet him now.
NATHAN.
Well, well, my child;
If not beneath the palms, be sure that we
Shall meet him somewhere else. Be satisfied.
Is not that Daja whom I see approaching?
RECHA.
She certainly has lost him.
NATHAN.
Wherefore so?
RECHA.
Her pace were quicker else.
NATHAN.
She has not seen us.
RECHA.
There, now she spies us.
NATHAN.
And her speed redoubles.
Recha, be calm!
RECHA.
What! would you have your child
Be cold and unconcerned about his fate
To whom her life is due?--a life to her
But dear because she owed it first to you.
NATHAN.
I would not wish you other than you are,
E'en if I knew that in your secret soul
Another and a different feeling throbs.
RECHA.
What means my father?
NATHAN.
Do you ask of me--
So tremblingly of me? What passes now
Within your soul is innocence and nature.
Nay, fear not, for it gives me no alarm.
But promise, if the heart shall ever speak
A plainer language, you will not conceal
One single of your wishes from my love.
RECHA.
Oh, the bare thought that I should ever wish

To hide them from my father, makes me shudder.
NATHAN.
Recha, enough of this. Now, what says Daja?
DAJA.
He's still beneath the palms, and presently
He'll reach yon wall. See! here he comes at last.
RECHA.
He seems irresolute which way to turn,
To left or right!
DAJA.
His custom is to seek
The convent walls, so he will pass this way.
What will you wager? Yes, he comes to us.
RECHA.
Right! Did you speak to him? How did he look?
DAJA.
As usual.
NATHAN.
Do not let him see you here.
Stand farther back, or to the house retire.
RECHA.
Just one look more. Ah! the trees hide him now.
DAJA.
Come, come away! Recha, your father's right.
Should he observe us he'll retire at once.
RECHA.
Alas! the trees----
NATHAN.
Now he emerges from them.
He can't but see you. Hence! I beg of you.
DAJA.
Come, Recha, come! I know a window whence
We may observe him better.
RECHA.
Come, then, come.
(They both retire.)
Scene
V.
Nathan
(who is presently joined by the Templar
).
NATHAN.
I almost shrink from meeting this strange fellow--
Recoil from his rough virtue! That one man
Should ever make another feel confused!

But see, he comes! he seems a noble youth;
Looks like a man. I like his daring eye,
His honest gait. Although the shell is bitter,
The kernel may not be so. I have seen
One like him somewhere. Pardon, noble Frank----
TEMPLAR.
What would you?
NATHAN.
Pardon me----
TEMPLAR.
What would you, Jew?
NATHAN.
The privilege of speaking to you.
TEMPLAR.
Well!
How can I help it? Quick, then--what's your wish?
NATHAN.
Patience! nor pass with such contempt and pride
One who must be your debtor evermore.
TEMPLAR.
How so? I almost guess. No; are you then----
NATHAN.
My name is Nathan, father to the maid
Your generous courage rescued from the flames.
I come to----
TEMPLAR.
If you come to render thanks,
Spare them. I have already been compelled
To bear too many thanks for this small act.
Besides, you owe me nothing. Could I know
The maiden was your daughter? I was bound--
It is a Templar's duty--to assist
All who need succour; and my life just then
Was a mere burden. It was a relief
To risk it for another, even though
The task were to preserve a Jewess' life.
NATHAN.
Great--great yet horrible--I understand
The turn. The modest greatness will assume
The hideous mask to ward off gratitude.
But though he may disdain our proffer'd thanks,
Is there no other tribute we can pay?
Sir Knight! if you were not a stranger here,
And not a pris'ner, I were not so bold.
But, come, what service can I render you?

TEMPLAR.
You!--nothing.
NATHAN.
I am rich.
TEMPLAR.
The richer Jew
Was ne'er in my esteem the better Jew.
NATHAN.
Is that a reason why you should not use
The better part of him--his wealth?
TEMPLAR.
Well, well,
I'll not refuse it wholly, for the sake
Of my poor mantle; when it is well worn,
And spite of darning will not hold together,
I'll come and borrow cloth or gold of you,
To make a new one. Nay, Sir, do not start;
The danger is not pressing--'tis not yet
Quite worthless; it is sound, and strong, and good.
Save in one corner, where an ugly spot
Is singed, and that is from a burn it got
When I bore off your daughter from the fire.
NATHAN (taking hold of the mantle)
.
'Tis strange, indeed, that such a spot as this
Should bear far better witness to the man
Than his own lips. This spot! Oh, I could kiss it.
Your pardon, Sir, in truth, I meant it not!
TEMPLAR.
What?
NATHAN.
'Twas a tear that fell.
TEMPLAR.
Well, 'tis no matter.
'Tis not the first. (This Jew doth puzzle me.)
NATHAN.
Would you but send this mantle to my daughter!
TEMPLAR.
Why?
NATHAN.
That she, too, may press it to her lips;
For at her benefactor's feet to fall
She now may hope in vain.
TEMPLAR.
But, Jew, your name?

Tis Nathan, is it not? You choose your words
With skill--I am confused. I did not think
NATHAN.
Feign, Templar, and dissemble as you may,
I see the truth. I see your generous heart,
Too honest and too good to be polite.
A grateful girl, all feeling, and her maid
Swift to obey--a father far from home,
You valued her fair fame, and would not see her.
You scorned to tempt lest you should victor prove.
For this too I must tender you my thanks.
TEMPLAR.
You know at least how Templars ought to feel.
NATHAN.
Why Templars only? and why ought to feel?
Is it because your rules and vows enjoin
These duties to your order? Sir, I know
How good men all should feel, and know as well
That every country can produce good men.
TEMPLAR.
You'll make distinctions?
NATHAN.
Yes, in colour, form,
And dress, perhaps.
TEMPLAR.
Ay, and in number too--
Here more--there less.
NATHAN.
The difference is not much.
Great men, like trees, have ever need of room;
Too many set together only serve
To crush each other's boughs. The middling sort,
Like us, are found in numbers, they abound;
Only let not one scar and bruise the other,
Let not the gnarl be angry with the stump,
Let not the upper branch alone pretend
Not to have started from the common earth.
TEMPLAR.
Well said. And yet what nation was the first
To scatter discord 'mongst their fellow-men?
To claim the title of "the chosen people?"
How now if I were not to hate them, but
To scorn this upstart nation, for their pride?
That pride which it bequeathed to Mussulman
And Christian, as if God were theirs alone.

You start to hear a Christian and a Templar
Talk thus. But when and where has all this rage,
This pious rage, to win the better God,
And force this better God on all the world,
Shown itself more, or in a blacker form,
Than here, and now? Who here, who now retains
The blinding scales upon his eyes--and yet
Let him be blind who will!--forget my words,
And leave me (is going).
NATHAN.
Templar! you but little know
How closer henceforth I shall cling to you.
We must, we must be friends. Despise my people--
We did not choose a nation for ourselves.
Are we our nation's? What then is a nation?
Were Jews or Christians such, ere they were men?
Ah! would that I had found in you one man
To whom it were enough to be a man.
TEMPLAR.
Thou hast so, Nathan! Yes, by Heaven, thou hast.
Thy hand. I blush to have mistaken thee.
NATHAN.
Now I feel proud. 'Tis only common souls
In whom we seldom err.
TEMPLAR.
Uncommon ones
We do not oft forget. Nathan, we must,
We must be friends.
NATHAN.
We are so. And my Recha
Will now rejoice. How bright the prospect grows
That dawns upon me! If you did but know her.
TEMPLAR.
I grow impatient, Nathan. But who now
Comes from your house? Methinks it is your Daja.
NATHAN.
Yes, and her look how full of care! God grant----
TEMPLAR.
That nothing may have chanced to our Recha!
Scene
VI.
Daja
(rushing in).
DAJA.
Nathan, dear Nathan!

NATHAN.
Well.
DAJA.
Forgive me, Knight,
That I must interrupt you.
NATHAN.
What has happened?
DAJA.
The Sultan sends for you--commands you straight
To speak with him. Protect us, Heaven! the Sultan!
NATHAN.
The Sultan sends for me! He would inspect
The goods--the precious wares that I have brought
From Persia. Say there's nothing yet unpacked.
DAJA.
No, no; 'tis not to look at anything;
He wants to speak to you in person, Nathan,
And orders you to come at once.
NATHAN.
I go.
Daja, return.
DAJA.
Knight, take it not amiss.
We were alarmed for what the Sultan might
Require of Nathan.
NATHAN.
That I soon shall know. (Exit Daja.)
Scene
VII.
Nathan
, the Templar
.
TEMPLAR.
Are you then not acquainted with him yet?
NATHAN.
Who, Saladin? Not yet. I've neither shunned
Nor sought to see him. And the public voice
Proclaims his fame so loud, that I could wish
Rather to take its language upon trust,
Than sift the truth. And yet if it be true
That he has spared your life----
TEMPLAR.
Yes, so it is.
The life I live, he gave.
NATHAN.

Then he bestows
A double, treble life on me. And thus
He flings a bond around me, which secures
My duty to his service; and henceforth
I burn to know his wishes. Now, for all
I am prepared; and further, will confess
'Tis for your sake alone that I am thus.
TEMPLAR.
Often I've sought to meet him, but as yet
Have found no means to render him my thanks.
The impress which his mind received of me
Was transient, and ere now has disappeared.
Who knows if he may still remember me?
And yet once more at least he must recall
Me to his thoughts--to fix my future lot!
'Tis not enough that by his gracious will
I still have of life; I've yet to learn
According to whose will I have to live.
NATHAN.
Therefore 'twere well I did not tarry now.
Perchance some happy word may give excuse
To speak of you. Now, pardon me, farewell!
I must away. When shall we meet again?
TEMPLAR.
Whenever 'tis permitted.
NATHAN.
When you will.
TEMPLAR.
To-day, then.
NATHAN.
And your name?
TEMPLAR.
My name was--is--
Conrad of Stauffen.
NATHAN.
Conrad of Stauffen! Stauffen!
TEMPLAR.
What is there in my name to wonder at?
NATHAN.
There are more races of that name, no doubt.
TEMPLAR.
Yes, many of the name were here--rot here,
My uncle even--I should say my father.
But wherefore is your eye so fixed on me?
NATHAN.

I know not; but I love to look on you.
TEMPLAR.
Therefore I take my leave. The searching eye
Will oft discover more than it desires.
I fear it, Nathan; so, farewell. Let time,
Not curious prying, make us better known. (Exit.)
NATHAN (looking after him with astonishment).
"The searching eye will oft discover more
Than it desires." As if he read my soul!
That, too, may chance to be. 'Tis not alone
His walk, his stature, but his very voice!
Leonard so bore himself--was even wont
To carry thus his sword upon his arm,
And thus to shade his eyebrow with his hand,
As if to hide the fire that fill'd his look.
So deeply graven images may seem
At times to lie asleep within the soul,
When all at once a single word--a tone--
Calls them to life again. Of Stauffen--right--
Filnek and Stauffen--I will soon know more.
But first to Saladin. Ha! Daja here--
And on the watch! Come nearer, Daja, come.
Scene
VIII.
Daja
, Nathan
.
NATHAN.
Well, both of you have something more at heart
Than to know what the Sultan wants with me.
DAJA.
And you can hardly blame her for it, sir.
You were beginning to converse with him
More trustingly yourself, when suddenly
The Sultan's message drove us from the window.
NATHAN.
Go tell her, Daja, she may soon expect
A visit from the Templar.
DAJA.
What! indeed!
NATHAN.
I think I may rely upon you, Daja.
Be on your guard, I beg, you'll not repent it.
Your conscience shall at length be satisfied,
But do not mar my plans. Inquire, explain,

But with reserve, with fitting modesty.
DAJA.
No need for such advice. I go, I go.
And you must follow; for, see, Hafi comes--
The Sultan sends a second messenger.
Scene
IX.
Nathan
, Al-Hafi
.
AL-HAFI.
Ha! are you there? I have been seeking you.
NATHAN.
Why in such haste? What can he want with me?
AL-HAFI.
Who?
NATHAN.
Saladin. But I am coming quickly.
AL-HAFI.
To whom? To Saladin?
NATHAN.
Has he not sent you?
AL-HAFI.
Me? no--but has he sent already?
NATHAN.
Yes.
AL-HAFI.
Then it is so.
NATHAN.
What's so?
AL-HAFI.
That----I'm not guilty,
God knows, I'm not to blame; 'tis not my fault.
I've done my best--belied, and slandered you--
To save you from it.
NATHAN.
Save me? and from what?
Be plain.
AL-HAFI.
From being made his Defterdar.
I pity you--I cannot stay to see it.
I fly this hour--you know the road I take.
Speak, then, if I can serve you; but your wants
Must suit a wretch that's wholly destitute.
Quick, what's your pleasure?

NATHAN.
Recollect yourself--
Your words are mystery. I know of nothing.
What do you mean?
AL-HAFI.
You'll take your money--bags?
NATHAN.
My money--bags!
AL-HAFI.
Ay, bring your treasures forth--
The treasures you must shower on Saladin.
NATHAN.
And is that all?
AL-HAFI.
Ah! shall I witness it,
How, day by day, he'll scoop and pare you down,
Till nothing but a hollow, empty shell,
A husk as light as film, is left behind.
Nathan, you've yet to learn how spendthrift waste
From prudent bounty's never empty stores
Borrows and borrows, till there's not a crumb
Left to keep rats from starving. Do not think
That he who wants your gold will heed advice.
When has the Sultan listened to advice?
Hear what befel me with him.
NATHAN.
Well--go on.
AL-HAFI.
He played just now at chess with Sittah. She
Is a keen player. I drew near and watched.
The game which Saladin supposed was lost,
Stood yet upon the board. He had given in,
I marked, and cried, "The game's not lost at all!"
NATHAN.
Oh! what a grand discovery for you.
AL-HAFI.
He needed only to remove his king
Behind the castle--and the check was saved.
Could I but show you----
NATHAN.
I believe it all!
AL-HAFI.
Then with the castle free, he must have won.
I saw it, and I called him to the board.
What do you think he did?

NATHAN.
He doubted you.
AL-HAFI.
Not only that--he would not hear a word--
And with contempt he overthrew the board.
NATHAN.
Indeed!
AL-HAFI.
He said he chose it--would be mate.
Is that to play the game?
NATHAN.
Most surely not.
'Twas rather playing with the game.
AL-HAFI.
And yet
The stakes were high.
NATHAN.
A trifle to the Sultan!
Money is nought to him. It is not that
Which galls, but not to hear Al-Hafi out--
Not to admire his comprehensive glance,
His eagle eye--'tis that demands revenge.
Say, am I right?
AL-HAFI.
I only tell this tale
That you may know how much his head is worth.
But I am weary of him. All the day
I am running round to every wretched Moor
To borrow--money for him--I who ne'er
Ask for myself, am now obliged to sue
For others--and, according to my creed,
To borrow is to beg, as, when you lend
Your money upon usury, you steal.
Among my Ghebers on the Ganges' shores
I shall need neither; there I shall not be
The tool or pimp of any; there alone
Upon the Ganges honest men are found.
You, Nathan, you alone of all I see
Are worthy on the Ganges' banks to live.
Then come with me; leave him the wretched gold
That he would strip you of--'tis all he wants.
Little by little he will ruin you;
'Tis better to be quit of all at once;
Come, then, and I'll provide you with a staff.
NATHAN.

Nay, that resource will still remain for us
As a last refuge. But I'll think of it.
AL-HAFI.
Nay, ponder not upon a thing like this.
NATHAN.
Then stay till I have seen the Sultan. Stay
Till I have bid farewell.
AL-HAFI.
The man who stays
To hunt for motives, to search reasons out,
Who cannot boldly and at once resolve
To live a free man's life, must be the slave
Of others till his death. But as you please.
Farewell! my path is here, and yours is there!
NATHAN.
But stay, Al-Hafi! till you have arranged
The state accounts.
AL-HAFI.
Pah! Nathan, there's no need;
The balance in the chest is quickly told,
And my account, Sittah, or you, will vouch.
Farewell!
(Exit.)
NATHAN (looking after him).
Yes, I will vouch it, honest, wild--
How shall I call him? Ah! the real beggar
Is, after all, the only real king. (Exit at opposite side.)
ACT III.
Scene
I.--A room in Nathan's
house
.
Recha
, Daja
.
RECHA.
Well, Daja, did my father really say
"That I might instantly expect him here?"
That surely meant that he would come at once,
And yet how many minutes have rolled by!
But I'll not dwell upon the moments gone,
I'll only live in those that are to come,
That one which brings him here must come in time.
DAJA.
But for the Sultan's ill-timed messenger

Nathan had brought him hither.
RECHA.
When he comes--
Oh! when this dearest of my inmost hopes
Shall be fulfilled--what then--what then?
DAJA.
What then?
Why then I trust the wish most dear to me
Will also be fulfilled.
RECHA.
And in its place
What wish shall take possession of my breast?
Which now forgets to heave, unless it pant
With some fond wish? Will nothing come? I shudder!
DAJA.
My wish shall then supplant the one fulfilled,
My wish to see you borne to Europe's shores
By hands well worthy of you.
RECHA.
You do err.
The very thought which makes you form this wish
Forbids it to be mine. Your native land
Attracts you, and has mine no charm for me?
Shall a remembrance of your cherished home,
Your absent kindred and your dearest friends,
Which years and distance have not yet effaced,
Rule in your soul with softer, mightier sway
Than what I know, and hear, and feel of mine.
DAJA.
'Tis vain to struggle, for the ways of Heaven
Are still the ways of Heaven. And who can say
If he who saved your life may not be doomed,
Through his God's arm, for whom he nobly fights.
To lead you to that people--to that land
To which you should belong by right of birth?
RECHA.
What are you saying, Daja? dearest Daja!
Indeed you have some strange and curious thoughts.
"His God!" whose God? To whom can God belong,
And how can God belong to any man,
Or need a human arm to fight his battles?
And who, among the scattered clods of earth
Can say for which of them himself was born,
Unless for that on which he was produced?
If Nathan heard thee! How has Nathan sinned,

That Daja seeks to paint my happiness
So far removed from his? What has he done,
That thus amongst the seeds of reason, which
He sowed unmixed and pure within my soul,
The hand of Daja must for ever seek
To plant the weeds, or flowers of her own land?
He has no wish to see upon this soil
Such rank luxuriant blossoms. I myself
Must own I faint beneath the sour--sick odour;
Your head is stronger and is used to it.
I find no fault with those of stronger nerves
Who can support it--mine, alas! give way.
Your angel too, how near befool'd was I
Through him; I blush whene'er I see my father.
DAJA.
As if, dear Recha, you alone were wise.
Folly! If I might speak----
RECHA.
And may you not?
Have I not listened gladly to your tales
About the valiant heroes of your faith?
Have I not freely on their deeds bestowed
My admiration--to their sufferings given
The tribute of my tears? Their faith, 'tis true,
Has never seemed to me their noblest boast,
But, therefore, Daja, I have only learnt
To find more consolation in the thought
That our devotion to the God of all
Depends not on our notions of that God.
My father has so often taught me this--
You have so often to this point agreed,
How can it be that you wish now alone
To undermine what you have built together?
But this is no discourse with which to wait
The friend whom we expect--and yet for me
'Tis of some moment whether he----But hark!
Hark! Some one comes this way.---If it were he!
Scene
II.
The Templar
, Daja
, Recha
.
(A servant ushers in the Templar
.)

This way, Sir Knight!--
(Recha
starts, composes herself, and is about to fall at his feet.)
'Tis he! my rescuer. Ah!
TEMPLAR.
'Twas only to avoid this scene that I
So long postponed my visit.
RECHA.
At the feet
Of this proud man, I will thank God alone,
And not the man. He does not want my thanks--
As little as the bucket does which proved
Itself so useful at the fire, and let
Itself be filled and emptied; so this man,
He too was thrust by chance amid the flames;
I dropped by chance into his open arms,
By chance remained there, like a fluttering spark
Upon his mantle--till--I know not what
Expelled us from the flames. What room is here
For thanks?--In Europe wine excites the men
To greater deeds--The Templar knows his duty,
Performs his task, as well-trained spaniels do,
Who fetch alike from water and from flames.
TEMPLAR (who has been surveying her with surprise and uneasiness).
O Daja, Daja! if in hasty hours
Of care and grief, this unchecked tongue of mine
Betrayed me into rudeness, why convey
To her each idle word that leaves my lips?
This is indeed too galling a revenge!
Yet, if henceforth, you will interpret better----
DAJA.
I question if these little stings, Sir Knight,
Were so shot forth as to have done you wrong.
RECHA.
How! you had cares, and were more covetous
Of them than of your life.
TEMPLAR.
Thou best of beings,
How is my soul with eye and ear at strife?
No, 'twas not she I rescued from the fire,
For who could know her and forbear the deed?
In truth, disguised by terror----
(He gazes on her as if entranced.)
RECHA.
But to me

You still appear the same as then you seemed.
(A pause, till she resumes in order to interrupt his reverie.)
Tell me, Sir Knight, where have you been so long?
And--I might almost ask--where are you now?
TEMPLAR.
I am where I, perhaps, ought not to be.
RECHA.
And been, perhaps, where you should not have been.
That is not well.
TEMPLAR.
I have been up the mountain--
What is the name?--ay! Sinai!
RECHA.
I am glad;
For, doubtless, you can tell me if 'tis true----
TEMPLAR.
If what is true? If holy people show
The spot where Moses stood before his God?
RECHA.
Oh no; not that. Wherever Moses stood
It was before his God. I know enough
About such things already. Is it true--
I wish to learn from you who have been there--
If it is not by far less difficult
To climb than to descend the holy mount?
For with all other mountains that I know,
'Tis quite the contrary. You turn away!
Why do you turn, Sir Knight? Nay, look at me.
TEMPLAR.
I wish to hear you rather.
RECHA.
I perceive,
Because you do not wish that I should see
You smile at my simplicity. You smile
That I have not some more important thing
To ask about the holy hill of hills.
Is it so?
TEMPLAR.
Must I meet those eyes again?
And now you cast them down, and check your smile.
How can I in those changeful features read
What I so plainly hear--the truth your words
So audibly declare, and yet would hide?
How truly did your father say to me,
"If you but knew her!"

RECHA.
Who said that to you?
TEMPLAR.
Your father, and of you he spoke the words.
DAJA.
Have I not said it to you many times?
TEMPLAR.
Where is your father now? with Saladin?
RECHA.
Doubtless he is.
TEMPLAR.
Still there! Oh, I forget.
He cannot still be there. He waits for me,
As hc appointed, near the cloister gate.
Forgive me, I must go in quest of him.
DAJA.
I will do that. Wait here, I'll bring him straight.
TEMPLAR.
O no, O no! He is expecting me.
Besides, you cannot tell what may have chanced.
'Tis not unlikely he may be engaged
With Saladin--you do not know the Sultan--
In some unpleasant----Danger may ensue
If I delay.
RECHA.
Danger! for whom? for what?
TEMPLAR.
Danger for me--for you--for him! unless
I go at once
(Exit.)
Sccnc
III.
Recha
, Daja
.
RECHA.
What is the matter, Daja?
So quick! what ails him--makes him fly from hence?
DAJA.
Let him alone. I think it no bad sign.
RECHA.
Sign! and of what?
DAJA.
That something vexes him.
It boils, but it must not boil over. Go,

'Tis your turn now.
RECHA.
My turn. You have become
Incomprehensible to me--like him.
DAJA.
Now you may pay him back with interest
All the unrest he once occasioned you.
But be not too vindictive--too severe.
RECHA.
Well, Daja, you must know your meaning best.
DAJA.
And are you then already calm once more?
RECHA.
In truth I am.
DAJA.
Confess at least, dear Recha,
That all this restlessness has brought you pleasure,
And that you have to thank his want of ease
For all the ease that you yourself enjoy.
RECHA.
I know not that, but I must still confess
That to myself it seems a mystery
How in this bosom, such a pleasing calm
Can suddenly succeed so rude a storm.
His countenance, his speech, his manner have----
DAJA.
By this time satisfied you.
RECHA.
No, not that.
DAJA.
Well, satisfied your more impatient want.
RECHA.
Well, well, if you must have it so.
DAJA.
Not I!
RECHA.
To me he must be ever dear. To me
He must remain more dear than life, although
My pulse no longer flutters at his name,
My heart no longer, when I think of him,
Beats with a fuller throb. What have I said?
Come, Daja, to the window once again
Which overlooks the palms.
DAJA.
I see 'tis not

Yet satisfied, that more impatient want.
RECHA.
Now, I shall see the palm--trees once again;
Not him alone amidst them.
DAJA.
Such a fit
Of coldness speaks of fevers yet to come.
RECHA.
Nay, I'm not cold, in truth I do not see
Less gladly that which I do calmly see.
Scene
IV.
(The Hall of Audience in Saladin's
Palace.)
Saladin
, Sittah
.
SALADIN (giving directions)
.
Bring the Jew here, as soon as he arrives.
He seems in no great haste.
SITTAH.
Nay, Saladin,
Perhaps he was not found at home.
SALADIN.
Ah, sister!
SITTAH.
You look as if some contest were at hand.
SALADIN.
Ay! and with weapons I'm not used to wield.
Must I then play the hypocrite--and frame
Precautions--lay a snare? Where learnt I that?
And for what end? To seek for money--money!
For money from a Jew? And to such arts
Must Saladin descend, that he may win
The most contemptible of paltry things?
SITTAH.
But paltry things, despised too much, are sure
To find some method of revenge.
SALADIN.
'Tis true!
What, if this Jew should prove an upright man,
Such as the Dervise painted him?
SITTAH.
Why, then,

Your difficulty ceases; for a snare
Implies an avaricious, cheating Jew,
And not an upright man. Then he is ours
Without a snare. 'Twill give us joy to hear
How such a man will speak--with what stern strength
He'll tear the net, or with what cunning skill
Untangle all its meshes, one by one.
SALADIN.
True, Sittah! 'twill afford me rare delight.
SITTAH.
What, then, need trouble you? For if he be,
Like all his nation, a mere cozening Jew,
You need not blush, if you appear to him
No better than he deems all other men.
But if to him you wear a different look,
You'll be a fool--his dupe!
SALADIN.
So I must, then,
Do ill, lest bad men should think ill of me.
SITTAH.
Yes, brother, if you call it doing ill
To put a thing to its intended use.
SALADIN.
Well, there is nothing woman's wit invents
It cannot palliate----
SITTAH.
How, palliate?
SALADIN.
Sittah, I fear such fine-wrought filagree
Will break in my rude hand. It is for those
Who frame such plots to bring them into play.
The execution needs the inventor's skill.
But let it pass.--I'll dance as best I can--
Yet sooner would I do it ill than well.
SITTAH.
Oh, brother, have more courage in yourself!
Have but the will, I'll answer for the rest.
How strange that men like you are ever prone
To think it is their swords alone that raise them.
When with the fox the noble lion hunts,
'Tis of the fellowship he feels ashamed,
But of the cunning, never.
SALADIN.
Well, 'tis strange
That women so delight to bring mankind

Down to their level. But, dear Sittah, go;
I think I know my lesson.
SITTAH.
Must I go?
SALADIN.
You did not mean to stay?
SITTAH.
No, not with you,
But in this neighb'ring chamber.
SALADIN.
What! to listen?
Not so, my sister, if I shall succeed.
Away! the curtain rustles--he is come.
Beware of lingering! I'll be on the watch.
(While Sittah
retires through, one door, Nathan
enters at another, and Saladin
seats himself.)
Scene
V.
Saladin
, Nathan
.
SALADIN.
Draw nearer, Jew--yet nearer--close to me!
Lay fear aside.
NATHAN.
Fear, Sultan, 's for your foes.
SALADIN.
Your name is Nathan?
NATHAN.
Yes.
SALADIN.
Nathan the Wise.
NATHAN.
No.
SALADIN.
But, at least the people call you so.
NATHAN.
That may be true. The people!
SALADIN.
Do not think
I treat the people's voice contemptuously.
I have been wishing long to know the man
Whom it has called the Wise.

NATHAN.
What, if it named
Him so in scorn? If wise means prudent only--
And prudent, one who knows his interest well?
SALADIN.
Who knows his real interest, you mean.
NATHAN.
Then, Sultan, selfish men were the most prudent,
And wise, and prudent, then, would mean the same.
SALADIN.
You're proving what your speeches contradict.
You know the real interests of man:
The people know them not--have never sought
To know them. That alone can make man wise.
NATHAN.
Which every man conceives himself to be.
SALADIN.
A truce to modesty! To meet it ever,
When we are seeking truth is wearisome (springs up).
So, let us to the point. Be candid, Jew,
Be frank and honest.
NATHAN.
I will serve you, prince,
And prove that I am worthy of your favour.
SALADIN.
How will you serve me?
NATHAN.
You shall have the best
Of all I have, and at the cheapest rate.
SALADIN.
What mean you? Not your wares?--My sister, then,
Shall make the bargain with you. (That's for the listener!)
I am not versed in mercantile affairs,
And with a merchant's craft I've nought to do.
NATHAN.
Doubtless you would inquire if I have marked
Upon my route the movements of the foe?
Whether he's stirring? If I may presume----
SALADIN.
Neither was that my object. On that point
I know enough. But hear me.
NATHAN.
I obey.
SALADIN.
It is another, a far different thing

On which I seek for wisdom; and since you
Are called the Wise, tell me which faith or law
You deem the best.
NATHAN.
Sultan, I am a Jew.
SALADIN.
And I a Mussulman. The Christian stands
Between us. Here are three religions, then,
And of these three one only can be true.
A man like you remains not where his birth
By accident has cast him; or if so,
Conviction, choice, or ground of preference,
Supports him. Let me, Nathan, hear from you,
In confidence, the reasons of your choice,
Which I have lacked the leisure to examine.
It may be, Nathan, that I am the first
Sultan who has indulged this strange caprice,
Which need not, therefore, make a Sultan blush.
Am I the first? Nay, speak; or if you seek
A brief delay to shape your scattered thoughts,
I yield it freely. (Has she overheard?
She will inform me if I've acted right.)
Reflect then, Nathan, I shall soon return.
(Exit.)
Scene
VI.
NATHAN (alone)
.
Strange! how is this? What can the Sultan want?
I came prepared for cash--he asks for truth!
Truth! as if truth were cash! A coin disused--
Valued by weight! If so, 'twere well, indeed!
But coin quite new, not coin but for the die,
To be flung down and on the counter told----
It is not that. Like gold tied up in bags,
Will truth lie hoarded in the wise man's head,
To be produced at need? Now, in this case,
Which of us plays the Jew? He asks for truth.
Is truth what he requires? his aim, his end?
Or does he use it as a subtle snare?
That were too petty for his noble mind.
Yet what is e'er too petty for the great?
Did he not rush at once into the house,
Whilst, as a friend, he would have paused or knocked?
I must beware. Yet to repel him now

And act the stubborn Jew, is not the thing;
And wholly to fling off the Jew, still less.
For if no Jew, he might with justice ask,
Why not a Mussulman?--That thought may serve.--
Others than children may be quieted
With tales well told. But see, he comes--he comes.
Scene
VII.
Saladin
, Nathan
.
SALADIN.
(Aside) (The coast is clear)--I am not come too soon?
Have you reflected on this matter, Nathan?
Speak! no one hears.
NATHAN.
Would all the world might hear!
SALADIN.
And are you of your cause so confident?
'Tis wise, indeed, of you to hide no truth,
For truth to hazard all, even life and goods.
NATHAN.
Ay, when necessity and profit bid.
SALADIN.
I hope that henceforth I shall rightly bear
One of my names, "Reformer of the world
And of the law!"
NATHAN.
A noble title, truly;
But, Sultan, ere I quite explain myself,
Permit me to relate a tale.
SALADIN.
Why not?
I ever was a friend of tales well told.
NATHAN.
Well told! Ah, Sultan! that's another thing.
SALADIN.
What! still so proudly modest? But begin.
NATHAN.
In days of yore, there dwelt in Eastern lands
A man, who from a valued hand received
A ring of priceless worth. An opal stone
Shot from within an ever-changing hue,
And held this virtue in its form concealed,
To render him of God and man beloved,

Who wore it in this fixed unchanging faith.
No wonder that its Eastern owner ne'er
Withdrew it from his finger, and resolved
That to his house the ring should be secured.
Therefore he thus bequeathed it: first to him
Who was the most beloved of his sons,
Ordaining then that he should leave the ring
To the most dear among his children; then,
That without heeding birth, the fav'rite son,
In virtue of the ring alone, should still
Be lord of all the house. You hear me, Sultan?
SALADIN.
I understand. Proceed.
NATHAN.
From son to son,
The ring at length descended to a sire
Who had three sons, alike obedient to him,
And whom he loved with just and equal love.
The first, the second, and the third, in turn,
According as they each apart received
The overflowings of his heart, appeared
Most worthy as his heir, to take the ring,
Which, with good-natured weakness, he in turn
Had promised privately to each; and thus
Things lasted for a while. But death approached,
The father now embarrassed, could not bear
To disappoint two sons, who trusted him.
What's to be done? In secret he commands
The jeweller to come, that from the form
Of the true ring, he may bespeak two more.
Nor cost nor pains are to be spared, to make
The rings alike--quite like the true one. This
The artist managed. When the rings were brought
The father's eye could not distinguish which
Had been the model. Overjoyed, he calls
His sons, takes leave of each apart--bestows
His blessing and his ring on each--and dies.
You hear me?
SALADIN (who has turned away in perplexity)
.
Ay! I hear. Conclude the tale.
NATHAN.
'Tis ended, Sultan! All that follows next
May well be guessed. Scarce is the father dead,
When with his ring, each separate son appears,

And claims to be the lord of all the house.
Question arises, tumult and debate--
But all in vain--the true ring could no more
Be then distinguished than----(after a pause, in which he awaits the Sultan's reply) the true faith now.
SALADIN.
Is that your answer to my question?
NATHAN.
No!
But it may serve as my apology.
I cannot venture to decide between
Rings which the father had expressly made,
To baffle those who would distinguish them.
SALADIN.
Rings, Nathan! Come, a truce to this! The creeds
Which I have named have broad, distinctive marks,
Differing in raiment, food, and drink!
NATHAN.
'Tis true!
But then they differ not in their foundation.
Are not all built on history alike,
Traditional or written? History
Must be received on trust. Is it not so?
In whom are we most likely to put trust?
In our own people? in those very men
Whose blood we are? who, from our earliest youth
Have proved their love for us, have ne'er deceived,
Except in cases where 'twere better so?
Why should I credit my forefathers less
Than you do yours? or can I ask of you
To charge your ancestors with falsehood, that
The praise of truth may be bestowed on mine?
And so of Christians.
SALADIN.
By our Prophet's faith,
The man is right. I have no more to say.
NATHAN.
Now let us to our rings once more return.
We said the sons complained; each to the judge
Swore from his father's hand immediately
To have received the ring--as was the case--
In virtue of a promise, that he should
One day enjoy the ring's prerogative.
In this they spoke the truth. Then each maintained
It was not possible that to himself

His father had been false. Each could not think
His father guilty of an act so base.
Rather than that, reluctant as he was
To judge his brethren, he must yet declare
Some treach'rous act of falsehood had been done.
SALADIN.
Well! and the judge? I'm curious now to hear
What you will make him say. Go on, go on!
NATHAH.
The judge said: If the father is not brought
Before my seat, I cannot judge the case.
Am I to judge enigmas? Do you think
That the true ring will here unseal its lips?
But, hold! You tell me that the real ring
Enjoys the secret power to make the man
Who wears it, both by God and man, beloved.
Let that decide. Who of the three is loved
Best by his brethren? Is there no reply?
What! do these love--exciting rings alone
Act inwardly? Have they no outward charm?
Does each one love himself alone? You're all
Deceived deceivers. All your rings are false.
The real ring, perchance, has disappeared;
And so your father, to supply the loss,
Has caused three rings to fill the place of one.
SALADIN.
O, charming, charming!
NATHAN.
And,--the judge continued:--
If you insist on judgment, and refuse
My counsel, be it so. I recommend
That you consider how the matter stands.
Each from his father has received a ring:
Let each then think the real ring his own.
Your father, possibly, desired to free
His power from one ring's tyrannous control.
He loved you all with an impartial love,
And equally, and had no inward wish
To prove the measure of his love for one
By pressing heavily upon the rest.
Therefore, let each one imitate this love;
So, free from prejudice, let each one aim
To emulate his brethren in the strife
To prove the virtues of his several ring,
By offices of kindness and of love,

And trust in God. And if, in years to come,
The virtues of the ring shall reappear
Amongst your children's children, then, once more,
Come to this judgment--seat. A greater far
Than I shall sit upon it, and decide.
So spake the modest judge.
SALADIN.
Oh God, O God!
NATHAN.
And if now, Saladin, you think you're he----
SALADIN.
(Approaches Nathan
, and takes his hand, which he retains to the end of the scene.)
This promised judge--I?--Dust! I?--Nought! oh God!
NATHAN.
What is the matter, Sultan?
SALADIN.
Dearest Nathan!
That judge's thousand years are not yet past;
His judgment-seat is not for me. But go,
And still remain my friend.
NATHAN.
Has Saladin
Aught else to say?
SALADIN.
No.
NATHAN.
Nothing?
SALADIN.
Truly nothing.
But why this eagerness?
NATHAN.
I could have wished
An opportunity to ask a boon.
SALADIN.
Wait not for opportunity. Speak now.
NATHAN.
I have been traveling, and am just returned
From a long journey, from collecting debts.
Hard cash is troublesome these perilous times,
I know not where I may bestow it safely.
These coming wars need money; and, perchance,
You can employ it for me, Saladin?
SALADIN (fixing his eyes upon Nathan
)

.

I ask not, Nathan, have you seen Al-Hafi?
Nor if some shrewd suspicion of your own
Moves you to make this offer.
NATHAN.
What suspicion?
SALADIN.
I do not ask--forgive me,--it is just,
For what avails concealment? I confess
I was about----
NATHAN.
To ask this very thing?
SALADIN.
Yes!
NATHAN.
Then our objects are at once fulfilled,
And if I cannot send you all my store,
The Templar is to blame for that. You know
The man. I owe a heavy debt to him.
SALADIN.
The Templar! Surely, Nathan, with your gold
You do not aid my direst foes?
NATHAN.
I speak
Of him whose life was spared by Saladin.
SALADIN.
Of what do you remind me? I had quite
Forgot the youth. Where is he? Know you him?
NATHAN.
Have you not heard, then, how your clemency
Through him has flowed to me? How, at the risk
Of the existence which your mercy gave,
He saved my daughter from the raging flames?
SALADIN.
Ha! did he so? He looked like one that would!
My brother, too--his image--would have done it.
Is he still here? Bring him to me at once.
I have so often spoken to my sister
Of this same brother, whom she never knew,
That I must let her see his counterfeit.
Go, fetch him. How a single noble deed,
Though but the offspring of the merest whim,
Gives birth to other blessings! Bring him to me.
NATHAN (loosing Saladin's
hand)

.
I'll go--the other matter then is settled. (Exit.)
SALADIN.
I wish I had but let my sister listen.
I'll go at once to her and tell it all.
(Exit on the opposite side.)
Scene
VIII.
The Place of Palms in the neighbourhood of the Convent, where the Templar awaits Nathan

.
TEMPLAR (walking to and fro, in conflict with himself.)
The panting victim here may rest awhile.
So far 'tis well. I dare not ask myself
What change has sprung within me, nor inquire
What yet may happen. Flight has proved in vain,
And, come what may, I could no more than flee,
The stroke was far too sudden to escape.
Long--much--I strove to keep aloof, in vain.
But once to see her, e'en against my will,
To see her, and to frame a firm resolve
Never to lose her. What, then, is resolve?
Resolve is purpose--action, while--in truth--
I was but passive. But to see her once,
And feel that I was woven into her being,
Was then and still remains the self-same thing.
To live apart from her--oh, bitter thought!--
Were death; and after death--where'er we were--
'Twould there be death too. Say, then, is this love?
And doth the Templar love? A Christian loves
A Jewish maiden! Well, and what of that?
This is the holy land; holy to me,
And dear, because I have of late renounced
Full many a prejudice. What says my vow?
In the same hour that made me prisoner
To Saladin. The head he gave me back,
Was it the old one? No. I'm newly framed,
I know no fragment of the ancient forms
That bound me once. My brain is clearer now,
More fit for my paternal home above.
Now I can think as once my father thought,
If tales of him are not untruly told--
Tales that were ne'er so credible as now,
When I am stumbling where my father fell.
Fell! yet 'twere better far to fall with men

Than stand with boys. His conduct guarantees
His approbation. And what need I more
Than Nathan's approbation? Of his praise
I cannot doubt. Oh, what a Jew is he!
And yet he would appear the simple Jew.
But, see, he comes--he comes in haste--delight
Beams from his eye. But who leaves Saladin
With other looks? Ho! Nathan!
Scene
IX.
Nathan
, the Templar
.
NATHAN.
Are you there?
TEMPLAR.
Your visit to the Sultan has been long.
NATHAN.
Not over long. My audience was delayed.
But, Conrad, this man well supports his fame--
His fame is but his shadow. But I must
Without delay inform you that he would----
TEMPLAR.
Say on.
NATHAN.
Would speak with you. So, come with me at once.
I have some brief commands to give at home,
Then to the Sultan.
TEMPLAR.
Nathan, I will ne'er
Enter your door again----
NATHAN.
Then you've been there
Already--spoken with her. Tell me all.
How do you like my Recha?
TEMPLAR.
Words would fail
To tell how much. I dare not trust myself
Alone with her again, unless you say
That I may gaze upon her form for ever.
NATHAN.
What can this mean?
TEMPLAR (after a short pause, embracing him suddenly)
.
My father!

NATHAN.
How, young man?
TEMPLAR (withdrawing himself as suddenly)
.
Call me your son! I do implore you, Nathan.
NATHAN.
Dear youth!
TEMPLAR.
And not your son! I pray you, Nathan,
Conjure you, by the strongest ties of Nature,
Let it content you now to be a man:
Repel me not.
NATHAN.
My dearest friend!
TEMPLAR.
Say son!
Why not your son? What, if in Recha's heart
Mere gratitude had paved the way for love,
And if we both but waited your assent
To crown our union! You are silent, sir!
NATHAN.
I am astonished at your words, young Knight.
TEMPLAR.
Astonished! Do I then astonish you
With your own thoughts, although you know them not
When uttered by my lips. Astonished, Nathan?
NATHAN.
Would that I knew what Stauffen was your father!
TEMPLAR.
What say you, Nathan? At a time like this,
Can you indulge such empty, curious thoughts?
NATHAN.
I knew a Stauffen once whose name was Conrad.
TEMPLAR.
What, if my father bore that very name?
NATHAN.
And did he so?
TEMPLAR.
I bear my father's name,
I am called Conrad.
NATHAN.
So! And yet the man
I knew was not your father, for, like you,
He was a Templar, and was never married.
TEMPLAR.

And what of that?
NATHAN.
How?
TEMPLAR.
He might still have been
My father.
NATHAN.
Nay, you jest.
TEMPLAR.
You're far too good.
What matters it? Does bastard wound your ear?
The race, good sir, is not to be despised.
But spare my pedigree, and I'll spare yours.
Great God! forbid my words should ever cast
The smallest doubt on your ancestral tree.
You can attest it backwards, leaf by leaf,
To Abraham. And from that point--I know it well,
Myself--can even swear to it.
NATHAN.
Your words are bitter. Do I merit this?
What have I e'er refused you? I have but
Forborn assent at the first word you spoke.
No more!
TEMPLAR.
Oh! true, no more. Forgive me, Nathan.
NATHAN.
Well, come with me, come.
TEMPLAR.
Whither? to your house?
That will I not--it burns. I'll wait you here.
Farewell. If I'm to see her once again,
I then shall see her often; and if not,
I have already seen her too--too much.
Scene
X.
The Templar
, Daja
.
TEMPLAR.
Too much, indeed! Strange that the human brain
So infinite of comprehension, should
At times with a mere trifle be engrossed,
Suddenly filled, and all at once quite full,
No matter what it teems with. But the soul
Soon calms again, and the fermenting stuff

Makes itself room, restoring life and order.
And is this, then, the first time that I love?
And was the glow to which I gave that name
Not love at all? And is this love alone
Which now with burning flame consumes my heart?
DAJA (who has crept up to his side)

.

Sir Knight! Sir Knight!
TEMPLAR.
Who calls? What, Daja, you!
DAJA.
Yes, I am here; I managed to slip by him.
But he can see us where we stand. Come nearer,
And place yourself with me behind this tree.
TEMPLAR.
Why so mysterious? What's the secret, Daja?
DAJA.
Yes, 'tis a secret which has brought me hither--
A twofold secret. Part is known to me,
The other part to you. Come, let us change:
First tell me yours, and then I'll tell you mine.
TEMPLAR.
Yes, willingly, when I have ascertained
What you call mine. But yours will throw a light
Upon the whole. Begin, then.
DAJA.
That's not fair;
You must begin, Sir Knight, and I will follow.
For be assured my secret's nothing worth,
Unless I hear yours first. Then lose no time,
For if I guess it, you've not trusted me;
My secret, then, will be my own, and yours
Worth nothing. But do you suppose, Sir Knight,
That you can hide such secrets from a woman?
TEMPLAR.
Secrets we often are unconscious of.
DAJA.
Perhaps. But I must prove myself your friend
And tell you all. Confess how happened it
That you so suddenly took leave of us,
And that with Nathan you will not return?
Has Recha, then, made no impression on you,
Or made too deep a one, perchance? Oh yes!
Too deep--too deep! You are a hapless bird
Whose fluttering wing the fatal twig has limed,

Confess it, plainly, with a word, you love--
Love her to madness, and I'll tell you then----
TEMPLAR.
To madness? Ah! you understand it well.
DAJA.
Well, grant the love, the madness I'll resign.
TEMPLAR.
Because, of course, there is no doubt of it.
A Templar love a Jewess!----
DAJA.
Why, it seems
Absurd. But often there's more fitness in
Some things than we can readily discern;
And 'twould not be the first time that our Lord
Had drawn us to Him by a secret path
Which we had ne'er discovered of ourselves.
TEMPLAR.
Solemnly spoken I (and if for our Lord
I substituted Providence, 'twere true).
You make me curious, far beyond my wont.
DAJA.
This is the land of miracles!
TEMPLAR.
Ay, true,
Of miracles! Can it be otherwise,
When all the world flocks hither? Dearest Daja,
You have your wish; so take it as confessed
That I do love her, nor can comprehend
How I can live without her.
DAJA.
Can this be?
Then swear, Sir Knight, to make her yours--to save
Her here on earth--to save her there for ever.
TEMPLAR.
How can I this? How can I swear to do
What stands not in my power.
DAJA.
'Tis in your power!
One single word brings it within your power.
TEMPLAR.
But will her father smile upon my suit?
DAJA.
Her father, truly! He shall be compelled.
TEMPLAR.
Compell'd! What, has he fallen among thieves?

Compell'd!
DAJA.
Then hear me. Nathan will consent:
He must consent.
TEMPLAR.
Consent! and must! Oh, Daja!
I have already tried to touch that chord;
It vibrates not responsive.
DAJA.
What! reject you?
TEMPLAR.
He answered me in such discordant tone
That I was hurt.
DAJA.
What say you? Did you breathe
The shadow of a wish to marry Recha.
And did not Nathan leap for joy? Did he
Draw coldly back--raise obstacles?
TEMPLAR.
He did.
DAJA.
Then I'll deliberate no moment more.
TEMPLAR (after a pause)

.

And yet you are deliberating still.
DAJA.
Nathan in all things has been ever good.
I owe him much. Did he refuse to listen?
God knows it grieves me to constrain him thus.
TEMPLAR.
I pray you, Daja, now to terminate
This dire uncertainty. But if you doubt
Whether the thing you would impart to me
Be right or wrong, worthy of shame or honour,
Then tell it not, and henceforth I'll forget
You have a secret it were well to hide.
DAJA.
Your words but spur me on to tell you all.
Then learn that Recha is no Jewess--that
She is a Christian maid.
TEMPLAR (coldly)

.

I wish you joy!
At last the tedious labour's at an end.
The birth-pangs have not hurt you. Still go on

With undiminished zeal, and people heaven
When you are fit no more to people earth.
DAJA.
How, Knight! and does the news I bring deserve
Such bitter taunts? Does it confer no joy
On you to hear that Recha is a Christian,
On you, her lover, and a Christian knight?
TEMPLAR.
And more especially since Recha is
A Christian of your making?
DAJA.
Think you so?
Then I would fain see him that may convert her.
It is her fate long since to have been that
Which she can now no more become.
TEMPLAR.
Explain,
Or leave me.
DAJA.
Well! she is a Christian maid,
Of Christian parents born--and is baptised.
TEMPLAR (hastily)

.
And Nathan!
DAJA.
Not her father.
TEMPLAR.
Nathan not
Her father? Are you sure of that?
DAJA.
I am;
The truth has cost me tears of blood. He's not.
TEMPLAR.
But as his daughter he has brought her up,
Brought up the Christian maiden as a Jewess?
DAJA.
Just so.
TEMPLAR.
And knows she aught about her birth?
Has she not learnt from him that she was born
A Christian and no Jewess?
DAJA.
Never yet.
TEMPLAR.
And he not only let the child grow up

In this mistaken notion, but he leaves
The woman in it.
DAJA.
Ay, alas!
TEMPLAR.
Oh, Nathan!
How can the wise, good Nathan lend himself
To stifle Nature's voice--to misdirect
The yearnings of a heart in such a way
Which, to itself abandoned, would have formed
Another bias, Daja? Ay, in truth,
The secret is of moment, and may have
Important issues. But I feel perplexed:
I know not how I ought to act. But go,
Let me have breathing time. He may approach,
He may surprise us suddenly. Farewell!
DAJA.
I tremble with affright.
TEMPLAR.
And I can scarce
Express my thoughts. But go; and should you chance
To meet him, say he'll find me at the Sultan's.
DAJA.
Let him not see that you have any thing
Against him. That 'twere well to keep reserved,
To give the proper turn to things at last.
It may remove your scruples, touching Recha.
But if you take her back to Europe, Knight,
You will not leave me here?
TEMPLAR.
We'll see, now go!
ACT IV.
Scene
I.--The Cloisters of the Convent
.
The Friar
, and presently afterwards the Templar
.
FRIAR.
Ay, ay! he must be right, the Patriarch!
And yet, of all his business, no great part
Has prospered in my hands. But why should he
Entrust such tasks to me? I have no wish
To play the knave, to wheedle and persuade,
To worm out secrets, and to thrust my hand

Into my neighbour's business. Not for this
Did I renounce the world, that I might be
Entangled with its cares for other men.
TEMPLAR (entering abruptly).
Good brother, are you here? I've sought you long.
FRIAR.
Me, sir?
TEMPLAR.
What, don't you recollect me, then?
FRIAR.
Ay! but, Sir Knight, I never thought to see
Your face again--and so I hoped in God.
God knows how much I hated the proposal
Which I was bound to make you, and He knows
How little I desired you should assent,
How in my inmost soul I was rejoiced
When you refused, without a moment's thought,
To do what had been shameful in a Knight.
But have you thought the matter o'er again?
TEMPLAR.
You seem to know what object brings me here.
FRIAR.
Have you, Sir Knight, reflected by this time,
That our good Patriarch is not much deceived
In thinking gold and glory may be won
By his commission? that a foe's a foe,
Were he our guardian angel seven times o'er?
Have you 'gainst flesh and blood weighed all these things,
And are you come to strike a bargain now?
TEMPLAR.
My dear good man, be patient; not for this
Am I come hither; not for aught like this
Do I desire to see the Patriarch.
On every point my thoughts remain unchanged;
Nor would I for the wealth of all this world
Forfeit that good opinion, which I won
From such an upright, honest man as you.
I merely come to ask the Patriarch
For counsel.
FRIAR (looking round timidly)

.

Counsel from the Patriarch!
What, you! a knight to ask a priest's advice!
TEMPLAR.
Mine is a priestly business.

FRIAR.
Yet the priests
Would scorn a knight's advice, were their affairs
Ever so knightly.
TEMPLAR.
Therefore they're allowed
To err sometimes, a privilege which I,
For one, don't greatly envy them; and yet,
If I were acting only for myself,
And were not bound to others, I should care
But little for advice. But in some things
'Twere better to go wrong by others' guidance
Than, by our own, go right. And I observe,
By this time, that religion's naught but party,
And he who in his own belief is most
Impartial, does but hold the standard up
Of his own creed, howe'er unconsciously.
Yet since 'tis so, it must be right.
FRIAR.
I'm silent.
In truth, I don't quite comprehend.
TEMPLAR.
And yet--
(Let me consider first what 'tis I want--
Decision or advice from sage or simple?)
Thanks, brother; yes, I thank you for your hint.
What is a patriarch? Be thou for once
My patriarch; for 'tis the Christian rather
Whom in the patriarch I would consult,
Than in the Christian the mere patriarch.
FRIAR.
Hold, hold, Sir Knight! no more of this, I find
That you mistake me. He who hath learnt much
Must needs have many cares. I know but one----
But hark, behold! here comes the very man!
'Tis he, so stay; he has perceived us both.
Scene
II.
The Patriarch
, after marching up one of the aisles with great pomp, approaches.
TEMPLAR.
I'd rather shun him--he is not my man--
A round, red smiling prelate! And what state!
FRIAR.
But you should see him at a festival,

Now he but comes from visiting the sick.
TEMPLAR.
Great Saladin will then have cause to blush.
PATRIARCH (coming forward, makes signs to the Friar)
.
Was that the Templar? What's his business here?
FRIAR.
I know not.
PATRIARCH (advancing, whilst the Friar
and his train retire.)
Well, Sir Knight, I'm truly glad
To meet so brave a youth. So very young,
Something may come of him, if Heaven assist.
TEMPLAR.
Not more than has already come of him,
But rather less, my reverend father.
PATRIARCH.
Well,
It is my prayer that so devout a Knight
May for the cause of Christendom and God
Be long preserved; nor can it fail to be,
If valour will give ear to aged words.
Then say, how can I serve you, Sir?
TEMPLAR.
With that
In which my youth's deficient--sound advice.
PATRIARCH.
Most gladly, if you'll follow my advice.
TEMPLAR.
Not blindly, though.
PATRIARCH.
Whose words are those? Indeed,
None should neglect to use the intellect
Bestowed by God, when it is suitable.
But is it always suitable? O no!
If God, through one of the celestial choir--
That is, through one of the blest ministers
Of His most sacred word--should condescend
To show some way by which the Church's weal,
Or else the general good of Christendom,
Might be secured, what man would venture then
To weigh the laws of intellect against
His will, who fashioned intellect itself?
Or measure the unchanged decrees of Heaven
By empty rules that suit this petty world?

But of all this enough. Now tell me, Knight,
Wherefore you seek our counsel?
TEMPLAR.
Reverend father!
Suppose a Jew possessed an only child--
A girl--whom he with fond parental care
Trained to each virtue, treasured as his soul,
Whilst she, with love as ardent as his own,
Repaid his love,--suppose it rumoured then
That she was not the daughter of this Jew,
But a poor orphan, purchased in her youth,
Or stolen, or found--or anything, but still
Of Christian birth, and in her youth baptised,
And that the Jew had reared her in his faith,
Allowed her to be thought a Jewish maid,
And firmly to believe herself his child,--
Say, reverend father, what should then be done?
PATRIARCH.
I shudder at the thought! But, worthy Sir,
Say, is this fact, or mere hypothesis?
That is, if your own head has framed the case,
Or has it happened--does it still exist?
TEMPLAR.
That's unimportant, and could not assist
Your reverence to pronounce upon the point.
PATRIARCH.
What! unimportant! See, Sir Knight, how apt
Proud reason is to err in sacred things.
'Tis of deep import; though, 'tis true, the case
May be the offspring of your sportive wit,
When we should straight dismiss it from our thoughts,
And I should then refer you to the stage
Where pros and cons like these are oft discussed
With loud applause. But if the object be,
By something better than a sleight of hand,
To sound my judgment, if the thing be fact,
And may have happened in our diocese,
Here in our dear Jerusalem itself,
Why then----
TEMPLAR.
What then?
PATRIARCH.
Then were it well, Sir Knight,
To execute at once upon the Jew
The penalty provided for the case,

By Papal and Imperial laws, against
So foul a crime, such dire iniquity.
TEMPLAR.
Indeed!
PATRIARCH.
The laws I mention have decreed
That if a Jew shall to apostasy
Seduce a Christian, he shall die by fire.
TEMPLAR.
Indeed!
PATRIARCH.
How much more when a Jew by force
Tears from baptismal bonds a Christian child?
For all that's done to children is by force,
Save what the Church shall order and perform.
TEMPLAR.
What if the child were steeped in misery,
And must have died, but for this bounteous Jew?
PATRIARCH.
It matters not: the Jew should still be burnt.
'Twere better to expire in misery,
Than live to suffer never-ending pains.
The Jew moreover should not have forestalled
The hand of God, whom had He willed to save,
Could save without him.
TEMPLAR.
Make him happy too,
In spite of him.
PATRIARCH.
It matters not, the Jew
Must still be burnt.
TEMPLAR.
That grieves me very much,
And all the more, as people say that he
Has reared the child not in his own belief,
So much as in no faith at all, and taught
Her neither more nor less of God than is
By reason asked.
PATRIARCH.
It matters not, the Jew
Must still be burnt--and for this very cause
Would merit threefold death. To rear a child
Without a faith! Not even teach a child
The greatest of all duties--to believe!
'Tis heinous, and I'm rapt in wonder, Knight,

That you yourself----
TEMPLAR.
Oh, reverend Sir, the rest
In the confessional, if God allow.
(Is going.)
PATRIARCH.
What, going! and not await my questioning!
Not name to me this infidel, this Jew!
Not find him out for me at once! But, hold!
A thought occurs. I'll to the Sultan straight.
According to the treaty we have sworn
With Saladin, he must protect our creed
With all the privileges, all the rights
That appertain to our most holy faith.
Thank God! we have retained the deed itself,
With seal and signature affixed, and we
Can readily convince him, make him feel
How full of peril for the state it is
Not to believe. All civil bonds are rent
Asunder, torn to pieces, Knight, when men
Have no belief. Away, away for ever
With such impiety!
TEMPLAR.
I much deplore
That I want time to relish this discourse,
This holy sermon. Saladin awaits
My coming.
PATRIARCH.
Ah, indeed!
TEMPLAR.
And I'll prepare
The Sultan for your presence, reverend Sir,
If you desire.
PATRIARCH.
Why, yes! for I have heard
You have found favour in the Sultan's sight.
I beg to be remembered with respect.
Zeal in the cause of God impels me on,
And all excesses are performed for Him.
Weigh that in kindness, then, most noble Sir!
But, tell me, was your case about the Jew
A problem merely?
TEMPLAR.
Problem!
(He retires.)

PATRIARCH.
(Of the facts,
I must have fuller knowledge. I must be
Better informed; 'twill be another job
For brother Bonafides.) Son, come hither!
(Speaks with the Friar as he retires.)
Scene
III.
Saladin's
Palace.
(Slaves are employed in bringing bags of gold, and piling them on the floor.)
Saladin
, Sittah
.
SALADIN.
In truth, this weary business ne'er will end;
Say, is it nearly done?
A SLAVE.
One half is done.
SALADIN.
Then take the rest to Sittah? Where's Al-Hafi?
He must take charge of what is here. But, hold,
Were it not best to send it to my father?
Here 'twill be quickly spent. I feel, in truth,
That I am growing miserly. At last
He must be skilful who gets much from me,
And till from Egypt further treasure comes,
Our poverty must be content to struggle.
Yet, at the Holy Sepulchre, the cost
Of all the Christian pilgrims must be paid;
They must, at least, not go with empty hands.
SITTAH.
Why, what is this? wherefore this gold to me?
SALADIN.
Recoup yourself with it, if aught is left,
Keep it in store.
SITTAH.
Are Nathan and the Knight
Not yet arrived?
SALADIN.
The former everywhere
Is seeking him.
SITTAH.
Behold what I have found
In turning o'er my ornaments and jewels (showing a small portrait).

SALADIN.
Ha! what is here! a portrait! yes, my brother!
'Tis he--'tis he! Was he--was he, alas!
Oh dear, brave youth! so early lost to me!
With thee at hand what had I not achieved!
Give me the portrait, Sittah. I recall
This picture well. He gave it to his Lilla--
Your elder sister--when one summer morn
He tore himself away reluctantly.
She would not yield, but clasped him in her arms.
'Twas the last morning that he e'er rode forth,
And I, alas! I let him ride alone.
Poor Lilla died of grief, and ne'er forgave
My error that I let him ride alone.
He ne'er returned.
SITTAH.
Poor brother!
SALADIN.
Say no more.
A few short years, and we shall ne'er return.
And then who knows? But 'tis not death alone
That blights the hopes and promises of youth,
They have far other foes, and oftentimes
The strongest, like the weakest, is o'ercome.
But be that as it may, I must compare
This portrait with the Templar, that I may
Observe how much my fancy cheated me.
SITTAH.
'Twas for that purpose that I brought it here.
But give it, and I'll tell thee if 'tis like:
We women are best judges of such things.
SALADIN (to the doorkeeper who enters)
.
Who's there? the Templar? Bid him come at once.
SITTAH.
Not to disturb you, or perplex him with
My curious questions, I'll retire awhile. (Throws herself upon the sofa, and lets her veil fall.)
SALADIN.
That's well. (And now his voice--will that be like?
For Assad's voice still slumbers in my soul!)
Scene
IV.
The Templar
and Saladin

.
TEMPLAR.
I am your prisoner, Sultan.
SALADIN.
You my prisoner!
Shall I refuse him liberty, whose life
I freely spared?
TEMPLAR.
It is my duty, Sire,
To hear, and not anticipate, your will.
Yet it but ill becomes my character
And station, Sultan, to be thus profuse
Of gratitude because you've spared my life--
A life which henceforth is at your command.
SALADIN.
Only forbear to use it to my hurt.
Not that I grudge my mortal enemy
Another pair of hands; but such a heart
As yours I do not yield him willingly.
You valiant youth! I have not gauged you ill:
In soul and body, you are truly Assad.
I fain would learn where you have been so long
Concealed. In what dim cavern you have slept?
What spirit, in some region of the blest,
Has kept this beauteous flower so fresh in bloom?
Methinks I could remind you of our sports
In days gone by; and I could chide you, too,
For having kept one secret from my ear,
For having dared one gallant deed alone.
I'm happy that so much of this deceit
At least is true, that in my sear of life
An Assad blooms for me once more. And you,
You too are happy, Knight!
TEMPLAR.
Whate'er you will--
Whatever be your thought--lies as a wish
Within mine inmost soul.
SALADIN.
We'll prove you, then.
Will you abide with me?--cling to my side,
Whether as Christian or as Mussulman,
In turban or white mantle? Choose your garb--
Choose for yourself. I never have desired
That the same bark should grow on every tree.
TEMPLAR.

Else, Saladin, you never had become
The hero that you are--who'd rather be
The gardener of the Lord.
SALADIN.
If thus you think
Of Saladin, we're half agreed, already----
TEMPLAR.
Nay, quite!
SALADIN (offering his hand)
.
One word!
TEMPLAR (taking it)
.
One man! and with this hand
Take more than you can e'er take back again.
Henceforth I'm wholly yours.
SALADIN.
This is too much--
For one day 'tis too much! Came he not with you?
TEMPLAR.
Who?
SALADIN.
Who? Nathan.
TEMPLAR.
No; I came alone.
SALADIN.
Oh, what a deed was thine! what happiness
That such a deed should serve so good a man!
TEMPLAR.
'Twas nothing.
SALADIN.
Why so cold, O valiant youth!
When God makes man His minister of good,
He need not be so cold, nor modestly
Wish to appear so cold.
TEMPLAR.
But in the world
All things have many sides, and who is he
Can comprehend how they may fit each other?
SALADIN.
Cling ever to what's noble, and praise God!
He knows how all things fit. But if you are
So scrupulous, young man, I must beware.
I too have many sides, and some of them
May seem to you not always made to fit.

TEMPLAR.
That grieves me; for suspicion, at the least,
Is not a sin of mine.
SALADIN.
Then, tell me, whom
Do you suspect? Not Nathan, surely? What!
Nathan suspected, and by you? Explain--
Afford me this first proof of confidence.
TEMPLAR.
I've nothing against Nathan. I am vexed,
But with myself alone.
SALADIN.
Why so?
TEMPLAR.
For dreaming
That any Jew can think himself no Jew.
I dreamt this waking.
SALADIN.
Tell me all your dream.
TEMPLAR.
You know that Nathan has a daughter, Sultan!
And what I did for her, I did--because
I did it. Far too proud to reap the thanks
I had not sown, from day to day I shunned
The maiden's sight. Her father was afar.
He comes, he hears, he seeks me, give me thanks;
Wishes that she might please me, and he talks
Of dawning prospects. Well, I hear it all,
I listen to him, go and see the maid--
O! such a maiden, Sultan. But, I blush.
SALADIN.
Why blush? Blush that a Jewish maid should win
Your admiration? 'Tis a venial fault.
TEMPLAR.
But oh! that, through her father's sweet discourse,
To this impression my o'er-hasty heart
Such weak resistance offered! Fool. I leaped
A second time into the flame, and then
I wooed, and was denied.
SALADIN.
Denied?--denied?
TEMPLAR.
The prudent father does not plainly say
No, to my suit--but he must first inquire--
He must reflect. Well, be it so. Had I

Not done the same? I looked about, inquired--
Reflected--ere I plunged into the flames
Where she was shrieking. Oh, by Heaven! it is
A splendid thing to be so circumspect!
SALADIN.
Nay, but you must concede somewhat to age.
His doubts will pass away, nor will he wish
You to become a Jew.
TEMPLAR.
Who knows?
SALADIN.
Who knows!
One who knows Nathan better than yourself.
TEMPLAR.
And yet the superstitions we have learned
From education, do not lose their power
When we have found them out; nor are all free
Whose judgment mocks the galling chains they wear.
SALADIN.
'Tis wisely said; but Nathan, surely Nathan----
TEMPLAR.
That superstition is the worst of all
Which thinks itself the easiest to be borne----
SALADIN.
'Tis possible. But Nathan----
TEMPLAR.
And to trust
To it alone a blind humanity
Till it is used to truth's more brilliant light.
To it alone----
SALADIN.
Well, well! But Nathan's fate
Is not to be so weak----
TEMPLAR.
I thought so once,
But what if this bright pattern to mankind
Were such a thorough Jew that he seeks out
For Christian children to bring up as Jews?
How then?
SALADIN.
Who speaks so of him?
TEMPLAR.
E'en the maid
For whom I'm so distressed, with hopes of whom
He seemed so glad to recompense the deed

He would not suffer me to do for naught.
This maid is not his daughter; no, she is
A kidnapped Christian child.
SALADIN.
Whom Nathan now
Refuses you!
TEMPLAR (earnestly)
.
Refuse or not refuse,
He is found out--the prating hypocrite
Is now found out; but on this Jewish wolf,
For all his philosophical sheep's garb,
Dogs I can loosen who will tear his hide.
SALADIN (earnestly)
.
Peace, Christian!
TEMPLAR.
What! peace, Christian? Wherefore so?
Shall Jew and Mussulman be free to boast
Their creeds, and shall the Christian be ashamed
To own his faith?
SALADIN (more earnestly)
.
Peace, Christian!
TEMPLAR (calmly)
.
Yes, I feel
What weight of blame lies in your calm reproof--
In that one word pronounced by Saladin.
Oh! that I knew what Assad would have done
Had he but fill'd my place!
SALADIN.
He had not done
Much better; nay, perhaps, had been more warm.
Where did you learn to bribe me with a word?
And yet, in truth, if all has happened so
As you narrate, it is not much like Nathan.
But Nathan is my friend, and of my friends
One must not quarrel with the other. So
Take counsel, act with prudence. Do not loose
On him the fanatics among your race.
Keep silence. All the clergy of your sect
Would call to me for vengeance upon him
With far more show of right than I could wish.
Let not revenge impel you to become

A Christian to the Jew or Mussulman.
TEMPLAR.
Thanks to the Patriarch's bloodthirsty rage,
Your counsel almost comes too late; and I
Had nearly proved his cruel instrument.
SALADIN.
How so? and did you see the Patriarch
Before you came to me?
TEMPLAR.
Yes, in the storm
Of passion--in the whirl of doubt----Forgive me.
I fear you will no longer find in me
One feature of your Assad.
SALADIN.
Yes, that fear
Is like him. But, methinks, I know full well
The weaknesses from which our virtues spring:
Attend to these--the former cannot hurt.
But go, seek Nathan, as he sought for you,
And bring him hither. Be but reconciled.
Are you in earnest, Knight, about this maid?
Be calm--she shall be yours. Nathan shall feel
That without swines-flesh he has dared to rear
A Christian child. Now, Templar, leave me. Go!
(Exit the Templar. Sittah
leaves the sofa.)
Scene
V.
Saladin
and Sittah
.
SITTAH.
'Tis strange, indeed.
SALADIN.
What say you now, my Sittah?
Was not our Assad once a handsome youth?
SITTAH.
If this were like him, and 'twere not the knight
Who had his portrait taken. But, dear brother,
How could you ever so forget yourself
As not to make inquiry for his parents?
SALADIN.
And more especially about his mother?
That was your meaning--eh?
SITTAH.

You are too quick.
SALADIN.
But nothing is more possible; for he,
My brother Assad, was so favoured by
The Christian ladies--handsome Christian ladies--
That a report once spread----But 'tis not right
We should refer to that. We'll be content
That he is here again, with all his faults,
The faults and wildness of his gentle heart--
That he is here again. Oh, Nathan must
Give him the maid. What think you?
SITTAH.
What, to him?
SALADIN.
Ay! for what claim has Nathan to the girl
If he is not her father? He, who saved
Her life, may properly assume the rights
Of him who gave existence to the maid.
SITTAH.
Then might not Saladin lay claim to her,
Withdrawing her from the unrightful owner?
SALADIN.
There is no need of that.
SITTAH.
No actual need,
But female curiosity suggests
That counsel to me. There are certain men
Of whom I feel impatient till I know
What maidens they can love.
SALADIN.
Well send for her.
SITTAH.
Brother, may I do that?
SALADIN.
But hurt not Nathan.
He must not think that we, by violence,
Would separate them.
SITTAH.
Fear it not.
SALADIN.
Farewell!
I must find out where this Al-Hafi is.
Scene
VI.
The hall in Nathan's

house, looking towards the palm-trees, as in the first Act. Part of the merchandise and treasures unpacked and displayed.

Nathan
and Daja
.

DAJA.
O, how magnificent are all these things!
How rich! they're such as none but you could give.
Where was this silver stuff with sprigs of gold
Woven? What might it cost? 'Tis what I call
A wedding garment. Is there any queen
Could wish aught richer?
NATHAN.
Why a wedding robe?
DAJA.
In buying it, you never thought of that.
But, Nathan, it must be so--it must, indeed--
'Twas made for that. See, here, the pure white ground,
Emblem of innocence; that branching gold,
Covering the virgin white on every side,
Emblem of wealth. Say, is it not divine?
NATHAN.
Why all this ingenuity of speech?
Over whose wedding dress would you display
This learning? Have you found a lover, Daja?
DAJA.
What, I?
NATHAN.
Who, then?
DAJA.
I, gracious Heaven?
NATHAN.
Who, then?
Whose wedding garment would you speak of, Daja?
All this is yours, 'tis meant for no one else.
DAJA.
What, mine! for me! I thought it was for Recha.
NATHAN.
No, what I bought for her is elsewhere packed;
'Tis in another bale. But, come, away
With all this rubbish.
DAJA.
Nathan, tempt me not,
For were these things the very costliest
In all the world, I'll touch not one of them

Till you have sworn to seize a happy chance
Which Heaven ne'er offers twice.
NATHAN.
What happy chance?
What must I seize?
DAJA.
Nathan, feign not such ignorance.
But, in one word--the Templar loves your Recha--
Give her to him, and then your sin, which I
Can hide no longer, will for ever cease.
The maid will then once more resume her place
Amongst the Christians, will again become
What she was born to, and what once she was;
And you, whom we can never thank enough
For all your goodness, will not then have heaped
More burning coals of fire upon your head.
NATHAN.
Still harping on the same old string again,
New tuned, but neither to accord nor hold.
DAJA.
How so?
NATHAN.
The Templar pleases me; 'tis true
I'd rather he, than any one, had Recha.
But patience.
DAJA.
Patience! and, say, is not that
The string you always harp on?
NATHAN.
Still, have patience
But for a few days longer. Ha! who comes?
A friar! Go ask him what his errand is.
DAJA (going)

.

What can he want?
NATHAN.
Give--give before he begs.
(Oh, that I knew how I could sound the Knight
Without betraying what my motive is!
For should I tell it, and my thoughts prove false,
I shall have staked the father's rights in vain.)
What is the matter?
DAJA.
He would speak with you.
NATHAN.

Let him approach. Leave us together, Daja.
Scene
VII.
Nathan
and the Friar
.
NATHAN.
(Aside. Gladly I would continue Recha's father!
And can I not be so, though I may cease
To bear the name? To her--at least to her--
I should be father still, if she but knew
How willingly I bore that title once.)
What can I do to serve you, pious brother?
FRIAR.
Not much; and yet it gives me pleasure, Nathan,
To see at least that you are still so well.
NATHAN.
You know me, then, it seems?
FRIAR.
Who knows you not?
You have impressed your name on many a hand--
It has been stamped on mine these many years.
NATHAN (feeling for his purse)
.
Come, brother, come; here's to refresh it.
FRIAR.
Thanks.
That would be robbing poorer men. I will
Take nothing; but I beg of you, permit
That I refresh your memory with my name;
For I can boast of having formerly
Placed something in your hand you should not scorn.
NATHAN.
Excuse me--I'm ashamed--what was it? Say,
And then take for atonement sevenfold
The value of the thing.
FRIAR.
Well, first of all,
Hear how this very day has brought to mind
The pledge I gave you.
NATHAN.
What! a pledge to me?
FRIAR.
Not long ago I led a hermit's life
On Quarantana, near to Jericho.

Some Arab thieves came and attacked my cell;
They robbed my oratory, forcing me
To follow them. But fortune favoured me.
I fled, came hither to the Patriarch,
And sought from him another calm retreat,
Where I might serve my God in solitude
Till death should bless me.
NATHAN.
Ah! I am on thorns.
Be quick! What pledge did you entrust to me?
FRIAR.
Yes, Nathan, presently. The Patriarch
Has promised I shall have a hermitage
On Tabor, when 'tis vacant; and meanwhile
Employs me in this convent as a brother,
And here I am at present. But I pine
For Tabor fifty times a day; for here
He makes me toil at work which I detest.
NATHAN.
Be speedy, I beseech you.
FRIAR.
Well, it chanced
Some one has whispered in his ear to-day
That a Jew lives hard by, who educates
A Christian as his daughter.
NATHAN.
How?
FRIAR.
Nay, hear.
He has commissioned me, if possible,
To find this Jew out for him; and he raves
Loudly and bitterly against the crime,
Which he pronounces as the actual sin
Against the Holy Ghost--that is, the sin
The greatest, which a sinner can commit.
But luckily we can't exactly tell
Its nature. But my conscience all at once
Was roused, and it occurred to me that I
Had once, perhaps, been guilty of this sin.
Do you remember, eighteen years ago,
When a knight's squire committed to your hands
A female infant but a few weeks old?
NATHAN.
What say you? Well, in fact there was----
FRIAR.

Ay, look--
Look well at me--for I'm that squire: 'twas I.
NATHAN.
What! you?
FRIAR.
And he from whom I brought the child
Was, if I recollect the matter right,
A Lord of Filneck--Wolf von Filneck.
NATHAN.
Right.
FRIAR.
Because the mother died not long before;
And he, the father, was obliged to fly
To Gaza suddenly. The helpless child
Could not accompany him, and therefore he
Committed it to you: that was my task.
I found you out at Daran.
NATHAN.
Right, quite right.
FRIAR.
It were no wonder had my memory
Deceived me. I have served so many lords.
The one who fled was not my master long,
He fell at Askalon. His heart was kind.
NATHAN.
Yes, yes, and I have much to thank him for.
Not once, but many times he saved my life.
FRIAR.
O, glorious! then the greater joy for you
To educate his daughter.
NATHAN.
You say well.
FRIAR.
Where is she now? She is not dead, I hope.
Let me not hear, I pray, that she is dead.
If no one else have found the secret out,
All is yet safe.
NATHAN.
Indeed!
FRIAR.
Oh, Nathan, trust me.
This is my way of thinking: if the good
That I propose to do is intertwined
With mischief, then I let the good alone;
For we know well enough what mischief is,

But not what is the best. 'Twas natural,
If you intended to bring up the child
With care, that you should rear it as your own.
And to have done this lovingly and well,
And be thus recompensed, is piteous.
It were perhaps more prudent, if the child
Had been brought up by some good Christian's hand,
In her own faith. But then you had not loved
Your dear friend's orphan child; and children need
Love--were it but the affection of a brute--
More at that age, than Christianity:
There's always time enough for that: and if
The maiden had grown up before your eyes,
Healthy and pious, she had then remained
The same as ever in her Maker's eyes.
For is not Christianity all built
Upon the Jewish creed? Oh oft, too oft,
It vexes me and costs me bitter tears,
To think that Christians will so constantly
Forget that Christ our Saviour was a Jew.
NATHAN.
Good brother, you shall be my advocate,
When hate and bigotry shall frown on me,
All for a deed--which you alone shall hear--
But take it with you to the tomb. As yet
E'en vanity has never tempted me
To breathe it to a soul; to you alone
It shall be told; for simple piety
Like yours can truly feel what man can do
Who places his full confidence in God.
FRIAR.
You're moved, and your eyes run o'er with tears.
NATHAN.
At Daran 'twas you met me with the child.
You had not heard that, a few days before,
The Christians murdered every Jew in Gath--
Woman and child. Amongst them was my wife--
Along with her, my seven hopeful sons.
All had sought shelter 'neath my brother's roof,
And there were burnt alive.
FRIAR.
Just God!
NATHAN.
You came.
Three nights in dust and ashes I had lain

Before my God and wept; and I at times
Arraigned my Maker, raged, and cursed myself
And the whole world together, and I swore
Eternal hate to Christianity.
FRIAR.
Who can condemn you? I believe it well.
NATHAN.
But by degrees returning reason came,
And spoke with gentle accent: "God is just!
And this was His decree. Now exercise
The lesson thou so long hast understood,
And which is surely not more difficult
To exercise than well to understand."
I rose and cried to God, "I will, I will!
Do Thou but aid my purpose." And, behold,
Just at that moment you dismounted. You
Gave me the child enfolded in your robe.
The words we spoke occur not to me now.
This much I recollect: I took the child;
I bore it to my bed; I kissed its cheek;
I flung myself upon my knees, and sobbed,
"My God, Thou hast restored me one of seven!"
FRIAR.
Nathan, you are a Christian. Yes, I swear
You are a Christian--better never lived.
NATHAN.
Indeed! the very thing that makes me seem
Christian to you, makes you a Jew to me.
But let us not distress each other thus,
'Tis time to act, and though a sevenfold love
Had bound me to this strange, this lovely maid,
Though the mere thought distracts me, that in her
I lose my seven dear sons a second time,
If Providence require her at my hands
I'm ready to obey.
FRIAR.
'Tis well! And thus
I thought to counsel you; but there's no need:
Your own good genius has forestalled my words.
NATHAN.
The first chance claimant must not tear her hence.
FRIAR.
Most surely not.
NATHAN.
And he who has no claim

Stronger than mine--at least he ought to have
Those prior claims which----
FRIAR.
Certainly,
NATHAN.
Those claims
Which are derived from nature and from blood.
FRIAR.
In my opinion, yes.
NATHAN.
Then name the man
As brother, or as uncle, bound to her,
I'll not withhold her from him; she was made
To be the ornament of any house,
The pride of any faith. I hope you know
More of your master and his creed than I.
FRIAR.
On that point, Nathan, I'm but ill informed,
I have already told you that I spent
Only some moments with him.
NATHAN.
Can you tell
The mother's name, at least? She was, I think,
A Stauffen?
FRIAR.
Possibly; nay, more--you're right.
NATHAN.
Conrad of Stauffen was her brother's name.
He was a Templar.
FRIAR.
Yes, I think he was:
But hold, I have a book that was my lord's.
I drew it from his bosom when he lay
Dead, and we buried him at Askalon.
NATHAN.
Well!
FRIAR.
There are prayers in it; 'tis what we call
A breviary. This, thought I, yet may serve
Some Christian man--not me, forsooth--for I
Can't read a word.
NATHAN.
No matter--to the point.
FRIAR.
The pages of this book are written all

In his own hand, and, as I'm told, contain
All that's important touching him and her.
NATHAN.
Go, run and fetch the book: 'tis fortunate!
I'll pay you for it with its weight in gold.
And with a thousand thanks besides. Go! run!
FRIAR.
I go--but what he wrote is Arabic.
(Exit)
NATHAN.
No matter, fetch it. What, if from this book
I can find means to keep this precious girl,
And win, to boot, a son-in-law like him!
I hardly hope--fate must decide. But who
Has told the Patriarch this? I must not fail
To ascertain. It surely was not Daja?
Scene
VIII.
Daja
and Nathan
.
DAJA (rushing in in agitation)
.
Only think, Nathan!
NATHAN.
What?
DAJA.
Well--only think:
The child was frightened when the message came!
NATHAN.
From whom? The Patriarch?
DAJA.
The Sultan's sister,
The Princess Sittah--
NATHAN.
Not the Patriarch?
DAJA.
No, Sittah. Can't you hear? The Princess sends,
And wishes Recha to be brought to her.
NATHAN.
Wishes for Recha! Sittah wishes thus?
'Tis Sittah, then--and not the Patriarch?
DAJA.
Why do you speak of him?
NATHAN.

Have you not heard
Some tidings of him lately? Have you seen
Nothing of him, and whispered nothing to him?
DAJA.
How could I so?
NATHAN.
Where are the messengers?
DAJA.
They stand without.
NATHAN.
I'll speak to them myself--
'Tis prudent; I shall see if nothing lurks
Behind this message, from the Patriarch. (Exit.)
DAJA.
Well, I have other fears. The only child,
As they suppose, of such a wealthy Jew,
Would for a Mussulman be no bad thing.
I'll wager that the Templar loses her,
Unless I risk a second step, and state
Plainly to Recha who she is. So, courage!
And to do this I must at once employ
The first brief moments when we are alone.
Chance serves: she waits for me, and on the way
An earnest hint will never prove amiss.
So now or never. All will soon be well. (Follows Nathan.)
ACT V.
Scene
I.--The room in Saladin's
Palace. The treasure still piled up

.
(Saladin
, and several Mamelukes.)
SALADIN (as he enters)

.
There lies the gold--and no one yet has seen
The Dervise. He will probably be found
Over the chess-board. Play can often make
A man forget himself. Then why not me?
But patience. What's the matter?
1ST MAMELUKE.
Oh, good news!
Joy, Sultan! joy. The Cairo caravan
Is safe arrived, and from the Nile it brings
The seven years' tribute.
SALADIN.

Bravo, Ibrahim!
You always were a welcome messenger,
And now at length--accept my heartfelt thanks
For the good tidings.
1ST MAMELUKE (waiting)
.
(Let me have them, then!)
SALADIN.
What are you waiting for? Go.
1ST MAMELUKE.
Nothing more
For my good news?
SALADIN.
What further?
1ST MAMELUKE.
Messengers
Of good are paid. Am I to be the first
Whom Saladin has learnt to pay with words?
The first to whom he proves ungenerous?
SALADIN.
Go, take a purse.
1ST MAMELUKE.
No, no--not now. Not if
You'd give them all to me.
SALADIN.
All? Hold, young man!
Come hither. Take these purses--take these two.
What, going? And shall I be conquered thus
In generosity? for surely 'tis
More difficult for this man to refuse
Than for the Sultan to bestow. Then, here
Here, Ibrahim! Shall I be tempted, just
Before my death, to be a different man?
Shall Saladin not die like Saladin?
Then wherefore has he lived like Saladin?
(Enter a second Mameluke.)
2ND MAMELUKE.
Hail, Sultan!
SALADIN.
If you come and bring the news----
2ND MAMELUKE.
That the Egyptian convoy is arrived.
SALADIN.
I know it.
2ND MAMELUKE.

Then I come too late.
SALADIN.
Too late?
Wherefore too late? There, for your tidings take
A purse or two.
2ND MAMELUKE.
Say three.
SALADIN.
You reckon well;
But take them.
2ND MAMELUKE.
A third messenger will come
Ere long, if he be able.
SALADIN.
Wherefore so?
2ND MAMELUKE.
He may perhaps, ere this, have brok'n his neck.
We three, when we had heard of the approach
Of the rich caravan, mounted our steeds,
And galloped hitherward. The foremost fell,
Then I was first, and I continued so
Into the town; but that sly fellow there,
Who knew the streets----
SALADIN.
But where is he who fell?
Go seek him out.
2ND MAMELUKE.
That I will quickly do,
And if he lives, one half of this is his.
(Exit.)
SALADIN.
Oh, what a noble fellow! who can boast
Such Mamelukes as these? And may I not,
Without conceit, imagine that my life
Has helped to make them so? Avaunt the thought!
That I should ever teach them otherwise.
3RD MAMELUKE.
Sultan!
SALADIN.
Are you the man who fell?
3RD MAMELUKE.
No, Sire.
I have to tell you that the Emir Mansor,
Who led the caravan, is just arrived.
SALADIN.

Then bring him quickly.--There he is already.
Scene
II.
The Emir Mansor
and Saladin
.
SALADIN.
Emir, you're welcome! What has happened to you,
Mansor? we have expected you for long.
MANSOR.
This letter will explain how, in Thebais,
Some discontents required the sabred hand
Of Abulkassen. But, since then, our march
Has been pressed forward.
SALADIN.
I believe it all.
But take, good Mansor--take, without delay,
Another escort if you will proceed,
And take the treasure on to Lebanon:
The greater part is destined for my father.
MANSOR.
Most willingly.
SALADIN.
And let your escort be
A strong and trusty one, for Lebanon
Is far from quiet, and the Templars there
Are on the stir again; be cautious, then
Come, I must see your troop, and order all.
(To a slave.) Say I shall presently return to Sittah.
Scene
III.
(The palm-trees before Nathan's
house.)
The Templar
, walking up and down.
TEMPLAR.
Into this house I never enter more:
He'll come to me at last. Yet, formerly,
They used to watch for me with longing eyes;
And now----The time may come he'll send to beg,
Most civilly, that I will get me hence,
And not pace up and down before his door!
No matter: though I feel a little hurt.
I know not what has thus embittered me:
He answered yes, and has refused me naught,

So far, and Saladin has pledged himself
To bring him round. Say, does the Christian live
Deeper in me than the Jew lurks in him?
Ah! who can truly estimate himself?
How comes it else that I should grudge him so
The trifling booty, which he took such pains
To rob the Christians of? No trifling theft!
No less than such a creature! And to whom
Does she belong? Oh, surely not to him,
The thoughtless slave, who floated the mere block
On to life's barren strand, then disappeared.
Rather to him, the artist, whose fine soul
Has from the block moulded this godlike form,
And graved it there. And yet in spite of him,
The Christian, who begot this beauteous maid,
Recha's true father must be still the Jew.
Were I to fancy her a Christian now,
Bereft of all the Jew has given to her--
Which only such a Jew could have bestowed--
Speak out, my heart--where would have been her charm'
It had been nothing--little; then her smile
Had been a pretty twisting of the mouth
And that which caused it were unworthy deemed
Of the enchantment blooming on her lips.
No: not her very smile! I've seen sweet smiles
Squandered on pride, on foppery, on lies,
On flatterers, on wicked wooers spent:
And did they charm me then? Did they awake
The wish to flutter out existence in
Their sunshine? And I'm angry now with him
Who gave this higher value to the maid?
And wherefore so? Do I deserve the taunt
With which I was dismissed by Saladin?
'Twas bad enough he should think thus of me.
How wicked, how contemptible, alas!
I must have seemed to him! And for a girl!
Conrad, this will not do. Avaunt such thoughts!
And what if Daja has been chattering
Of things not easy to be proved? But see,
He comes, engaged in converse; and with whom?
With him, the Friar. Then he knows all: perhaps
He has betrayed him to the Patriarch.
O Conrad! what vile mischief hast thou done!
O! that one spark of love, that wayward passion,
Should so inflame the brain! But, quick! resolve;

What's to be done? Stay, step aside awhile;
Perhaps the Friar will leave him. Let us see.
Scene
IV.
Nathan
and the Friar
.
NATHAN (approaching him)
.
Good brother, once more, thanks.
FRIAR.
The same to you.
NATHAN.
Why thanks from you? Because I'm wayward, and
Would force upon you what you cannot use?
FRIAR.
The book you have did not belong to me.
It is the maid's, is all her property,
Her only patrimony--save yourself.
God grant you ne'er have reason to repent
Of what you've done for her!
NATHAN.
Impossible!
That cannot be. Fear not.
FRIAR.
Alas! alas!
These Patriarchs and Templars----
NATHAN.
Cannot work
Such evil as to force me to repent.
But are you sure it is a Templar who
Urges the Patriarch?
FRIAR.
It is none else;
A Templar talked with him just now, and all
I hear confirms the rumour.
NATHAN.
But there is
Only one Templar in Jerusalem,
And him I know. He is a friend of mine,
A noble, open-hearted youth.
FRIAR.
The same.
But what one is at heart, and what one must
Appear in active life, are not the same.

NATHAN.
Alas! 'tis true. And so let every one
Act as he will, and do his best, or worst.
With your book, brother, I defy them all!
I'm going straightway with it to the Sultan.
FRIAR.
Then God be with you! Here I take my leave.
NATHAN.
What! without seeing her? But come again,
Come soon--come often. If the Patriarch
To-day learns nothing. Well! no matter now!
Tell him the whole to-day, or when you will.
FRIAR.
Not I. Farewell!
(Exit.)
NATHAN.
Do not forget us, brother!
O God! I could sink down upon my knees,
Here on this spot! Behold, the knotted skein
Which has so often troubled me, at last
Untangles of itself. I feel at ease,
Since henceforth nothing in this world remains
That I need hide. Henceforth, I am as free
Before mankind, as in the sight of God.
Who only does not need to judge us men
By deeds, which oftentimes are not our own.
Scene
V.
Nathan
and the Templar
.
(The latter advancing towards him from the side.)
TEMPLAR.
Hold, Nathan, hold! Take me along with you.
NATHAN.
Who calls? You, Templar! Where can you have been
That you could not be met with at the Sultan's?
TEMPLAR.
We missed each other; do not be displeased.
NATHAN.
Not I, but Saladin.
TEMPLAR.
You had just gone.
NATHAN.
Oh, then, you spoke with him. I'm satisfied.

TEMPLAR.
Yes; but he wants to talk with us together.
NATHAN.
So much the better. Come with me; I go
Direct to him.
TEMPLAR.
Say, Nathan, may I ask
Who left you even now?
NATHAN.
What! don't you know?
TEMPLAR.
Was it that worthy fellow, the good friar,
Whom the old Patriarch employs at will
To work his ends?
NATHAN.
The same--the very same.
TEMPLAR.
'Tis a prime hit to make simplicity
The workman of deceit.
NATHAN.
Yes, if he use
The fool, and not the pious man.
TEMPLAR.
This last
The Patriarch ne'er trusts.
NATHAN.
Depend on this,
That man will not assist the Patriarch
To a wicked end.
TEMPLAR.
Well, so I think myself.
But has he told you aught of me?
NATHAN.
Of you?
He scarcely knows your name.
TEMPLAR.
That's like enough.
NATHAN.
He spoke to me about a Templar, who----
TEMPLAR.
Who what?
NATHAN.
But then he never mentioned you.
TEMPLAR.
Who knows? Come tell me, Nathan, all he said.

NATHAN.
Who has accused me to the Patriarch?
TEMPLAR.
Accused you! With his leave, that is untrue.
No! Hear me, Nathan! I am not the man
E'er to deny my actions. What I've done
I've done--and there's an end. Nor am I one
Who would maintain that all I've done is right.
But should one fault condemn me? Am I not
Resolved on better deeds for time to come?
And who is ignorant how much the man
Who wills it may improve? Then hear me, Nathan:
I am the Templar talked of by the Friar,
Who has accused--you know what maddened me,
What set my blood on fire within my veins--
Fool that I was! I had almost resolved
To fling myself both soul and body, straight
Into your arms. But how was I received?
How did you meet me, Nathan? Cold--or worse.
Lukewarm--far worse than cold. With cautious words,
Well weighed and measured, Nathan, you took care
To put me off, and with calm questions, asked
About my parentage, and God knows what,
You sought to meet my suit. I cannot now
Dwell on it and be patient. Hear me further.
While in this ferment, Daja suddenly
Drew near to me and whispered in my ear
A secret which cleared up the mystery.
NATHAN.
What was it?
TEMPLAR.
Hear me to the end. I thought
The treasure you had from the Christians stolen,
You would not promptly to a Christian yield;
And so the project struck me, with good speed,
To bring you to extremities.
NATHAN.
Good speed?
Good, good? pray where's the good!
TEMPLAR.
But hear me out.
I own my error; you are free from guilt;
That prating Daja knows not what she says.
She's hostile to you, and she seeks to twine
A dangerous snare around you. Be it so.

I'm but a crazed enthusiast, doubly mad,
Aiming at far too much, or much too little.
That may be also true. Forgive me, Nathan.
NATHAN.
If you conceive thus of me----
TEMPLAR.
Well, in short.
I saw the Patriarch--but named you not.
'Twas false to say so, for I only told
The case in general terms, to sound his mind.
And that I also might have left undone,
For knew I not the Patriarch to be
An arrant, subtle knave? And might I not
As well have told you all the case at first?
Or was it right in me to risk the loss
Of such a father to the hapless maid?
But what has happened now? The Patriarch,
Ever consistent in his villainy,
Has all at once restored me to myself.
For hear me, Nathan, hear me! Were he now
To learn your name, what more could then occur?
He cannot seize the maid, if she belong
To some one else, and not to you alone.
'Tis from your house alone she can be dragged
Into a convent: grant her, then, I pray,
Grant her to me! Then come the Patriarch!
He'll hardly dare to take my wife from me.
Oh! give her to me. Be she yours or not--
Your daughter--Christian--Jewess--'tis all one--
Or be she nothing--I will ne'er inquire,
Or in my lifetime ask you what she is,
'Tis all alike to me.
NATHAN.
Do you then think
That to conceal the truth I am compelled?
TEMPLAR.
No matter.
NATHAN.
I have ne'er denied the truth
To you, or any one whom it concerned
To know the fact, that she's of Christian birth,
And that the maid is my adopted child.
Why I have not informed her of the truth,
I need explain to none but to herself.
TEMPLAR.

Nathan; no need of that, it were not well
That she should see you in a different light;
Then spare her the discovery. As yet
She's yours alone--no other's--to bestow.
Then grant her to me, Nathan, I implore--
Grant her to me: I only, I alone,
Can rescue her a second time--and will.
NATHAN.
Yes, you could once have saved her, but alas!
'Tis now too late.
TEMPLAR.
Too late! ah! say not so.
NATHAN.
Thanks to the Patriarch.
TEMPLAR.
Why, thanks to him?
Why should we thank the Patriarch! For what?
NATHAN.
That now we know her relatives, and know
Into whose hands Recha may be restored.
TEMPLAR.
Let him give thanks who shall have better cause
To thank him.
NATHAN.
But you must receive her now
From other hands than mine.
TEMPLAR.
Alas, poor maid!
O hapless Recha! what has chanced to thee,
That what to other orphans had appeared
A real blessing, is to thee a curse!
But, Nathan, where are these new relatives?
NATHAN.
Where are they?
TEMPLAR.
Ay, both where and who are they?
NATHAN.
Her brother is discovered, and to him
You must address yourself.
TEMPLAR.
Her brother! Ha!
And what is he--a soldier or a priest?
Tell me at once what I've to hope from him.
NATHAN.
I hear he's neither--or he's both. As yet

I do not know him thoroughly.
TEMPLAR.
What more?
NATHAN.
He is a gallant fellow, and with him
Recha may be content.
TEMPLAR.
But he's a Christian.
At times I know not what to make of you.
Take it not ill, good Nathan, that I ask,
Must she not henceforth play the Christian,
Associate with Christians, and at last
Become the character she long has played?
Will not the tares at length grow up and choke
The pure wheat you have sown? And does not that
Affect you? Yet you say she'll be content
When with her brother.
NATHAN.
As I think and hope.
For should she e'er have need of anything,
Has she not you and me?
TEMPLAR.
What can she need
When with her brother. Gladly he'll provide
His dear new sister with a thousand robes,
With dainties, and with toys and finery.
And what could any sister wish for more--
Unless, perhaps, a husband? And him too,
Him too the brother, in due time, will find;
And the more Christian he, the better!--Nathan,
How sad to think the angel you have formed,
Should now be marred by others!
NATHAN.
Be assured
He'll always prove deserving of our love.
TEMPLAR.
Nay speak not so; of my love, speak not so,
For it can brook no loss, however small,
Not e'en a name. But, hold! Has she as yet
Any suspicion of these late events?
NATHAN.
'Tis possible, and yet I know not how.
TEMPLAR.
It matters not; she must, in either case,
First learn from me what fate is threat'ning her.

My purpose not to speak with her again,
And ne'er to see her more, till I should call
Your Recha mine, is gone. I take my leave.
NATHAN.
Nay, whither would you go?
TEMPLAR.
At once to her,
To learn if she be bold enough at heart,
To fix upon the only course that now
Is worthy of her.
NATHAN.
Name it.
TEMPLAR.
It is this:
That henceforth she should never care to know
Aught of her brother or of you.
NATHAN.
What more?
TEMPLAR.
To follow me--even if it were her fate
To wed a Mussulman.
NATHAN.
Stay, Templar, stay!
You will not find her. She's with Sittah now,
The Sultan's sister.
TEMPLAR.
Wherefore, and since when?
NATHAN.
If you desire to see her brother, come,
Follow me straight.
TEMPLAR.
Her brother, say you? Whose?
Recha's, or Sittah's?
NATHAN.
Both--ay, both, perhaps.
But come this way, I pray you. Come with me.
(Nathan
leads the Templar
away.)
Scene
VI.--Sittah's
harem
.
Sittah
and Recha

engaged in conversation.
SITTAH.
How I am pleased with you, sweet girl. But, come,
Shake off these fears, and be no more alarmed,
Be happy, cheerful. Let me hear you talk.
RECHA.
Princess!
SITTAH.
Nay, child, not princess! Call me friend,
Or Sittah--or your sister--or dear mother,
For I might well be so to you--so good,
So prudent, and so young! How much you know,
How much you must have read!
RECHA.
Read, Sittah! now
You're mocking me, for I can scarcely read.
SITTAH.
Scarce read, you young deceiver!
RECHA.
Yes, perhaps
My father's hand; I thought you spoke of books.
SITTAH.
And so I did--of books.
RECHA.
They puzzle me
To read.
SITTAH.
Indeed!
RECHA.
I speak, in veriest truth.
My father hates book-learning, which he says,
Makes an impression only on the brain
With lifeless letters.
SITTAH.
Well, he's right in that.
And so the greater part of what you know----
RECHA.
I've learnt from his own mouth, and I can tell
The when, the where, and why he taught it me.
SITTAH.
So it clings closer, and the soul drinks in
The full instruction.
RECHA.
Yes, and Sittah, too,
Has not read much.

SITTAH.
How so? I am not vain
Of having read, and yet why say you so?
Speak boldly. Tell the reason.
RECHA.
She's so plain--
So free from artifice--so like herself.
SITTAH.
Well!
RECHA.
And my father says 'tis rarely books
Work that effect.
SITTAH.
Oh, what a man he is,
Dear Recha!
RECHA.
Is he not?
SITTAH.
He never fails
To hit the mark.
RECHA.
Yes, yes; and yet this father----
SITTAH.
What ails you, love?
RECHA.
This father----
SITTAH.
Oh my God!
You're weeping.
RECHA.
And this father--it must forth--
My heart wants room, wants room----
(Throws herself in tears at Sittah's
feet.)
SITTAH.
What ails you, Recha?
RECHA.
Yes, I must lose this father!
SITTAH.
Lose him--never!
Why so? Be calm. Courage! it must not be.
RECHA.
Your offer to be friend and sister to me
Will now not be in vain.
SITTAH.

Yes, I am both.
Arise, arise, or I must call for help.
RECHA.
O pardon! I forget, through agony,
With whom I speak. Tears, sobbing, and despair
Are naught with Sittah. Reason, calm and cool,
Is over her alone omnipotent.
No other argument avails with her.
SITTAH.
Well, then?
RECHA.
My friend and sister, suffer not
Another father to be forced on me.
SITTAH.
Another father to be forced on you!
Who can do that, or wish to do it, love?
RECHA.
Who but my good, my evil genius, Daja?
She can both wish it and perform the deed.
You do not know this good, this evil Daja.
May God forgive her, and reward her, too,
For she has done me good and evil, both.
SITTAH.
Evil? Then she has little goodness left.
RECHA.
Oh, she has much.
SITTAH.
Who is she?
RECHA.
Who? a Christian,
Who cared for me in childhood's early years.
You cannot know how little she allowed
That I should miss a mother's tender cares--
May God reward her for it!--but she has
Worried and tortured me.
SITTAH.
Wherefore, and how?
RECHA.
Poor woman, she's a Christian, and from love
Has tortured me: a warm enthusiast,
Who thinks she only knows the real road
That leads to God.
SITTAH.
I understand you now.
RECHA.

And one of those who feel in duty bound
To point it out to every one who strays
From the plain path, to lead, to drag them in.
And who can censure them? for if the road
They travel is the only one that's safe,
They cannot, without pain, behold their friends
Pursue a path that lead to endless woe,
Else, at the self-same time, 'twere possible
To love and hate another. Nor does this
Alone compel me to complain aloud.
Her groans, her prayers, her warnings, and her threats
I could have borne much longer willingly.
They always called up good and wholesome thoughts.
Who is not flattered to be held so dear,
And precious by another, that the thought
Of parting pierces him with lasting pain?
SITTAH.
This is most true.
RECHA.
And yet this goes too far,
And I have nothing to oppose to it--
Patience, reflection, nothing.
SITTAH.
How? to what?
RECHA.
To what she has disclosed to me.
SITTAH.
Say, when?
RECHA.
'Tis scarce an instant. Coming hither
We passed a Christian temple on our way;
She all at once stood still, seemed inly moved,
Raised her moist eyes to heaven, then looked on me.
"Come," she exclaimed at length, "come straight on here,
Through this old fane." She leads, I follow her.
My eyes with horror overrun the dim
And tottering ruin: all at once she stops
By a low ruined altar's sunken steps.
O, how I felt, when there, with streaming eyes
And wringing hands, down at my feet she fell!
SITTAH.
Good child!
RECHA.
And, by the Holy Virgin, who had heard
So many suppliants' prayers, and had performed

Full many a wonder there, she begged, implored
With looks of heart-felt sympathy and love,
That I would now take pity on myself,
And pardon her for daring to unfold
The nature of the Church's claims on me.
SITTAH.
I guessed as much.
RECHA.
I'm born of Christian blood,
Have been baptised, and am not Nathan's child!
Nathan is not my father! God, O God!
He's not my father, Sittah! Now, behold,
I'm once more prostrate at your feet.
SITTAH.
Arise!
Recha, arise! behold, my brother comes.
Scene
VII.
Saladin
, Sittah
, and Recha
.
SALADIN.
What is the matter, Sittah?
SITTAH.
She has swooned.
SALADIN.
Who is she?
SITTAH.
Don't you know?
SALADIN.
'Tis Nathan's child.
What ails her?
SITTAH.
Look up, Recha! 'tis the Sultan.
RECHA (crawling to Saladin's feet).
No, I'll not rise--not rise nor even look
Upon the Sultan's countenance, nor wonder
At the bright lustre of unchanging truth
And goodness on his brow and in his eye,
Before----
SITTAH.
Rise, rise!
RECHA.
Before he promises----

SALADIN.
Come, come! I promise, whatsoe'er your prayer.
RECHA.
'Tis only this--to leave my father to me,
And me to him. As yet I cannot tell
Who seeks to be my father: who it is
Can harbour such a wish I'll ne'er inquire.
Does blood alone make fathers--blood alone?
SITTAH.
Who can have been so cruel as to raise
This dire suspicion in my Recha's breast?
Say, is it proved? beyond all doubt made clear?
RECHA.
'Tis proved, for Daja had it from my nurse,
Whose dying lips entrusted it to her.
SALADIN.
Dying! she raved. And even were it true,
A father is not made by blood alone;
Scarcely the father of a savage beast--
Blood only gives the right to earn the name.
Then fear no more, but hear me. If there be
Two fathers who contend for thee, leave both,
And claim a third! O! take me for your father!
SITTAH.
Oh, do so, Recha, do so!
SALADIN.
I will be
A good, kind father to you. But, in truth
A better thought occurs. Why should you need
Two fathers? They are mortal, and must die.
'Twere better, Recha, to look out betimes
For one to start with you on equal terms,
And stake his life for thine. You understand?
SITTAH.
You make her blush!
SALADIN.
Why that was half my scheme.
Blushing becomes plain features, and will make
A beauteous cheek more beauteous. My commands
Are giv'n to bring your father, Nathan, here.
Another comes as well. You'll guess his name?
Hither they come! Will you allow it, Sittah?
SITTAH.
Brother!
SALADIN.

And when he comes, maid, you must blush
To crimson.
RECHA.
Sittah! wherefore should I blush?
SALADIN.
You young dissembler, you will else grow pale!
But as thou wilt and canst. (A female slave enters, and approaches Sittah
.) What, here so soon?
SITTAH.
Well, let them enter. Brother, here they are!
Scene
VIII.
Nathan
, the Templar
, and the others.
SALADIN.
Welcome, my dear good friends! Nathan, to you
I must first mention, you may send and fetch
Your moneys when you will.
NATHAN.
Sultan----
SALADIN.
And now
I'm at your service.
NATHAN.
Sultan----
SALADIN.
For my gold
Is now arrived; the caravan is safe:
These many years I have not been so rich.
Now, tell me what you wish for, to achieve
Some splendid speculation? You in trade,
Like us, have never too much ready cash.
NATHAN.
Why speak about this trifle first? I see
An eye in tears (going towards Recha
). My Recha, you have wept.
What have you lost? Are you not still my child?
RECHA.
My father!
NATHAN.
That's enough! We're understood
By one another! But look up--be calm,
Be cheerful! If your heart is still your own,
And if no threatened loss disturb your breast,

Your father is not lost to you!
RECHA.
None, none!
TEMPLAR.
None! Then I'm much deceived. What we don't fear
To lose, we ne'er have loved, and ne'er have wished
To be possessed of. But 'tis well, 'tis well!
Nathan, this changes all! At your command,
We come here, Sultan. You have been misled
By me, and I will trouble you no more!
SALADIN.
Rash, headlong youth! Must every temper yield
To yours!--and must we all thus guess your mind?
TEMPLAR.
But, Sultan, you have heard and seen it all.
SALADIN.
Well, truly, it was awkward to be thus
Uncertain of your cause!
TEMPLAR.
I know my fate.
SALADIN.
Whoe'er presumes upon a service done,
Cancels the benefit. What you have saved
Is, therefore, not your own. Or else the thief,
Urged by mere avarice through flaming halls,
Were like yourself a hero. (Advancing towards Recha
to lead her to the Templar
.) Come, sweet maid!
Be not reserved towards him. Had he been so,
Were he less warm, less proud, he had held back,
And had not saved you. Weigh the former deed
Against the latter, and you'll make him blush!
Do what he should have done! confess your love!
Make him your offer! and if he refuse,
Or e'er forget how infinitely more
You do for him than he has done for you--
For what, in fact, have been his services,
Save soiling his complexion? a mere sport--
Else has he nothing of my Assad in him,
But only wears his mask. Come, lovely maid.
SITTAH.
Go, dearest, go! this step is not enough
For gratitude; it is too little.
NATHAN.
Hold!

Hold, Saladin! hold, Sittah!
SALADIN.
What would you?
NATHAN.
It is the duty of another now
To speak.
SALADIN.
Who questions that? Beyond all doubt
A foster--father has a right to vote
First, if you will. You see I know the whole.
NATHAN.
Not quite. I speak not, Sultan, of myself.
There is another and a different man
Whom I must first confer with, Saladin.
SALADIN.
And who is he?
NATHAN.
Her brother.
SALADIN.
Recha's brother?
NATHAN.
E'en so.
RECHA.
My brother! Have I then a brother?
TEMPLAR (starting from his silent and sullen inattention)
.
Where is this brother? Not yet here! 'Twas here
I was to meet him.
NATHAN.
Patience yet awhile.
TEMPLAR (bitterly)
.
He has imposed a father on the girl;
He'll find a brother for her now!
SALADIN.
Indeed,
That much was wanting. But this mean rebuke,
Christian, had ne'er escaped my Assad's lips.
NATHAN.
Forgive him: I forgive him readily.
Who knows what in his youth and in his place
We might ourselves have thought? (Approaching him in
a very friendly manner) Suspicion, knight,
Follows upon reserve. Had you at first
Vouchsafed to me your real name----

TEMPLAR.
How! what!
NATHAN.
You are no Stauffen.
TEMPLAR.
Tell me who I am.
NATHAN.
Conrad of Stauffen, not.
TEMPLAR.
Then what's my name?
NATHAN.
Leo of Filneck.
TEMPLAR.
How?
NATHAN.
You start!
TEMPLAR.
With reason.
But who says this?
NATHAN.
I, who can tell you more.
Meanwhile, observe, I tax you not with falsehood.
TEMPLAR.
Indeed!
NATHAN.
It may be both names fit you well.
TEMPLAR.
I think so. (Aside) God inspired him with that thought.
NATHAN.
Your mother was a Stauffen: and her brother
(The uncle to whose care you were consigned,
When, by the rigour of the climate chased,
Your parents quitted Germany, to seek
This land once more) was Conrad. He, perhaps,
Adopted you as his own son and heir.
Is it long since you travelled hither with him?
Does he still live?
TEMPLAR.
What shall I answer him?
He speaks the truth. Nathan, 'tis so indeed;
But he himself is dead. I journeyed here,
With the last troops of knights, to reinforce
Our order. But inform me how this tale
Concerns your Recha's brother.
NATHAN.

Well, your father----
TEMPLAR.
What! did you know him too?
NATHAN.
He was my friend.
TEMPLAR.
Your friend! Oh, Nathan, is it possible?
NATHAN.
Oluf of Filneck did he style himself;
But he was not a German.
TEMPLAR.
You know that?
NATHAN.
He had espoused a German, and he lived
For some, time with your mother there.
TEMPLAR.
No more
Of this, I beg. But what of Recha's brother?
NATHAN.
It is yourself.
TEMPLAR.
What, I? am I her brother?
RECHA.
He, my brother?
SALADIN.
Are they so near akin?
RECHA (approaching the Templar)
.
My brother!
TEMPLAR (stepping back)
.
I, your brother?
RECHA (stopping and turning to Nathan)
.
No, in truth,
It cannot be. His heart makes no response.
O God! we are deceivers.
SALADIN (to the Templar
)
.
Say you so?
Is that your thought? All is deceit in you:
The voice, the gesture, and the countenance,
Nothing of these is yours. How! will you not
Acknowledge such a sister? Then begone!

TEMPLAR (approaching him humbly).
Oh! do not misinterpret my surprise.
Sultan, you never saw your Assad's heart
At any time like this. Then do not err,
Mistake not him and me. (Turning to Nathan
.) You give me much,
Nathan, and also you take much away,
And yet you give me more than you withdraw--
Ay, infinitely more. My sister, sister! (embraces Recha
.)
NATHAN.
Blanda of Filneck.
TEMPLAR.
Blanda, ha! not Recha?
Your Recha now no more! Have you resigned
Your child? Give her her Christian name once more,
And for my sake discard her then. Oh, Nathan,
Why must she suffer for a fault of mine?
NATHAN.
What mean you, oh, my children, both of you?
For sure my daughter's brother is my child
Whenever he shall wish.
(While they embrace Nathan, Saladin
uneasily approaches Sittah
.)
SALADIN.
What say you, sister? Sittah.
SITTAH.
I'm deeply moved----
SALADIN.
And I half tremble when
I think of the emotion that must come:
Prepare yourself to bear it as you may.
SITTAH.
What! How!
SALADIN.
Nathan, a word--one word with you.
(He joins Nathan
, while Sittah
approaches the others to express her sympathy, and Nathan
and Saladin
converse in a low tone.)
Hear, hear me, Nathan. Said you not just now
That he----
NATHAN.

That who?
SALADIN.
Her father was not born
In Germany. You know then whence he came?
And what he was?
NATHAN.
He never told me that.
SALADIN.
Was he no Frank, nor from the Western land?
NATHAN.
He said as much. He spoke the Persian tongue.
SALADIN.
The Persian! need I more? 'Tis he! 'twas he!
NATHAN.
Who?
SALADIN.
Assad, my brother Assad, beyond doubt.
NATHAN.
If you think so, then be assured from this:
Look in this book (handing him the breviary).
SALADIN.
Oh, 'tis his hand! once more
I recognise it.
NATHAN.
They know naught of this:
It rests with you to tell them all the truth.
SALADIN (turning over the leaves of the breviary)
.
They are my brother's children. Shall I not
Acknowledge them and claim them? Or shall I
Abandon them to you? (Speaking aloud.) Sittah, they are
The children of my brother and of yours. (Rushes to embrace them.)
SITTAH (following his example)
.
What do I hear? Could it be otherwise?
SALADIN (to the Templar
)
.
Proud youth! from this time forward you are bound
To love me. (To Recha
.) And henceforth, without your leave
Or with it, I am what I vowed to be.
SITTAH.
And so am I.
SALADIN (to the Templar

)

.

My son! my Assad's son!

TEMPLAR.

I of your blood! Then those were more than dreams
With which they used to lull my infancy--
(Falls at Sultan's
feet.)

SALADIN (raising him)

.

There, mark the rascal! though he knew something
Of what has chanced, he was content that I
Should have become his murderer! Beware.
(The curtain falls whilst they repeatedly embrace each other in silence.)

END OF VOL. I.

LONDON: PRINTED BY WILLIAM CLOWES AND SONS, STAMFORD STREET
AND CHARING CROSS.

York Street, Covent Garden,
November, 1877.

A
CLASSIFIED CATALOGUE
OF
SELECTED WORKS
PUBLISHED BY
GEORGE BELL AND SONS.

CONTENTS:

TRAVEL AND ARCHEOLOGY.

ANCIENT ATHENS; its History, Topography, and Remains. By T. H. Dyer, LL.D
. Super-royal 8vo. copiously Illustrated. 1l. 5s.

'Dr. Dyer's volume will be a work of reference to the student of Greek History and literature, of the greatest interest and value.'--Spectator.

DESERT OF THE EXODUS. Journeys on Foot in the Wilderness of the Forty Years' Wanderings, undertaken in connexion with the Ordnance Survey of Sinai and the Palestine Exploration Fund. By E. H. Palmer, M.A.
, Lord Almoner's Professor of Arabic, and Fellow of St. John's College, Cambridge. With Maps and numerous Illustrations. 2 vols. 8vo. 1l. 8s.

'A work which the biblical student will highly prize for the strong light which it sheds upon a most important portion of Scripture history, but which cannot be read without interest and delight by every one who is capable of taking an intelligent interest in manners and customs widely removed from our own.'--Saturday Review.

HISTORY OF EGYPT. From the Earliest Times till its Conquest by the Arabs, A.D

. 640. By S. Sharpe

. With numerous Illustrations, Maps, c. 6th Edition. 2 vols. post 8vo. 10s.

NINEVEH AND ITS PALACES. By J. Bonomi, F.R.S.L

. New Edition, revised and considerably enlarged. With upwards of 300 Engravings. Post 8vo. 5s.

HISTORY OF POMPEII: its Buildings and Antiquities. An Account of the City, with full description of the Remains and Recent Excavations, and also an Itinerary for Visitors. By T. H. Dyer, LL.D

. With nearly 300 Wood Engravings, a large Map, and a Plan of the Forum. 4th Edition, bringing the work down to 1874. Post 8vo. 7s. 6d.

ROME AND THE CAMPAGNA. A Historical and Topographical Description of the Site, Buildings and Neighbourhood of ancient Rome. By the Rev. R. Burn

, late Fellow and Tutor of Trinity College, Cambridge. With 85 Engravings by Jewitt, and numerous Maps and Plans. An Appendix and additional Plan illustrating recent Excavations have lately been added. Demy 4to. 3l. 3s.

BIOGRAPHY.

BARBAULD (MRS.) A Memoir of, including Letters and Notices of her Family and Friends. By her great-niece, Anna Letitia Le Breton

. With Portrait. Demy 12mo. 5s.

BOSWELL'S JOHNSON, and JOHNSONIANA

. Including his Tour to the Hebrides, Tour in Wales, c. Edited, with large Additions and Notes, by the Rt. Hon. J. W. Croker

. The second and most complete Copyright Edition, with upwards of 40 Engravings on Steel. Post 8vo. 5 vols. 20s.

BRYAN. A Biographical and Critical Dictionary of Painters and Engravers. With a List of Ciphers, Monograms, and Marks. By M. Bryan

. A New Edition by G. Stanley

. Imp. 8vo. 2l. 2s.

----A SUPPLEMENT

of RECENT

and LIVING PAINTERS

. By H. Ottley

. Imp. 8vo. 12s.

COLERIDGE (S. T.) Biographia Literaria, and two Lay Sermons. Post 8vo. 3s. 6d.

COOPER (THOMPSON). A New Biographical Dictionary. By T. Cooper, F.S.A

. 1 vol. 8vo. 12s.

FOSTER (JOHN), The Life of. 2 vols. post 8vo. 3s. 6d. each.

GOETHE, Autobiography of (Wahrheit und Dichtung aus Meinem Leben). 2 vols. post 8vo. 3s. 6d. each.

GOETHE. Conversations with Eckermann and Soret. Post 8vo. 3s. 6d.

GOETHE. Correspondence with Schiller. 2 vols. post 8vo. 7s.

GOLDSMITH (O.) The Life of, together with The Sketch-Book. By Washington Irving

. Post 8vo. 3s. 6d. The Life alone, in paper wrapper, 1s. 6d.

IRVING (W.) Life and Letters. By his Nephew, P. E. Irving

. In 2 vols. post 8vo. 3s. 6d. each.

LUTHER, Michelet's Life of. Translated by W. Hazlitt

. Post 8vo. 3s. 6d.

MAHOMET AND HIS SUCCESSORS

. By Washington Irving

. Post 8vo. 3s. 6d.

MICHAEL ANGELO AND RAPHAEL, their Lives and Works. By Duppa and Quatremere de Quincy

. With 13 Engravings on Steel. Post 8vo. 5s.

NELSON, The Life of. By R. Southey

. With additional Notes and numerous Illustrations. Post 8vo. 5s.

RICHTER (J. P. F.) Autobiography and short Memoir, with the Levana. Post 8vo. 3s. 6d.

WASHINGTON, The Life of. By W. Irving

. With Portrait. In 4 vols. post 8vo. 3s. 6d. each.

WELLINGTON, The Life of. By An Old Soldier

, from the materials of Maxwell. Eighteen Engravings. Post 8vo. 5s.

WESLEY (JOHN), The Life of. By R. Southey

. New and Complete Edition. With Portrait. Post 8vo. 5s.

By the late Sir A. Helps, K.C.B.

BRASSEY (T.) The Life and Labours of the late. With Illustrations. 5th Edition, 10s. 6d.

HERNANDO CORTES, The Life of, and The CONQUEST OF MEXICO

. 2 vols. Crown 8vo. 15s.

COLUMBUS, The Life of. The Discoverer of America. 5th Edition. Crown 8vo. 6s.

PIZARRO, The Life of. With Some Account of his Associates in the Conquest of Peru. 2nd Edition. Crown 8vo. 6s.

LAS CASAS, The Life of, the Apostle of the Indies. 3rd Edition. Crown 8vo. 6s.

HISTORY.

MODERN EUROPE, from the Fall of Constantinople to the Founding of the German Empire, A.D. 1453-1871. By Thomas Henry Dyer, LL.D

. 2nd Edition, revised throughout and continued by the Author. In 5 vols. demy 8vo. 2l. 12s. 6d.

KINGS OF ROME, History of the. By T. Dyer, LL.D

. With a Prefatory Dissertation on the Sources and Evidences of Early Roman History. Demy 8vo. 16s.

'It will mark or help to mark an era in the history of the subject to which it is devoted. It is one of the most decided as well as one of the ablest results of the reaction which is now in progress against the influence of Niebuhr.'--Pall Mall Gazette.

DECLINE OF THE ROMAN REPUBLIC. From the Destruction of Carthage to the Consulship of Julius Cæsar. By George Long, M.A

. 5 vols. 8vo. 14s. per vol.

'If any one can guide us through the almost inextricable mazes of this labyrinth, it is Mr. Long. As a chronicler, he possesses all the requisite knowledge, and what is nearly, if not quite as important, the necessary caution. He never attempts to explain that which is hopelessly corrupt or obscure: he does not confound twilight with daylight; he warns the reader repeatedly that he is standing on shaking ground; he has no framework of theory into which he presses his facts.'--Saturday Review.

LIFE OF THE EMPEROR KARL THE GREAT. Translated from the contemporary History Of Eginhard

, with Notes and Chapters on Eginhard--the Franks--Karl--and the Breaking-up of the Empire. With a Map. By William Glaister, M.A., B.C.L.

, University College, Oxford. Crown 8vo. 4s. 6d.

HISTORY OF ENGLAND, during the Early and Middle Ages. By C. H. Pearson, M.A.

, Fellow of Oriel College, Oxford. 2nd Edition, much enlarged. Vol. I. 8vo. 16s. Vol. II. 8vo. 14s.

HISTORICAL MAPS OF ENGLAND during the first Thirteen Centuries. With Explanatory Essays and Indices. By C. H. Pearson, M.A

. Imp. folio. 2nd Edition. 31s. 6d.

THE BARONS' WAR. Including the Battles of Lewes and Evesham. By W. H. Blaauw, M.A

. 2nd Edition, with Additions and Corrections by C. H. Pearson

, M.A. Demy 8vo. 10s. 6d.

THIRTY YEARS' PEACE, 1815-45, A History of the. By Harriet Martineau

. 4 vols. post 8vo. 3s. 6d. each.

QUEENS OF ENGLAND, from the Norman Conquest to the Reign of Queen Anne. By Agnes Strickland

. Library Edition, with Portraits, Autographs, and Vignettes, 8 vols. post 8vo. 7s. 6d. each. Cheap Edition, 6 vols. 5s. each.

MARY, QUEEN OF SCOTS, The Life of. By A. Strickland

. 2 vols. post 8vo. cloth gilt, 11s.

PHILOSOPHY.

ELEMENTS OF THOUGHT. By Isaac Taylor

, Post 8vo. 4s.

HOME EDUCATION. By the same Author. Fcap. 8vo. 5s.

ELEMENTS OF MORALITY, including Polity. By W. Whewell, D.D

. 4th Edition. In 1 vol. 8vo. 15s.

MORAL PHILOSOPHY. Lectures on the History of, in England. By W. Whewell, D.D

. Crown 8vo. 8s.

MANUAL OF HUMAN CULTURE. By M. A. Garvey, LL.B

. Crown 8vo. 7s. 6d.

LOCKE. PHILOSOPHICAL WORKS

, containing an Essay on the Human Understanding, c., with Notes and Index by J. A. St. John

. Portrait. In 2 vols. Post 8vo. 7s.

INTELLECTUAL DEVELOPMENT OF EUROPE

. A History of the. By J. W. Draper, M.D., LL.D

. 2 vols. Post 8vo. 10s.

COMTE'S PHILOSOPHY OF THE SCIENCES

. Edited by G. H. Lewes

. Post 8vo. 5s.

KANT. CRITIQUE OF PURE REASON

. Translated by J. M. D. Meiklejohn

. Post 8vo. 5s.

HEGEL. LECTURES ON THE PHILOSOPHY OF HISTORY

. Translated by J. Sibree, M.A

. Post 8vo. 5s.

THEOLOGY.

ARTICLES OF RELIGION, History of the. To which is added a Series of Documents from A.D. 1536 to A.D. 1615. Together with Illustrations from contemporary sources. By the late C. Hardwick, M.A.

, Archdeacon of Ely. 3rd Edition. Revised by the Rev. F. Procter, M.A.

, Author of 'A History of the Book of Common Prayer,' with additional matter. Post 8vo. 5s.

THE CREEDS, History of. By J. Rawson Lumby, M.A.

, Tyrwhitt's Hebrew Scholar, Crosse Divinity Scholar. Crown 8vo. 7s. 6d.

PEARSON (BP.) ON THE CREED. Carefully printed from an Early Edition. With Analysis and Index. Edited by E. Walford, M.A

. Post 8vo. 5s.

COMMON PRAYER. Historical and Explanatory Treatise on the Book of. By W. G. Humphry, B.D.

, Prebendary of St. Paul's and Vicar of St. Martin-in-the-Fields. 5th Edition, revised and enlarged. Fcap. 8vo. 4s. 6d.

COMMON PRAYER, Rational Illustrations of the Book of. By C. Wheatly

, M.A. Post 8vo. 3s. 6d.

AN INTRODUCTION TO THE OLD TESTAMENT

. By F. Bleek

. Translated from the German by G. H. Venables

, under the supervision of the Rev. E. Venables

. In 2 vols. 10s.

COMPANION TO THE GREEK TESTAMENT

. For the use of Theological Students and the Upper Forms in Schools. By A. C. Barrett, M.A.

, Caius College. 3rd Edition, enlarged and improved. Fcap. 8vo. 5s.

By F. H. Scrivener, D.C.L., Prebendary of Exeter.

NOVUM TESTAMENTUM GRÆCUM, TEXTUS STEPHANICI

, 1550. Accedunt variæ lectiones editionum Bezæ, Elzeviri, Lachmanni, Tischendorfii, et Tregellesii. 16mo. 4s. 6d. With wide Margin for Notes, 4to. 12s.

A PLAIN INTRODUCTION TO THE CRITICISM OF THE NEW TESTAMENT

. With 40 Facsimiles from Ancient Manuscripts. Containing also an Account of the Egyptian Versions by Canon Lightfoot, D.D

. For the Use of Biblical Students. New Edition. Demy 8vo. 16s.

SIX LECTURES ON THE TEXT OF THE NEW TESTAMENT

and the ancient Manuscripts which contain it. Chiefly addressed to those who do not read Greek. With facsimiles from MSS. c. Crown 8vo. 6s.

BOOK OF PSALMS; a New Translation, with Introductions and Notes, Critical and Explanatory. By the Rev. J. J. Stewart Perowne, D.D.

, Canon Residentiary of Llandaff, and Hulsean Professor of Divinity, Cambridge. 8vo. Vol. I. 3rd Edition, 18s. Vol. II. 3rd Edition, 16s. An abridged Edition for Schools and Private Students. Crown 8vo. 10s. 6d.

A COMMENTARY ON THE GOSPELS AND EPISTLES

for the Sundays and other Holy Days of the Christian Year. By the Rev. W. Denton, A.M.

, Worcester College, Oxford, and Incumbent of St. Bartholomew's, Cripplegate. In 5 vols. 18s. each.

A COMMENTARY ON THE ACTS OF THE APOSTLES

. In 2 vols. Vol. I. 18s. Vol. II. 14s. These Commentaries originated in Notes collected by the compiler to aid in the composition of expository sermons. They are derived from all available sources, and especially from the wide but little-known field of theological comment found in the 'Schoolmen' of the Middle Ages. They are recommended to the notice of young Clergymen, who frequently, while inexperienced, are called upon to preach to educated and intelligent congregations.

BIBLE-ENGLISH. Chapters on Words and Phrases in the Authorized Version of the Holy Scriptures and the Book of Common Prayer, no longer in common use; illustrated from contemporaneous writers. By the Rev. T. Lewis O. Davies, M.A.

, Vicar of St. Mary Extra, Southampton. Small crown 8vo. 5s.

'Everyone who takes an interest in the history of the English Language, and indeed everyone who is not absolutely inattentive to the words spoken around him, may turn to Mr. Davies's little book with the certainty of finding both useful information and agreeable entertainment in its pages.'--Pall Mall Gazette.

LIFE OF JESUS CHRIST; in its Historical Connexion and Development. By A. Neander

. From the 4th German Edition. Post 8vo. 3s. 6d.

LIFE AND EPISTLES OF ST. PAUL. By T. Lewin

, Esq., M.A., F.S.A., Trinity College, Oxford, Barrister-at-law, Author of 'Fasti Sacri,' 'Siege of Jerusalem,' 'Cæsar's Invasion,' 'Treatise on Trusts,' c. With upwards of 350 Illustrations finely engraved on Wood, Maps, Plans, c. In 2 vols. 3rd Edition, revised. Demy 4to. 2l. 2s.

'Nothing but a careful inspection of the work itself can give the reader an adequate idea of the thoroughness with which Mr. Lewin has carried out his plan--a plan which may be described as the giving of all information possibly attainable about every person or place connected directly or even indirectly with St. Paul.'--Spectator.

FASTI SACRI; or, a Key to the Chronology of the New Testament. By the same Author. 4to. 21s.

ANALOGY OF RELIGION, Natural and Revealed, and Sermons with Notes. By Bp. Butler

. Post 8vo. 3s. 6d.

HOLY LIVING AND DYING. By Bp. Jeremy Taylor

. With portrait. Post 8vo. 3s. 6d.

THOMAS A KEMPIS. On the Imitation of Christ. A New Translation. By the Rt. Rev. H. Goodwin

, Bishop of Carlisle. 3rd Edition. With fine Steel Engraving after Guido, 5s.; without the Engraving, 3s. 6d. Cheap Edition, 1s. cloth; 6d. sewed.

For Confirmation Candidates.

THE CHURCH TEACHER'S MANUAL OF CHRISTIAN INSTRUCTION

. Being the Church Catechism expanded and explained in Question and Answer, for the use of Clergymen, Parents, and Teachers. By the Rev. M. F. Sadler

. 16th Thousand. Fcap. 8vo. 2s. 6d.

'It is impossible to overrate the service to religious instruction achieved by this compact and yet pregnant volume.... We owe many boons to Mr. Sadler, whose sermons and theological lectures and treatises have wrought much good in matters of faith. This Catechetical Manual is second to none of such.'--English Churchman.

CATECHETICAL HINTS AND HELPS. A Manual for Parents and Teachers on giving Instruction in the Catechism of the Church of England. 3rd Edition, enlarged. Fcap. 8vo. 2s. 6d.

'Perhaps the most thoroughly practical little book on its subject we have ever seen. Its explanations, its paraphrases, its questions, and the mass of information contained in its appendices, are not merely invaluable in themselves, but they are the information actually wanted for the purpose of the teaching contemplated. We do not wonder at its being in its third edition.'--Literary Churchman.

THE WINTON CHURCH CATECHIST. Questions and Answers on the Teaching of the Church Catechism. 32mo. cloth, 3s. Also in Four Parts, 6d. or 9d. each.

LIFE AFTER CONFIRMATION. By J. S. Blunt

. 18mo. 1s.

CONFIRMATION DAY. Being a Book of Instruction for Young Persons how they ought to spend that solemn day. By the Rt. Rev. H. Goodwin, D.D.

, Bp. of Carlisle. 8th Thousand. 2d., or 25 for 3s. 6d.

By the Rev. M. F. Sadler, Rector of Honiton.

THE ONE OFFERING; a Treatise on the Sacrificial Nature of the Eucharist. 3rd Edition. Fcap. 8vo. 2s. 6d.

'A treatise of singular clearness and force, which gives us what we did not really possess till it appeared.'--Church Times.

'It is by far the most useful, trustworthy, and accurate book we have seen upon the subject.'--Literary Churchman.

'The subject of the Holy Eucharist is ably and fully treated, and in a candid spirit, by Mr. Sadler in these pages.'--English Churchman.

JUSTIFICATION OF LIFE: its Nature, Antecedents, and Consequences. Fcap. 8vo.

[In the press.]

THE LOST GOSPEL AND ITS CONTENTS; or, the Author of 'Supernatural Religion' Refuted by Himself. By Rev. M. F. Sadler

, Rector of Honiton. Demy 8vo. 7s. 6d.

THE SACRAMENT OF RESPONSIBILITY: or, Testimony of the Scripture to the Teaching of the Church on Holy Baptism. Fcap. 8vo. cloth, 2s. 6d. Also, Cheap Edition, 25th Thousand, fcap. 8vo. sewed, 6d.

'An exceedingly valuable repertory of arguments on the questions it refers to.'--English Churchman.

CHURCH DOCTRINE--BIBLE TRUTH. Fcap. 8vo. 18th Thousand, 3s. 6d.

'Some writers have the gift of speaking the right word at the right time, and the Rev. M. F. Sadler is pre-eminently one of them. "Church Doctrine--Bible Truth," is full of wholesome truths fit for these times.... He has power of putting his meaning in a forcible and intelligible way, which will, we trust, enable his valuable work to effect that which it is well calculated to effect, viz. to meet with an appropriate and crushing reply one of the most dangerous misbeliefs of the time.'--Guardian.

THE SECOND ADAM AND THE NEW BIRTH; or, the Doctrine of Baptism as contained in Holy Scripture. Fcap. 8vo. 7th Edition, price 4s. 6d.

'The most striking peculiarity of this useful little work is that its author argues almost exclusively from the Bible. We commend it most earnestly to clergy and laity, as containing in a small compass, and at a trifling cost, a body of sound and Scriptural doctrine respecting the New Birth, which cannot be too widely circulated.'--Guardian.

PARISH SERMONS. Trinity to Advent. Fcap. 8vo. 2nd Edition, 6s.

PLAIN SPEAKING ON DEEP TRUTHS. Sermons preached at St. Paul's Church, Bedford. Fcap. 8vo. 4th Edition, 6s.

ABUNDANT LIFE, and other Sermons. Fcap. 8vo. 6s.

THE COMMUNICANT'S MANUAL; being a Book of Self-examination, Prayer, Praise, and Thanksgiving. 8th Thousand. Royal 32mo. roan, gilt edges, price 2s.; cloth, 1s. 6d. Cheap Edition, for distribution, 25th Thousand, 8d. A larger Edition, on fine paper, and Rubrics. Fcap. 8vo. 2s. 6d.; morocco, 7s.

SCRIPTURE TRUTHS. A Series of Ten Plain, Popular Tracts upon subjects now universally under discussion, 9d. per set, sold separately. No. 1. Reasons for Infant Baptism. 2. On Eucharistic Worship. 3. On the Priesthood of the Christian Ministry. 4. On Confirmation. 5. Reasons for receiving the Holy Communion. 6. On the Doctrine of the Holy Communion. 7. On Baptism and Conversion. 8. Some Objections to receiving the Holy Communion considered. 9. On the First Truths of the Christian Faith. 10. On Faith and Justification.

STANDARD PROSE WORKS.

ADDISON. Works. With Notes by Bishop Hurd

, and numerous unpublished Letters. With Portrait and eight steel Engravings. 6 vols. cloth, gilt, post 8vo. 4s. each.

BACON'S (LORD) ESSAYS AND HISTORICAL WORKS

, with Introduction and Notes by J. Devey, M.A

. Post 8vo. 3s. 6d.

BURKE. Works. In 8 vols. post 8vo. cloth, gilt, 4s. each.

COLERIDGE (S. T.) THE FRIEND

. A Series of Essays on Morals, Politics, and Religion. Post 8vo. 3s. 6d.

COLERIDGE (S. T.) BIOGRAPHIA LITERARIA

, and Two Lay Sermons. Post 8vo. 3s. 6d.

CRAIK (G. L.) THE PURSUIT OF KNOWLEDGE UNDER DIFFICULTIES

. Illustrated. Post 8vo. 5s.

EMERSON (R. W.) WORKS, comprising Essays, Lectures, Poems, and Orations. In 2 vols. post 8vo. 3s. 6d. each.

FIELDING (H.) TOM JONES

, the History of a Foundling. Roscoe's

Edition revised. With Illustrations by G. Cruikshank

. In 2 vols. 7s.

FIELDING (H.) JOSEPH ANDREWS

, and Roscoe's

Biography of the Author revised. With Illustrations by G. Cruikshank

. Post 8vo. 3s. 6d.

FIELDING (H.) AMELIA

. Roscoe's

Edition revised. With Cruikshank's Illustrations. Post 8vo. 5s.

HAZLITT'S (W.) LECTURES

, c. 6 vols. 3s. 6d. each.

IRVING (W.) WORKS. In 11 vols. Post 8vo. 3s. 6d. each. [See also p. 3.]

LAMB (C.) ESSAYS OF ELIA, AND ELIANA

. New Edition, post 8vo. 3s. 6d.

LUTHER (M.) TABLE-TALK

. Translated by W. Hazlitt

. With Life and Portrait. Post 8vo. 3s. 6d.

MANZONI (ALESSANDRO). THE BETROTHED

(I promessi Sposi). The only complete English translation. With numerous Woodcuts, 5s.

PEPYS'S DIARY. With Life and Notes by Richard Lord Braybrooke

. 4 vols. post 8vo. cloth, gilt, 5s. 6d. per vol.

PROUT (FATHER). RELIQUES

. New Edition, revised and largely augmented. Twenty-one spirited Etchings by Maclise

. 1 vol. 7s. 6d.

RICHTER (J. P. F.) AUTOBIOGRAPHY AND LEVANA

. Translated. Post 8vo. 3s. 6d.

RICHTER (J. P. F.) FLOWER, FRUIT, AND THORN PIECES

. A Novel. Translated by Alex. Ewing

. 3s. 6d.

WALTON. THE COMPLETE ANGLER

. Edited by E. Jesse

. With an account of Fishing Stations, c., and 203 Engravings. 5s.; or with 26 additional page Illustrations on Steel, 7s. 6d.

POETRY AND DRAMA

SHAKESPEARE. Edited by S. W. Singer

. With a Life by W. W. Lloyd

. Uniform with the Aldine Edition of the Poets. 10 vols. 2s. 6d. each. In half morocco, 5s.

CRITICAL ESSAYS ON THE PLAYS. By W. W. Lloyd

. Uniform with the above, 2s. 6d.; in half morocco, 5s.

SHAKESPEARE'S PLAYS AND POEMS. With Notes and Life by Charles Knight

, and 40 Engravings on Wood by Harvey

. Royal 8vo. cloth, 10s. 6d.

---- (Valpy's

Cabinet Pictorial Edition), with Glossarial Notes, Digests, c., and 171 Outline Plates. 15 vols. Fcap. 8vo. 2l. 5s.

---- (Pocket Volume Edition). Comprising all his Plays and Poems. Edited from the First Folio Edition by T. Keightley

. 13 vols. royal 32mo. in a cloth box, price 21s.

SHAKESPEARE. DRAMATIC ART OF

The History and Character of the Plays. By Dr. Ulrici

. Translated by L. D. Schmitz

. 2 vols. post 8vo. 3s. 6d. each.

CHAUCER. Robert Bell's

Edition. Revised. With Preliminary Essay by the Rev. W. W. Skeat

. M.A. 4 vols. 3s. 6d. each.

EARLY BALLADS AND SONGS OF THE PEASANTRY OF ENGLAND

. Edited by Robert Bell

. Post 8vo. 3s. 6d.

GREENE, MARLOWE

, and BEN JONSON

. Poems of. Edited by Robert Bell

. 1 vol. post 8vo. 3s. 6d.

PERCY'S RELIQUES OF ANCIENT ENGLISH POETRY. Reprinted from the Original Edition, and Edited by J. V. Prichard

. In 2 vols. 7s.

MILTON'S (J.) POETICAL WORKS. With Memoir and Notes, and 120 Engravings. In 2 vols. post 8vo. 5s. each.

GOLDSMITH. POEMS. Illustrated. 16mo. 2s. 6d.

SHERIDAN'S DRAMATIC WORKS. With Short Life, by G. C. S. and Portrait. Post 8vo. 3s. 6d.

ALFIERI. The Tragedies of. In English Verse. Edited by E. A. Bowring

, C. B. 2 vols. post 8vo. 7s.

CAMOENS' LUSIAD. Mickle's

Translation revised. Post 8vo. 3s. 6d.

DANTE. THE DIVINE COMEDY. Translated by the Rev. H. F. Cary

. Post 8vo. 3s. 6d.

This and the following one are the only editions containing the author's last corrections and emendations.

---- The Popular Edition, neatly Printed in Double Columns. Royal 8vo. sewed, 1s. 6d.; cloth, 2s. 6d.

---- Translated into English Verse by J. C. Wright, M.A

. With Portrait and 34 Engravings on Steel, after Flaxman. 5th Edition, post 8vo. 5s.

PETRARCH. SONNETS, TRIUMPHS, AND OTHER POEMS. Translated into English Verse. With Campbell's Life of the Poet. Illustrated. Post 8vo. 5s.

MOLIÈRE. DRAMATIC WORKS. In prose. Translated by C. H. Wall

. In 3 vols. post 8vo. 3s. 6d. each. Also fine-paper Edition, large post 8vo. 7s. 6d. each.

Translated by E. A. Bowring, C.B.

POEMS OF GOETHE. 2nd Edition (including Hermann and Dorothea). Post 8vo. 3s. 6d.

POEMS OF SCHILLER. 2nd Edition. Post 8vo. 3s. 6d.

POEMS OF HEINE. 2nd Edition. Post 8vo. 5s.

By Professor Conington, M.A.

HORACE'S ODES AND CARMEN SÆCULARE. Translated into English Verse. 7th Edition. Fcap. 8vo. 5s. 6d.

---- SATIRES AND EPISTLES. Translated into English Verse. 3rd Edition. 6s. 6d.

By C. S. Calverley.

VERSES AND TRANSLATIONS. 5th Edition. Fcap. 8vo. 5s.

FLY LEAVES. 6th Edition. Fcap. 8vo. 3s. 6d.

TRANSLATIONS INTO ENGLISH AND LATIN. Crown 8vo. 7s. 6d.

THEOCRITUS, into English Verse. Crown 8vo. 7s. 6d.

By Adelaide Anne Procter.

LEGENDS AND LYRICS. Illustrated Edition, with Portrait, and Introduction by Charles Dickens

. 4th Thous. 21s.

---- First Series. Introduction by Charles Dickens, and Portrait of the Author. 29th Thousand. Fcap. 8vo. 6s.

---- Second Series. 23rd Thousand. Fcap. 8vo. 5s.

ENGLISH SONGS AND LYRICS. By Barry Cornwall

. New Edition. Fcap. 8vo. 6s.

SONGS, BALLADS, AND STORIES. By W. Allingham

. Crown 8vo. gilt edges, 10s. 6d.

ALDINE SERIES OF THE BRITISH POETS.

The Editors of the various authors in this Series have in all cases endeavoured to make the collections of Poems as complete as possible, and in many instances copyright Poems are to be found in these editions which are not in any other. Each volume is carefully edited, with Notes where necessary for the elucidation of the Text, and a Memoir. A Portrait also is added in all cases where an authentic one is accessible. The volumes are printed on toned paper in fcap. 8vo. size, and neatly bound in cloth gilt, price 5s. each.

*** A Cheap Reprint of this Series, neat cloth, 1s. 6d. per volume.

AKENSIDE. KIRKE WHITE.

BEATTIE. MILTON. 3 vols.

BURNS. 3 vols. PARNELL.

BUTLER. 2 vols. POPE. 3 vols.

CHAUCER. 6 vols. PRIOR. 2 vols.

CHURCHILL. 2 vols. SHAKESPEARE'S POEMS.

COLLINS. SPENSER. 5 vols.

COWPER, including his Translations. 3 vols. SURREY.

SWIFT. 3 vols.

DRYDEN. 5 vols. THOMSON. 2 vols.

FALCONER. WYATT.

GOLDSMITH. YOUNG. 2 vols.

GRAY.

The following volumes of a New Series have been issued, 5s. each.

CHATTERTON. 2 vols.

CAMPBELL. THE COURTLY POETS, from RALEIGHT to WOTTON.

WILLIAM BLAKE. GEORGE HERBERT.

ROGERS. KEATS.

REFERENCE.

STUDENTS' GUIDE to the University of Cambridge. 3rd Edition, revised and corrected. Fcap. 8vo. 6s. 6d.

KING'S INTEREST TABLES. 25th Edition, 7s. 6d.

KENT'S COMMENTARY on International Law. New Edition, revised, with additional Notes and Cases, by J. T. Abdy, LL.D. Crown 8vo. [Immediately.]

THE EPIGRAMMATISTS. Selections from the Epigrammatic Literature of Ancient, Mediæval, and Modern Times. With Notes, c. by Rev. H. P. Dodd, M.A. 2nd Edition, enlarged. Post 8vo. 6s.

LATIN AND GREEK QUOTATIONS. A Dictionary of. Including Proverbs, Maxims, Mottoes, Law Terms, Phrases, c. By H. T. Riley. Post 8vo. 5s. With Index Verboram, 6s.

BRYAN'S DICTIONARY OF PAINTERS. See p. 2.

COOPER'S BIOGRAPHICAL DICTIONARY. See p. 2.

DR. RICHARDSON'S DICTIONARY OF THE ENGLISH LANGUAGE. Combining Explanation with Etymology, and copiously illustrated by Quotations from the best authorities. New edition, with a Supplement. In 2 vols. 4to. 4l. 14s. 6d.; half-bound in russia, 5l. 15s. 6d.; russia, 6l. 12s. The Supplement separately. 4to. 12s. An 8vo edition, without the Quotations, 15s.; half russia, 20s.; russia, 24s.

The following are the only authorised and unabridged Editions of WEBSTER'S DICTIONARY containing the valuable Etymological Notes and Derivations of Dr. Mahn, of Berlin, who devoted five years to the Revision of the Work.

WEBSTER'S GUINEA DICTIONARY of the English Language, including scientific, biblical, and Scottish terms and phrases, with their pronunciations, alternative spellings, derivations, and meanings. In 1 vol. 4to. with nearly 1600 pages and 3000 Illustrations. Strongly bound in cloth, 21s.; half calf, 30s.; calf or half russia, 1l. 11s. 6d.; russia, 2l.

WEBSTER'S COMPLETE DICTIONARY, containing all that appears in the above, and also a valuable Appendix, and 70 pages of Illustrations grouped and classified, rendering it a complete Literary and Scientific Reference Book. 1 vol. 4to. strongly bound in cloth, 1l. 11s. 6d.; half calf, 2l.; calf or half russia, 2l. 2s.; russia, 2l. 10s.

'Certainly the best practical English Dictionary extant.'--Quarterly Review.

NATURAL HISTORY.

THE LIBRARY OF NATURAL HISTORY. Containing Morris' British Birds--Nests--Eggs--British Butterflies--British Moths--Bree's Birds of Europe--Lowe's Works on British and Exotic Ferns, Grasses and Beautiful Leaved Plants--Hibberd's Plants--Maund's Botanic Garden--Tripp's British Mosses--Gatty's Seaweeds--Wooster's Alpine Plants, and Couch's Fishes--making in all 43 Volumes, in super-royal 8vo. containing upwards of 2550 full--page Plates, carefully coloured.

Complete Lists sent post free on application.

SOWERBY'S BOTANY. Containing a Description and Life--size Drawing of every British Plant. Edited and brought up to the present standard of scientific knowledge, by T. Boswell (formerly Syme), LL.D., F.L.S., c. With Popular Descriptions of the Uses, History, and Traditions of each Plant, by Mrs. Lankester, Author of 'Wild Flowers worth Notice,' 'The British Ferns,' c. The Figures by J. C. Sowerby, F.L.S., J. De C. Sowerby, F.L.S., and J. W. Salter, A.L.S., F.G.S., and John Edward Sowerby. Third Edition, entirely revised, with descriptions of all the species by the Editor. In 11 vols. 22l. 8s. cloth; 24l. 12s. half morocco; and 28l. 3s. 6d. whole morocco. Volumes sold separately.

SOWERBY'S FERNS AND FERN-ALLIES OF GREAT BRITAIN. With 80 Plates by J. E. Sowerby. The Descriptions, Synonyms, c, by C. Johnson. Royal paper, Coloured Plates, 25s.

COTTAGE GARDENER'S DICTIONARY. With a Supplement, containing all the new plants and varieties down to the year 1869. Edited by G. W. Johnson. Post 8vo. cloth, 6s. 6d.

BOTANIST'S POCKET-BOOK. By W. R. Hayward. Containing the Botanical name, Common name, Soil or Situation, Colour, Growth, and time of Flowering of all plants, arranged in a tabulated form. 2nd Edition, revised. Fcap. 8vo. 4s. 6d.

MY GARDEN; its Plan and Culture. Together with a General Description of its Geology, Botany, and Natural History. By A. Smee, F.R.S., with more than 1300 Engravings on Wood. 4th Thousand, imp. 8vo. 21s.

"'My Garden' is indeed a book which ought to be in the hands of everyone who is fortunate enough to possess a garden of his own; he is certain to find some things in it from which he may profit."--Nature.

NATURAL HISTORY OF SELBORNE. With Notes by Sir William Jardine and Edward Jesse, Esq. Illustrated by 40 highly-finished Engravings; or, with the Plates coloured, 7s. 6d.

HISTORY OF BRITISH BIRDS. By R. Mudie. With 28 Plates. 2 vols. 7s. 6d. each.

ART AND ORNAMENT.

TURNER'S PICTURESQUE VIEWS IN ENGLAND AND WALES. With Descriptive Notices. 96 Illustrations, reproduced in Permanent Photography. In 3 vols. imp. 4to. Vol. I. Landscapes, 40 Plates, 2l. 12s. 6d.; Vol. II. Castles and Abbeys, 32 Plates, 2l. 2s.; Vol. III. Coast Scenery, 24 Plates, 1l. 11s. 6d.

TURNER'S CELEBRATED LANDSCAPES. Sixteen Autotype Reproductions of the most important Works of J. M. W. Turner, R.A. With Memoir and Descriptions. Imp. 4to. 2l. 2s.

THE RAFFAELLE GALLERY. Permanent Reproductions in Autotype of Engravings of the most celebrated Works of Raffaelle Sanzio d'Urbino. With Descriptions, c. Imp. quarto, 2l. 2s.

FLAXMAN. CLASSICAL COMPOSITIONS, comprising the Outline Illustrations to Homer's 'Iliad' and 'Odyssey,' the 'Tragedies' of Æschylus, the 'Theogony' and 'Works and Days' of Hesiod, engraved by Piroli of Rome, and William Blake. Imp. 4to. half bound morocco, 4l. 14s. 6d. The four parts, separately, 21s. each.

---- THE DRAWINGS OF. Thirty-two large Plates, comprising the entire Series of the Flaxman Drawings in the Gallery of University College, London, reproduced by the Autotype Process of Permanent Photography. Edited, with a descriptive letterpress and copious Introduction, by Sidney Colvin, M.A., Fellow of Trinity College and Slade Professor in the University of Cambridge. Large folio, in portfolio, 10l. 10s.

MEMOIRS OF SIR EDWIN LANDSEER. Being a New Edition of 'The Early Works of Sir Edwin Landseer.' Revised and enlarged by F. G. Stephens. With 24 Illustrations in Photography. Imp. 8vo. 1l. 5s.

NOTES ON IRISH ARCHITECTURE. By the late Earl Of Dunraven. Edited by M. Stokes, Associate of the Scottish Society of Antiquaries. With numerous Woodcuts and fine Photographic Illustrations. Imp. 4to. Vol. I. 4l. 4s.; Vol. II. 4l. 4s.

MOUNTAINS AND LAKES Of Switzerland AND ITALY. 64 Picturesque Views in Chromolithograph, from Original Sketches by C. C. Pyne. With a Map of Routes and Descriptive Notes by Rev. J. Mercier. 2nd Edition. Crown 4to. 2l. 2s.

RIVIERA, THE. Pen-and-Pencil Sketches from Cannes to Genoa. By Dean Alford. With 12 Chromolithographic Illustrations and numerous Woodcuts, from Drawings by the Author. Imp. 8vo. 21s.

CRUIKSHANK (G.) A COMPLETE CATALOGUE OF THE ENGRAVED WORKS OF. Including Etchings on Steel, Copper, c., and Woodcuts executed between the years 1805 and 1870. Compiled by G. W. Reid, Keeper of the Prints and Drawings in the British Museum. With a large number of Illustrations, chiefly from the Original Plates and Blocks. In 3 vols. royal 4to. 12l. 12s.

FLAXMAN. LECTURES ON SCULPTURE, as delivered before the President and Members of the Royal Academy. By J. Flaxman, R.A. With 53 Plates. New Edition, 6s.

HEATON (MRS.) A CONCISE HISTORY OF PAINTING FOR STUDENTS AND GENERAL READERS. By Mrs. Heaton. With Illustrations. 8vo. 15s.

DRAWING COPIES. By P. H. Delamotte, Professor of Drawing at King's College, London. 96 Original Sketches in Architecture, Trees, Figures, Foregrounds, Landscapes, Boats, and Sea--pieces. Royal 8vo. Oblong, half-bound, 12s.

HANDBOOK TO THE DEPARTMENT OF PRINTS AND DRAWINGS IN THE BRITISH MUSEUM. With Introduction and Notices of the various Schools, and a Frontispiece after Raffaelle. By Louis Fagan, of the Department of Prints and Drawings, British Museum. Medium 8vo. 8s.; sewed, 9s. in cloth.

By Eliza Meteyard.

MEMORIALS OF WEDGWOOD. A Series of Plaques, Cameos, Vases, c., selected from various Private Collections, and executed in Permanent Photography. With Introduction and Descriptions. Imp. 4to. 3l. 3s.

WEDGWOOD AND HIS WORKS: a Selection of his choicest Plaques, Medallions, Vases, c, from Designs by Flaxman and others, in Permanent Photography, with a Sketch of his Life and of the Progress of his Art Manufacture. Imp. 4to. 3l. 3s.

CATALOGUE OF WEDGWOOD'S MANUFACTURES. With Illustrations. Half-bound 8vo. 10s. 6d.

WEDGWOOD HANDBOOK. A Manual for Collectors: Treating of the Marks, Monograms, and other Tests of the Old Period of Manufacture; also including the Catalogues with Prices obtained at various Sales, together with a Glossary of Terms. 8vo. 10s. 6d.

OLD DERBY CHINA FACTORY. The Workmen and their Productions. Containing Biographical Sketches of the chief Artist-workmen, the various Marks used, Facsimiles from the old Derby Books, and original Price Lists of more than 400 Figures and Groups, c. With 12 Coloured Plates and numerous Woodcuts. By John Haslem

. Imp. 8vo. 31s. 6d.

'That which has been done so well by Miss Meteyard for Etruria, by Mr. Binns for Worcester, and by Mr. Owen for Bristol, has now been done for the Derby works with at least equal zeal, intelligence, and ability, by Mr. Haslem.'--Staffordshire Advertiser.

FOR YOUNG PEOPLE.

AUNT JUDY'S MAGAZINE. Edited by H. K. F. Gatty

. A High-class Illustrated Magazine for Young People. 8d. Monthly.

The CHRISTMAS VOLUME for 1877 contains Stories by Mrs. Ewing, Ascott R. Hope, Flora Masson, and others. Translations from the German, French, and Swedish--Short Stories--Fairy Tales--Papers on Historical Subjects--Natural History Articles. Short Biographies of Eminent Persons--Verses--A Christmas Play by Douglas Straight--Acrostics--Correspondence--Book Notices, and numerous Illustrations. Imp. 16mo. Handsomely bound, price 8s. 6d.

Former Volumes may still be had, some at reduced prices.

By Mrs. Alfred Gatty.

PARABLES FROM NATURE. With Notes on the Natural History; and numerous large Illustrations by eminent Artists. 4to. cloth gilt, 21s. Also in 2 vols. 10s. 6d. each.

---- 16mo. with Illustrations. First Series, 17th Edition, 1s. 6d. Second Series, 10th Edition, 2s. The two Series in 1 vol. 3s. 6d. Third Series, 6th Edition, 2s. Fourth Series, 4th Edition, 2s. The two Series in one vol. 4s. Fifth Series, 2s.

WORLDS NOT REALIZED. 16mo. 4th Edition, 2s.

PROVERBS ILLUSTRATED. 16mo. With Illustrations. 4th Edition, 2s.

A BOOK OF EMBLEMS. Drawn by F. Gilbert

. With Introduction and Explanations. Imp. 16mo. 4s. 6d.

WAIFS AND STRAYS OF NATURAL HISTORY. With Coloured Frontispiece and Woodcuts. Fcap. 3s. 6d.

THE POOR INCUMBENT. Fcap. 8vo. 1s. and 1s. 6d.

AUNT SALLY'S LIFE. With Six Illustrations. Square 16mo. 3rd Edition, 3s. 6d.

THE MOTHER'S BOOK OF POETRY. Selected and Arranged by Mrs. A. Gatty

. Crown 8vo. 3s. 6d.; or with Illustrations, elegantly bound, 7s. 6d.

A BIT OF BREAD. By Jean Macé

. Translated by Mrs. Alfred Gatty

. 2 vols. fcap. 8vo. Vol. I. 4s. 6d. Vol. II. 3s. 6d.

The Uniform Edition. Fcap. 8vo. 3s. 6d. each volume.

PARABLES FROM NATURE. 2 vols. With Portrait.

DOMESTIC PICTURES AND TALES. With 6 Illustrations.

THE HUMAN FACE DIVINE, and other Tales. With Illustrations. 3rd Edition.

WORLDS NOT REALIZED, and Proverbs Illustrated.

THE FAIRY GODMOTHERS, and other Tales. With Frontispiece. 7th Edition, 2s. 6d.

THE HUNDRETH BIRTHDAY, and other Tales. With Illustrations by Phiz

. New Edition.

AUNT JUDY'S TALES. Illustrated. 7th Edition.

AUNT JUDY'S LETTERS; a Sequel to 'Aunt Judy's Tales.' Illustrated. 5th Edition.

MRS. ALFRED GATTY'S PRESENTATION BOX for Young People, containing the above volumes, neatly bound, and enclosed in a cloth box. 31s. 6d.

By Mrs. Ewing.

'Everything Mrs. Ewing writes is full of talent, and also full of perception and common sense.'--Saturday Review.

A GREAT EMERGENCY, and other Tales. With 4 Illustrations. Fcap. 8vo. 5s. [Just published.]

THE BROWNIES, and other Tales. Illustrated by George Cruikshank

. 3rd Edition. Imp. 16mo. 5s.

'Mrs. Ewing gives us some really charming writing. While her first story most prettily teaches children how much they can do to help their parents, the immediate result will be, we fear, anything but good. For if a child once begins "The Brownies," it will get so deeply interested in it, that when bed-time comes it will altogether forget the moral, and will weary its parents with importunities for just a few minutes more to see how everything ends. The frontispiece, by the old friend of our childhood, George Cruikshank, is no less pretty than the story.'--Saturday Review.

MRS. OVERTHEWAY'S REMEMBRANCES. Illustrated with 10 fine Full-page Engravings on Wood, after Drawings by Pasquier

and Wolf

, and Edition, cloth gilt, 3s. 6d.

'It is not often nowadays the privilege of a critic to grow enthusiastic over a new work; and the rarity of the occasion that calls forth the delight is apt to lead one into the sin of hyperbole. And yet we think we shall not be accused of extravagance when we say that, without exception, "Mrs. Overthewny's Remembrances" is the most delightful work avowedly written for children that we have ever read. There are passages in this book which the genius of George Eliot would be proud to own. It is full of a peculiar, heart-stirring pathos of its own, which culminates in the last pages, when Ida finds that her father is not dead. The book is one that may be recurred to often, and always with the same delight. We predict for it a great popularity.'-- Leader.

MELCHIOR'S DREAM, and other Tales. Illustrated. 3rd Edition. Fcap. 8vo. 3s. 6d.

"'Melchior's Dream' is an exquisite little story, charming by original humour, buoyant spirits, and tender pathos."--Athenæum.

A FLAT IRON FOR A FARTHING; or, Some Passages in the Life of an Only Son. With 12 Illustrations by H. Allingham

. 5th Edition. Small 8vo. 5s.

'Let every parent and guardian who wishes to be amused, and at the same time to please a child, purchase "A Flat Iron for a Farthing; or, some Passages in the Life of an Only Son," by J. H Ewing. We will answer for the delight with which they will read it themselves, and we do not doubt that the young and fortunate recipients will also like it. The story is quaint, original, and altogether delightful.'--Athenæum.

'A capital book for a present. No child who is fortunate enough to possess it will be in a hurry to put it down, for it is a book of uncommon fascination. The story is good, the principles inculcated admirable, and some of the illustrations simply delicious.'--John Bull.

LOB-LIE-BY-THE-FIRE; or, the Luck of Lingborough. And other Tales. Illustrated by George Cruikshank

. 2nd Edition. Imp. 16mo. 5s.

'A charming tale by another of those clever writers, thanks to whom the children are now really better served than their neighbours.'--Spectator.

'Mrs. Ewing has written as good a story as her "Brownies," and that is saying a great deal. "Lob-lie-by-the-fire" has humour and pathos, and teaches what is right without making children think they are reading a sermon.'--Saturday Review.

SIX TO SIXTEEN: A Story for Girls. With 10 Illustrations by Mrs. Allingham

. 3rd Edition. Small post 8vo. 5s.

'The homely good sense and humour of the bulk of the story are set off by the pathos of its opening and its close, and a soft and beautiful light, as of dawn and sunset, is thrown round the substantial English ideal of what a girl's education ought to be, which runs through the tale.'--Spectator.

'It is a beautifully told story, full of humour and pathos, and bright sketches of scenery and character. It is all told with great naturalness, and will amuse grown-up people quite as much as children. In reading the story, we have been struck especially by characteristic bits of description, which show very happily the writer's appreciation of child life.'--Pall Mall Gazette.

'We have rarely met, on such a modest scale, with characters so ably and simply drawn ... The merits of the volume, in themselves not small, are much enhanced by some clever illustrations from the pencil of Mrs. Allingham.'--Athenæum.

'The tone of the book is pleasant and healthy, and singularly free from that sentimental, not to say "mawkish," stain which is apt to disfigure such productions. The illustrations by Mrs. Allingham add a special attraction to the little volume.'--Times.

'It is scarcely necessary to say that Mrs. Ewing's book is one of the best of the year.'--Saturday Review.

'There is in it not only a great deal of common sense, but there is true humour.... We have not met a healthier or breezier tale for girls for a long period.'--Academy.

JAN OF THE WINDMILL; a Story of the Plains. With 11 Illustrations by Helen Allingham. Crown 8vo. 8s. 6d.

'A capital story, which, like all that Mrs. Ewing gives us, will be read with pleasure Some well-drawn illustrations materially increase the attractiveness of the volume.'--City Press.

By Mrs. O'Reilly.

'Mrs. O'Reilly's works need no commendation ... the style is so good, the narrative so engrossing, and the tone so excellent.'--John Bull.

LITTLE PRESCRIPTION, and other Tales. With 6 Illustrations by W. H. Petherick and others. 16mo. 2s. 6d.

'A worthy successor of some charming little volumes of the same kind.... The tale from which the title is taken is for its grace and pathos an especial favourite.'--Spectator.

'Mrs. O'Reilly could not write otherwise than well, even if she were to try.'--Morning Post.

CICELY'S CHOICE, A Story for Girls. With a Frontispiece by J. A. Pasquier. Fcap. 8vo. gilt edges, 3s. 6d.

'A pleasant story.... It is a book for girls, and grown people will also enjoy reading it.'--Athenæum.

'A pleasant, well-written, interesting story, likely to be acceptable to young people who are in their teens.'--Scotsman.

GILES'S MINORITY; or, Scenes at the Red House. With 8 Illustrations. 16mo. 2s. 6d.

'In one of our former reviews we praised "Deborah's Drawer." "Giles's Minority" no less deserves our goodwill. It is a picture of school-room life, and is so well drawn that grown-up readers may delight in it. In literary excellence this little book is above most of its fellows.'--Times.

DOLL WORLD; or, Play and Earnest. A Study from Real Life. With 8 Illustrations. By C. A. Saltmarsh. 16mo. 2s. 6d.

'It is a capital child's book, and it has a charm for grown-up people also, as the fairy haze of "long-ago" brightens every page. We are not ashamed to confess to the "thrilling interest" with which we followed the history of "Robertina" and "Mabel."'--Athenæum.

DEBORAH'S DRAWER. With 9 Illustrations. 16mo. 2s. 6d.

'Any godmamma who wishes to buy an unusually pretty and artistically-written gift-book for an eight-year-old pet cannot do better than spend a florin or two on the contents of "Aunt Deborah's Drawer."'--Athenæum.

DAISY'S COMPANIONS; or, Scenes from Child Life. A Story for Little Girls. With 8 Illustrations. 3rd Edit. 16mo. 2s. 6d.

'If anybody wants a pretty little present for a pretty (and good) little daughter, or a niece or grand-daughter, we cannot recommend a better or tastier one than "Daisy's Companions."'--Times.

Captain Marryats Books for Boys.

Uniform Illustrated Edition, neatly bound in cloth, post 8vo. 3s. 6d. each; gilt edges, 4s. 6d.

POOR JACK. With Sixteen Illustrations after Designs by Clarkson Stanfield, R.A.

THE SETTLERS IN CANADA. With Illustrations by Gilbert

and Dalziel

.

THE MISSION; or, Scenes in Africa. With Illustrations by John Gilbert

.

THE PRIVATEERSMAN. Adventures by Sea and Land in Civil and Savage Life One Hundred Years Ago. Illustrated with Eight Steel Engravings.

THE PIRATE, AND THREE CUTTERS. With Memoir of the Author, and 20 Steel Engravings by Clarkson Stanfield, R.A

.

Cheap Edition, without Illustrations, 1s. 6d.

MASTERMAN READY; or, the Wreck of the Pacific. Embellished with Ninety-three Engravings on Wood.

A BOY'S LOCKER. A Smaller Edition of Captain Marryat's Books for Boys, in 12 vols. Fcap. 8vo. in a compact cloth box, 21s.

By Hans Christian Andersen.

FAIRYTALES AND SKETCHES. Translated by C. C. Peachey, H. Ward, A. Plesner, c. With 104 Illustrations by Otto Speckter and others. Crown 8vo. 6s.

'The translation most happily hits the delicate quaintness of Andersen--most happily transposes into simple English words the tender precision of the famous story-teller; in a keen examination of the book we scarcely recall a single phrase or turn that obviously could have been bettered.'--Daily Telegraph.

TALES FOR CHILDREN. With 48 Full-page Illustrations by Wehnert, and 57 Small Engravings on Wood by W. Thomas. A new Edition. Crown 8vo. 6s.

This and the above volume form the most complete English Edition of Andersen's Tales.

LATER TALES. Translated from the Danish by Augusta Plesner and H. Ward. With Illustrations by Otto Speckter, W. Cooper, and other Artists. Cloth gilt, 3s. 6d.

WONDERWORLD. A Collection of Fairy Tales, Old and New. Translated from the French, German, and Danish. With 4 Coloured Illustrations and numerous Woodcuts by L. Richter, Oscar Pletsch, and others. Royal 16mo. cloth, gilt edges, 3s. 6d.

'It will delight the children, and has in it a wealth of wisdom that may be of practical service when they have grown into men and women.'--Literary World.

GUESSING STORIES; or, The Surprising Adventures of the Man with the Extra Pair of Eyes. By the late Archdeacon Freeman. 3rd Edition, 2s. 6d.

GRIMM'S GAMMER GRETHEL; or, German Fairy Tales and Popular Stories. Translated by Edgar Taylor. Numerous Woodcuts after G. Cruikshank's designs. Post 8vo. 3s. 6d.

LITTLE PLAYS FOR LITTLE PEOPLE; with Hints for Drawing-room Performances. By Mrs. Chisholm, Author of 'Rana, the Story of a Frog.' 16mo. with Illustrations, 2s. 6d.

ROBINSON CRUSOE. With a Biographical Account of Defoe. Illustrated with 70 Wood Engravings, chiefly after Designs by Harvey; and 12 Engravings on Steel after Stothard. Post 8vo. 5s.

THE WIDE, WIDE WORLD. By E. Wetherell. With 10 Illustrations. Post 8vo. 3s. 6d.

UNCLE TOM'S CABIN. By H. B. Stowe. Illustrated. Post 8vo. 3s. 6d.

KIRSTIN'S ADVENTURES. A Story of Jutland Life. By the Author of 'Casimir the Little Exile,' c. With Illustrations. Crown 8vo. 3s. 6d.

'There is so much true art and natural talent in the book that we are half inclined to take it away from the boys and girls for whom it is written.'--Times.

KATIE; or, the Simple Heart. By D. Richmond, Author of 'Annie Maitland.' Illustrated by M. I. Booth. 2nd Edition. Crown 8vo. 3s. 6d.

'The family life which surrounds Katie is both pretty and natural. The tone is good, and the plot--we speak from experience--engages a child's interest with almost too keen a sympathy.'--Guardian.

QUEENS OF ENGLAND from the Norman Conquest. By A. Strickland. An Abridged Edition, with Portrait of Matilda of Flanders. In 1 vol. crown 8vo. cloth, 6s. 6d.

GLIMPSES INTO PET-LAND. By the Rev. J. G. Wood, M.A., F.L.S. With Frontispiece. Fcap. 3s. 6d.

FRIENDS IN FUR AND FEATHERS. By Gwynfryn. Illustrated with 8 Full-page Engravings by F. W. Keyl, c. 5th Edition. Handsomely bound, 3s. 6d.

'We have already characterised some other book as the best cat-and-dog book of the season. We said so because we had not seen the present little book, which is delightful. It is written on an artistic principle, consisting of actual biographies of certain elephants, squirrels, blackbirds, and what not, who lived in the flesh; and we only wish that human biographies were always as entertaining and instructive.'--Saturday Review.

INSECT ARCHITECTURE. By Rennie. Edited by the Rev. J. G. Wood, Author of 'Homes Without Hands.' Post 8vo. with nearly 200 Illustrations, 5s.

THE ENTERTAINING NATURALIST. By Mrs. Loudon. Revised and enlarged by W. S. Dallas, F.L.S. With nearly 500 Illustrations. Post 8vo. 5s.

ANECDOTES OF DOGS. By Edward Jesse. With Illustrations. Post 8vo. cloth, 5s. With 34 Steel Engravings after Cooper, Landseer, c. 7s. 6d.

NATURAL HISTORY OF SELBORNE. By Gilbert White. Edited by Jesse. Illustrated with 40 Engravings. Post 8vo. 5s.; or, with the Plates Coloured, 7s. 6d.

CHARADES, ENIGMAS, AND RIDDLES. Collected by a Cantab. 5th Edition, enlarged. Illustrated. Fcap. 8vo. 1s.

POETRY-BOOK FOR SCHOOLS, illustrated with 37 highly finished Engravings by C. W. Cope, R.A., W. Helmsley, S. Palmer, F. Skill, G. Thomas, and H. Weir. Crown 8vo. gilt, 2s. 6d.; cloth, 1s.

GILES WITHERNE; or, the Reward of Disobedience. A Village Tale for the Young. By the Rev. J. P. Parkinson, D.C.L. 6th Edition. Illustrated by the Rev. F. W. Mann. Super-royal 16mo. 1s.

THE PILGRIM'S PROGRESS. By John Bunyan. With 281 Engravings from Designs by William Harvey. Post 8vo. 3s. 6d.

OLD NURSERY RHYMES AND CHIMES. Collected and arranged by a Peal of Bells. Fcap. 4to. Ornamental binding, 2s. 6d.

NURSERY CAROLS. By the Rev. Dr. Monsell, Rector of St. Nicholas, Guildford, with upwards of 100 Illustrations by Ludwig Richter and Oscar Pletsch. Imp. 16mo. 3s. 6d.

'At once a poet and a child lover, full of fun and yet disposed gently to instil what is good, Dr. Monsell is inimitable in this particular department.'--John Bull.

LONDON:
GEORGE BELL SONS, York Street,
Covent Garden.

CPSIA information can be obtained at www.ICGtesting.com
230268LV00002B/112/P

9 781153 661409